10 00

CHURCH HISTORY
IN THE AGE OF SCIENCE

CHURCH HISTORY IN THE AGE OF SCIENCE

HISTORIOGRAPHICAL PATTERNS
IN THE UNITED STATES
1876–1918

by Henry Warner Bowden

THE UNIVERSITY OF
NORTH CAROLINA PRESS
CHAPEL HILL

Library of Congress Catalog Card Number 72–156134
ISBN 0–8078–1176–9
Manufactured in the United States of America
Printed by Kingsport Press, Inc., Kingsport, Tennessee

For
JEANNETTE EVELYNN
and
WARNER HILL BOWDEN
With love and marked gratitude

&CONTENTS

ᴤPREFACE

This collection of essays grew out of an attempt to understand the methods and goals of church historians within the general context of professional historical study. In viewing present-day discussions about the possible uniqueness of church history and the diversified objectives and results some scholars wish to attain, it was apparent that the origins of the debate were rooted in an earlier period. Working back into the intellectual developments of nineteenth-century American historiography, it soon became clear that ideas about empirical science were a pervasive factor in the minds of leading authors. Despite the fact that they were unable to agree upon a comprehensive definition of scientific history, and even knowing that several scholars included here did not wish to be forced into circumstances where scientific epistemology was the controlling ideal, their work is more intelligible when viewed as responses to this general conception. The ideas of individual historians in this period are best interpreted by using the popular acceptance of scientific standards as a common background.

An overarching interpretive framework is useful to some extent, but the work of each man retained an integrity that frustrated attempts to reduce them simply to variations on a single theme or even representatives of conflicting schools of thought. Early in the investigation I proceeded on the hypothesis that ideas about secular and church history could be compared by studying their institutional embodiment, the American Historical Association and the American Society of Church History. That proved unworkable because, even though each group began with a fairly definite ideology, many different sets of ideas quickly found a home in both organizations. There is little evidence that the major professional associations tried to perpetuate any specific set of ideas about historical research or the ends history was meant to serve. The context surrounding differing historiographical theories cannot be defined in institutional terms. It is more feasible to concentrate on the intellectual and social differences of specific authors. Some light may be shed on the early years of the AHA and the ASCH, but the studies are primarily intended to illuminate the ideas of separate thinkers who responded to the new paradigms thought to be resident in natural science.

The following collection of essays is concerned with analyzing different ways in which church history was written in this country during a limited time period. Discussions of each thinker are not intended as full-length intellectual biographies. They are offered as selective treatments of the manner in which each man thought he could meet the scholarly demands of his profession. These historians were also leaders of the AHA or the ASCH, and they participated in the increased emphasis on research in higher education. A discussion touching all these points gives more cohesion to the various agents involved. What follows is an attempt to outline some of the major issues in historiography as they were debated in a context dominated by the rubrics of scientific empiricism. It is interesting to follow this debate because the issues are germane to fundamental attitudes which every professional historian brings to his material. None of the basic issues have been resolved, and historians would do well to practice their craft with knowledge of alternative approaches.

These studies are based on the assumption that historical writings, like other forms of cultural expression, are themselves historical documents. Writers of history always respond to dominant aspects of the intellectual milieu in which they form ideas about fact and value. At one level, the student of historical writings is concerned simply with reviewing the differences between published works on similar topics, pointing out the improvements achieved by more comprehensive research and revision. He is concerned more fundamentally, however, to explain how such divergent views could be expressed regarding the same persons and events. He searches for reasons why those differing histories, as products of deliberate thought, were given credence and why a particular interpretation was sometimes found more acceptable to the community of critical scholars. That larger task of probing beneath the surface of finished historical volumes can contribute to the history of ideas in our nation. As one student in the field recently described this objective, "Historiography can be seen as a category of intellectual history which relates historical works to the periods in which they were written and attempts to uncover their basic assumptions, revealing more immediately the limitations of the historical discipline, suggesting new questions to be asked, new avenues to be explored, new techniques, new metaphors, new models to be utilized."[1]

In light of these basic assumptions one can treat historical writing as a class of primary sources, using it as a means of discovering the general pattern of thought held by respective authors. With that end in view, the student of historiography appreciates R. G. Collingwood's provocative suggestion that "the important question about any statement contained in a source is not whether it is true or false, but what it means."[2] If histories are accepted as sources and their various truth-claims momentarily left unjudged, there is room and time enough for investigating levels of meaning found therein. The ostensible meaning which the author intended to convey is rather easily discerned, but it is more important to determine the reasons and conditions which brought him to that understanding. Those are the elements that help explain the age as well as the man. The student of historiography may limit himself to such a task in the manner thought by Reinhold Niebuhr to resemble Rorschach analysis. Any historian, like the patient, observes materials presented to him and then records his own understanding of the data; the analyst in both cases is concerned primarily with what the person under observation says he sees. The analyst regards any correlation between interpretation and the actual ink spots or historical sources to be less important than what the observer reports. In each of the cases an interpretation made by the spokesman, historians for our choice, can be seen as pointing to a state of mind as well as describing a configuration of objective data.[3] And it is the mind of the historian, not his accuracy about facts of historical phenomena, that chiefly concerns the historiographical analyst. Though the following essays concentrate on published materials of various historians, whenever other manuscripts could contribute to a more basic understanding of a scholar's intellectual framework, they were utilized. These studies attempt to make both the mind of the man understand-

1. David J. O'Brien, "American Catholic Historiography: A Post Conciliar Evaluation," *Church History* 37 (March 1968): 80.
2. Robin G. Collingwood, *The Idea of History* (New York: Galaxy Press, 1956), p. 260.
3. Reinhold Niebuhr, *The Irony of American History* (New York: Charles Scribner's Sons, 1952), p. 151.

able through his work and his total historiographical effort meaningful through an adequate knowledge of the mind which produced it.

On one level these essays examine the impact of scientific thinking on American ideas about history, indicating the force of that impact on a special system of ideas. They trace a shift in attitudes about the goal and methods of acceptable historical writing in the latter part of the nineteenth century and then, using church historiography as a basis for determining the religious sympathies of the writers, they disclose a gradual development away from traditional confessionalism in theological circles toward an orientation more secular and contemporaneous. The specific questions which give some coherence to these individual writers can be summarized in the following way: Is church history a unique discipline, distinct from other historical studies? Does the act of choosing the church as a topic of study influence in any way the research methods or modes of interpretation used by the investigator? Must one believe the truths of Christian churches before studying them, or can anyone, regardless of his religious persuasion, write an adequate account of a church's past? Does church history fall necessarily under a larger and more comprehensive theological outlook, or do the results of historical study stand independent of any possible consequences they might have for theology?

Church historiography is interesting in itself, but in a large sense its problems are common to every branch of historical inquiry. It makes clear the issues facing every historian regarding impartial investigation, faithfulness to documentary evidence, discovery of positive or negative bias and curtailing it. Perhaps church history best illustrates these problems because interpolations have been relatively more prevalent there, and some churchmen continue to defend the subject as if it were different from other historical pursuits. There will probably always be some church historians who begin by defining the church as a special institution and argue on that basis that studies must take its uniqueness into account. But those theological spokesmen are only making explicit the problems each historian must face, whatever his topic happens to be. All historians must notice the effect of cultural factors on their definition of a subject, their conception of acceptable evidence and the insights they bring to bear on the material. Without this critical appreciation of the difficulties involved in making declarative sentences, a valuable dimension will be lacking in their finished work.

Though many earlier ideas are incorporated into this history, the general beginning point is the year 1876 when Herbert Baxter Adams participated in his first history seminar at Johns Hopkins University, the first real university in the United States. As professor of history at that institution and as secretary of the American Historical Association, Adams more than any other single man helped define the concept of scientific history. That term meant different things to several historians, but all of them shared a modicum of three views which challenged the dominant conception of what constituted a proper approach to church history. Too many individuals ascribed too many differing ideas to the general notion of "scientific history" for a comprehensive, fully representative discussion ever to be accomplished. The cluster of ideas introduced in chapter 1 were prevalent among founders of the AHA, and they provide the best set of lenses through which to observe other historians.

The first characteristic of this popular but catchall phrase, scientific history, was an iconoclastic attitude that insisted on revising every area of historical knowledge. This derived from the overall self-consciousness of the American age of science which was described, rather dramatically, by one contemporary who contrasted his generation with those of less accomplishment:

This century . . . has been . . . an age of ideas, an era of seeking and finding the like of which was never known before. . . . In their mental habits, in their methods of inquiry, and in the data at their command, "the men of the present day who have fully kept pace with the scientific movement are separated from the men whose education ended in 1830 by an immeasurably wider gulf than has ever before divided one progressive generation of men from their predecessors."[4]

The second common element has been termed "empiricism" because it resisted a priori assumptions and demanded that historical knowledge be derived objectively from the available research data. The third viewpoint complemented the others by declaring that natural phenomena, tangible observable evidence, were the only source upon which scientific history could be based. According to the dictum of British historian, Henry T. Buckle, their method followed the pattern

---

4. John Fiske, *The Idea of God as Affected by Modern Knowledge* (Boston: Houghton Mifflin Co., 1886), pp. 56–57. The quotation which Fiske cited was from his own work, *Outlines of Cosmic Philosophy* (1874), 1:230.

of "applying to the history of Man those methods of investigation which have been found successful in other branches of knowledge," that is, in the natural sciences.[5] Scientific historians thought they could transfer the procedures of the laboratory into their own research and thereby produce lasting and reliable history. None of them succeeded in becoming absolutely objective; neither did they write history without strong preconceptions, but their professed ideals set the tone of American historiography for over a quarter of a century.

The prevailing viewpoint in church historiography during the early decades of this period was embodied in the work of Philip Schaff. In each of the three areas listed above, he resisted the values associated with empirical science, and thus he stood against the developing consensus of American scholars. His main contention was similar to that of his Roman Catholic counterpart, John G. Shea: the church was a holy institution, and its history was necessarily an account of providential acts among men. Both writers found it difficult to be iconoclastic or to believe that historical evidence could speak for itself without an overarching theological pattern for interpretation. From that point of view they denied that naturalistic explanations supplied an adequate account of the events and experiences which constituted the church's past. Schaff insisted that church history was a distinctly religious discipline, and he played a major role in founding the American Society of Church History in 1888. Two reasons for organizing the ASCH were to further Schaff's interests in the discipline as a distinctive mode of study and also to use its offices to facilitate ecumenical understanding in the United States.

By 1896 it had become evident that many church historians were impressed with the standards set by scientific history and that they had adopted those new ideas as their own. Ephraim Emerton at Harvard and Williston Walker at Yale denied Schaff's ideas and pursued scholarly objectives that would align their subject with general historical studies. Other writers like Arthur C. McGiffert, Walter Rauschenbusch, and Frank Hugh Foster contributed to the demise of Schaff's theological synthesis, but they did so in order to replace it with new theological viewpoints rather than with an empirical naturalism. Their work indicated a continued interest in church historiography which

5. In H. Stuart Hughes, *History as Art and as Science* (New York: Harper & Row, 1964), pp. 8–9.

blended careful investigative procedures with insights derived from religious commitment. But their works, harboring more contemporaneous interests as they did, represented another departure from Schaff's outmoded ideology. When the ASCH was revived in 1906, it bore little resemblance to the earlier organization. It embodied neither a concerted methodological approach nor a consensus about the theological value of church history. The year 1918 seems natural for bringing this study to a close because that was when Rauschenbusch died, Emerton resigned his professorship, and McGiffert reduced the pace of his research to become president of Union Theological Seminary. During the forty-year period American church historiography developed from a theologically oriented perspective into a wide spectrum of viewpoints about the nature of the craft. Those changes constitute an important chapter in the history of ideas, both religious and secular, in the United States.

Parts of chapters 1, 2, and 4 have appeared in a shortened form in *Church History* 36 (September 1967); an earlier version of chapter 3 was printed in *Catholic Historical Review* 54 (July 1968); sections of chapter 7 were included in *Foundations* 9 (July–September 1966). The material in this volume incorporates those earlier essays in a substantially rewritten form.

It is always a pleasure to acknowledge the help received while living several years with a specific intellectual problem. I should like to thank Miss Frieda Thies of Johns Hopkins University for facilitating my study of the Herbert B. Adams papers. Miss Florence E. Blakely of Duke University cooperated in every way she could to provide photocopies of the J. C. C. Newton notes on Adams's lectures. William M. Robarts of Union Theological Seminary aided research by allowing me to see the small collection of Schaff manuscripts housed in New York City. Paul Desjardins, S.J., of Saint Mary's College, Montreal, provided valuable information on both John Shea and Felix Martin. George H. Williams of Harvard Divinity School aided me in searching for evidence regarding Ephraim Emerton's nebulous past. Frederick Arnold and Miss Eleanor Weld of Princeton University's Firestone Library have been repeatedly helpful in locating rare publications and in making them available for study. Edward C. Starr of the American Baptist Historical Society placed the entire Rauschenbusch collection at my disposal. Max Stackhouse, now at Andover

Newton Theological Seminary, allowed me to copy relevant parts of the Fetter lecture notes for my research. Finally, the Rutgers University Research Council granted a fellowship in the summer of 1967 which made possible the acquisition of many works by John G. Shea; it has also provided funds to help defray the expense of publishing this manuscript.

I have benefited from private conferences with several leading scholars in the field of church history. Lefferts A. Loetscher of Princeton Seminary helped greatly in outlining the plan of study, while James H. Nichols of the same institution read several chapters and made suggestions which led to substantial changes in the work. John William Ward, now of Amherst College, helped over a period of years to bring the early sections of the work into their final form. Two of my major professors at Princeton University, Horton M. Davies and George F. Thomas, have influenced my thinking to an extent greater than my ability to thank them. But I am most indebted to John F. Wilson who made invaluable suggestions and criticisms throughout the course of my work, both while a graduate student and in subsequent discussions. One can only hope that the cumulative effect of their comments will have served to improve the chapters which follow.

CHURCH HISTORY
IN THE AGE OF SCIENCE

I &HISTORY
AS A SCIENCE

American universities were the agents that brought new ideas about historical study and writing to this country, and those ideas brought about a revolution in historiography. Increased pressure for relevant education stemming from various segments of society made it necessary for colleges in the United States to expand and adapt themselves to an increasing number of new fields. By the 1870s prominent educational architects were aware that a new age was at hand, an age of industrialization and increasing social complexity that called for leaders better acquainted with scientific theory, improved technology, economics, and the dynamics of social change. Education was believed to be a means of building up a generation of responsible citizens capable of dealing with problems arising in an age of science. The modernized curriculum was adapted to include prominently the subjects of physical science, political science, and social science. In the last quarter of the nineteenth century when scientism reached its peak as a pervasive influence, scholars even spoke of "historical science" and invested that category with emphases, values, and presuppositions that mark it as a distinctive pattern of ideas.

During those years there were at least two working definitions of scientific history, and the scholars who subscribed to them cannot be classified rigidly into a single school.[1] But even with these differences in mind, it is still feasible to discuss them under one heading because all types of scientific historians shared the major categories outlined below. The enthusiasm generated by that new aggregation of practicing historians gave students a sense of mission ordinarily reserved for these embarking on a crusade. One such reminisced that those were years of "great awakening in the American historical world, as effective in its way as was the corresponding awakening already taking place in the field of the natural sciences. It was a time of exhilaration

1. W. Stull Holt, "The Idea of Scientific History in America," *Journal of the History of Ideas* 1 (June 1940) : 352–62.

and almost religious fervor among the younger scholars, who saw new spheres of opportunity opening before them. . . ."[2] It will be useful to compare the dominant ideas clustered around the general term, "scientific history," with current theological approaches to historical material. Eventually the former triumphed, and the submergence of the latter is proper subject for a chapter in post–Civil War American intellectual history.

Previous to the emergence of scientific historians in the United States there were two general attitudes about the proper mode of writing history. The more popular of the two was basically literary and was practiced by such luminaries as George Bancroft, Francis Parkman, and William Prescott. They all worked on the principle that re-creation of the past required sympathetic imagination and genuine literary skill. Each took pains to create an emotional relationship with past events, to engage readers with the idea of participating in a continuing historical drama and to cause them to "imagine [an earlier epoch] in its former wholeness and the life that it contained." In such literary ventures they usually made a superficial distinction between their own work and what they called "historical romance," but, despite their fidelity to documents, they admired and emulated no author more than Sir Walter Scott.[3] Of course, historians of that persuasion, who formed what we may call the "romantic school," did not avoid hard work in archives nor did they knowingly falsify the record. Several became distinguished for their conscientious sifting of documentary materials, but too often strict accuracy and careful judgment were sacrificed to style. The key element to good history for them was lively and colorful narrative, and thus history was ultimately defined as a literary art.[4] In addition to emphasizing artistic qualifications, the romantic historian also judged the past in the light of vague, though widely held, convictions about historical progress. Writers like Bancroft believed in a "dynamic Providence whose infinite wisdom has established the laws of the moral world and controlled the direction of history. . . . Every event . . . re-

2. Charles M. Andrews, "These Forty Years," *American Historical Review* 30 (January 1925): 233–34.
3. David Levin, *History as Romantic Art: Bancroft, Prescott, Motley, and Parkman* (Stanford: Stanford University Press, 1959), pp. 8, 11.
4. John S. Bassett, *The Middle Group of American Historians* (New York: Macmillan Co., 1917), pp. 220–21.

flected one of these laws, and . . . there was an essential harmony among the separate incidents of history. History was the unfolding of a vast, Providential plan. . . ."[5] It was the duty of romantic historians to employ their literary ability in arranging the apparently disconnected events into their "essential harmony" with the guiding principles of the "Providential plan" for civilization. Fundamental themes like the promise of inevitable progress for those endowed with natural goodness, the right of national self-determination and America's destiny as leader of those free nations, the theory of Teutonic superiority and the value of representative, archetypical figures in historical movements—all figured heavily in their narratives.[6]

Concurrent with that popular literary school of writers there developed a point of view defining historical activity much more narrowly. This latter contingent restricted its activities because adherents were skeptical of their capacity for sympathetic understanding of bygone ages and critical of deriving unlimited information from the few surviving documents.[7] So their main concern for collecting and arranging in natural order as much material about the past as possible was based on the assumption that no later spokesman could measure up to eyewitnesses and no interpretation could equal the unembellished reproduction of authentic records.

Though the romantic historian maintained some popularity until the end of the century (in part because of the longevity of the principal writers) an increased reliance on the critical use of documentary evidence heralded the decline of romanticism as early as the 1850s. Although the builders of archives did not share all the ideas that characterized scientific historians, they were similar to the later group in the basic respect for objective facts as "the most accurate, dependable and valuable form of knowledge available to man."[8] The irrefutable, dispassionate character of primary source materials carried such weight with this second group of historians, whom we may call "archivists," that they became reluctant to interject any private observations at all. Jared Sparks, Peter Force, and Edmund B. O'Cal-

5. In Levin, *History as Romantic Art*, pp. 25–26.
6. Ibid., p. 87.
7. Bassett, *Middle Group*, p. 315.
8. Stow Persons, *American Minds: A History of Ideas* (New York: Henry Holt & Co., 1958), pp. 221–22.

laghan restricted themselves to critical selections of data, publishing them in large volumes compiled along thematic or chronological lines. Their work never suggested the free character portraits or striking national dramas which were the staple features of romantic writing.[9]

It is important to notice that the crucial difference between romanticists and archivists did not involve questions about interpreting documents in the light of various political ideals. The deciding factor was whether one *ought* to interpret documentary evidence freely under any circumstances. The romanticists felt justified in surveying source material and then producing narratives which glorified heroic contests, excoriated deceit and tyranny, or lauded the democratic process. The archivists, on the other hand, were convinced that the canons of reliable history prevented them from taking such liberties. Thus Bancroft's history of the United States was considered poor writing not because it was written from a liberal viewpoint and "voted for Jackson," but because it presumed to vote at all. Archivists criticized romanticists for going too far beyond what the evidence would allow, but they did not try to supply a more subdued discussion of those same themes strictly within bounds of the record. The important point is that they considered it illegitimate to move beyond, read into, or extrapolate from the pristine documents themselves.

The development of the new universities in the United States held promise that the latest learning and best procedures would be brought to bear on problems facing contemporary society. The first American institution devoted primarily to graduate instruction, as distinguished from the more prosaic aims of college curricula, was the Johns Hopkins University which opened in 1876. Daniel Coit Gilman, its first president, aided by a far-sighted board of trustees, created a vigorous institution which pioneered in several new educational fields for a crucial decade.[10] Hopkins' special quality lay in its attempt "to bring together a competent corps of professors . . . teachers in the largest sense . . . to add something by their writings and discoveries

9. John Higham, Leonard Krieger, and Felix Gilbert, eds., *History* (Englewood Cliffs, N.J.: Prentice-Hall, 1965), p. 94.

10. See for example the speech of Charles W. Eliot at the twenty-fifth anniversary of Johns Hopkins University in which he acknowledges that leadership, in Fabian Franklin, *The Life of Daniel Coit Gilman* (New York: Dodd, Mead & Co., 1910), p. 389.

to the world's stock of literature and science."[11] That quality tended to make Johns Hopkins and those patterned after it places of new learning and champions of a dual purpose which strove, in the words of Gilman, for "the advancement of individual scholars who by their excellence will advance the sciences they pursue, and society where they dwell."[12] Students in the new university setting sought to get beyond the traditional stock of information and to advance scientific truth, while concurrently professors who had shown an ability to investigate and discover new truths were appointed to posts of intellectual leadership. Their responsibilities as lecturers were modest enough to permit research, and the authorized subject matter was exciting enough to challenge all participants to do their best work.[13] The keynotes were innovation, discovery, and breakthrough. That attitude was put more succinctly by Andrew D. White, first president of Cornell, when he said his university was intended "to afford an asylum for Science—where truth shall be sought for truth's sake, where it shall not be the main purpose of the Faculty to stretch or cut sciences exactly to fit 'Revealed Religion.' "[14]

While attention to history had increased along with the general concern for higher education before the Civil War, not until the 1880s were courses in history developed within American colleges. "One would naturally suppose, remarked Charles W. Eliot, president of Harvard after 1869, "that the history of the United States and England, at least, would hold an important place in the programmes of American schools. . . ." But far from holding a significant position in the schools, history was hardly considered at all. Eliot's survey in the early 1880s showed that "the great majority [of colleges had] . . . no requirement in history for admission, and [employed] no

11. A statement made by one of the original trustees, G. W. Brown, in Hugh Hawkins, *Pioneer: A History of the Johns Hopkins University, 1874–1889* (Ithaca: Cornell University Press, 1960), p. 6.

12. In W. Carson Ryan, *Studies in Early Graduate Education,* Bulletin 30 (New York: Carnegie Foundation for the Advancement of Teaching, 1939), p. 28; see also pages 30–32 for considerations of the social utility of advanced education.

13. Daniel C. Gilman, "The Johns Hopkins University, 1876–1891," *Johns Hopkins University Studies in Historical and Political Science,* 9th ser. 3–4 (1891): 208–9 (hereafter cited as *JHUS*).

14. In Carl L. Becker, *Cornell University: Founders and the Founding* (Ithaca: Cornell University Press, 1943), p. 156.

teacher of history whatever."[15] Similarly, Andrew White pointed out that if anyone wished to acquire a historical understanding of events as recent as the Civil War, he was obliged to travel to Paris or Berlin and consult with scholars there.[16] In 1880 there were no more than eleven professors of history in American colleges, but given the monumental lethargy toward introducing historical studies, that achievement must have seemed quite heartening.

One notable result of the emerging university ethos was a gradual identification of the historiographical enterprise with professional status and its procedural norms with scientific standards. As professors of history gradually assumed a secure place in universities, they complied with the expectation of original investigation and the subsequent publication of findings. Earlier in the century histories had been produced by clergymen, judges, or men of independent means who devoted either their leisure to historical pursuits or their total energies to the production of historical literature. But in the 1870s and 1880s it became increasingly the case that historians occupied professional chairs and university regulars virtually monopolized the published results of historical inquiry. Such eminent editors and writers as Herbert Baxter Adams, Moses Coit Tyler, and Charles Kendall Adams influenced the trend and set precedents for later professional historians. They also created a new kind of student: one who was sufficiently well informed to teach history and who had, at the same time, mastered the new research techniques well enough to write history in the new genre.

Historical study slowly won a place within an educational system traditionally based on classical languages, but the factors contributing to an appreciation of the utility of history by a mercantile society have not been adequately identified. New ideas about the methodological approach to historical materials are relatively easy to identify: they were directly influenced by principles championed within universities and by the general acceptance of scientific standards of excellence. As history came to be recognized as a legitimate part of university curricula, and as the universities became identified as citadels of

15. Charles W. Eliot, "What is a Liberal Education?" *Century Magazine* 28 (June 1884) : 207.

16. Andrew D. White, "Sanitary Science and Public Instruction," *Popular Science Monthly* (February 1874), p. 421.

science (thus committed to explicit norms regarding research and accuracy), the result was a true renaissance of historiography. Some observers of that renaissance, noting that historical studies were shaped according to scientific criteria, have concluded that the problems faced by historians and the solutions they proposed were not intellectual but rather institutional in nature. In this view historians are thought to have appropriated scientific terminology in order to vindicate their profession and place it on a par with the natural sciences. The adoption of new linguistic patterns did not seem to indicate that historians were actually trying to practice their craft with methods and values much different from their predecessors.[17] But such a viewpoint does not do justice to the thinking of the historians themselves or understand the sincerity with which they sought scientific credentials. The period was one in which the aims and methods of historical study changed from romanticism and antiquarianism to research interests the new historians considered more accurate and more relevant to the nation's cultural heritage. The medium in which one may see those ideas at work was both a pedagogical device and a research technique: the history seminar.

SEMINARS AND THE HISTORICAL LABORATORY

It was easier to justify using the newly imported seminar as a method of instruction than it had been to defend the study of history as a serious academic discipline. The seminar—or "seminary" as it was sometimes clumsily transliterated from the Latin *seminarium*—was readily accepted because of prestige already gained through European usage. The ideal seminar was both a technical device and a method designed to help raw graduate students sharpen their analytical acuity by probing, assessing, and comparing notes on primary source material. Seminars provided a setting in which professors and apprentices might thoroughly investigate topics, destroy misconceptions, revise weak hypotheses, and arrive at definitive interpretations. Such goals

17. J. H. Randall, Jr., and George Haines IV, "Controlling Assumptions in the Practice of American Historians," *Theory and Practice in Historical Study: A Report of the Committee on Historiography,* Bulletin 54 (New York: Social Science Research Council, 1946), p. 25. Another discussion that sheds more light on the beginnings of these ideas is by Donald E. Emerson, "Hildreth, Draper, and 'Scientific History,' " in *Historiography and Urbanization: Essays in Honor of W. Stull Holt,* ed. Eric Goldman (Baltimore: Johns Hopkins Press, 1914), pp. 139–70.

presupposed unprecedented criteria for accuracy, thoroughness, caution in statement, and solid documentation. We can understand how significant a departure scientific historians were in American historiography when we see that their methodological approach in seminars "was deliberately modeled after the laboratory approach of the natural sciences. Research was to begin with the detailed examination of physical objects that could be measured, weighed, analyzed, and compared, and thus humanistic and social studies were to become 'scientific.' "[18] Those strictures produced skilled researchers, and their attachment to seminar training has made it almost a prerequisite in the education of new historians.

The historical *seminarium* in continental universities had originally stemmed from philological investigations which, in turn, had derived from ecclesiastical pedagogy. The old scholastic method of advancing philosophical inquiry by disputing original theses provided a basic framework for investigating new areas of study whenever they came into their own. Around 1830 Leopold von Ranke, who had been trained chiefly in philological seminars at Leipzig, began applying that method to historical topics. Those first history seminars at Berlin, which Ranke called *exercitationes historicae,* began as private sessions with a few advanced students. As they scrutinized the medieval documents which constituted his private library, Ranke explored not only various subjects, he drilled his students in the exacting methods of analyzing sources and showed them how to evaluate the integrity of fragmentary evidence. Those modest beginnings were crucial in establishing a new school of German historiography.[19]

American historians of the scientific school revered Ranke as their patriarch and the exemplar of their craft. Herbert B. Adams spoke for them all when he described the German master as

the best type of the truly scientific historian, for his principle was to tell things exactly as they occurred. He held strictly to the facts in the case. He did not attempt to preach a sermon, or point to a moral, or adorn a tale, but simply to tell the truth as he understood it. He did not believe it the historian's duty to point out divine providence in human history.

18. Jurgen Herbst, *The German Historical School in American Scholarship: A Study in the Transfer of Culture* (Ithaca: Cornell University Press, 1965), p. 37.
19. For a good discussion of early German seminars, see Herbert B. Adams, "Seminary Libraries and University Extension," *JHUS* 5 (1887): 443–44.

. . . Without presuming to be a moral censor, Ranke endeavored to bring historical truth in all its purity before the eyes of the world and to avoid . . . false coloring.[20]

The significance of Adams's statement lies in its indicating more about the values and ideals of American historians than about Ranke himself. Most scientific historians ignored the ultimate philosophical aims of Ranke's approach and concentrated entirely on the masterful analysis to which he subjected historical documents.[21] Thus they appropriated only part of Ranke to support their own conceptions of what constituted proper historical research.[22]

By the 1860s most major German universities sponsored history seminars, and American students who traveled to the land of *Geisteswissenschaft* for further preparation in historical or political science inevitably confronted the new method of study. Several men who influenced thinking about the new science of historical research in the United States were trained in German seminars and afterward paid tribute to their academic mentors.

Charles Kendall Adams was one such scholar who illustrates the influence of German seminars in the United States. As professor of history at the University of Michigan, he traveled to Europe in 1867 and spent an eighteen-month sabbatical attending lectures at Leipzig, Munich, Heidelberg, and Berlin. After learning all he could about the methods of research and instruction in those institutions, he returned to Michigan and put his newly acquired techniques to work, frankly admitting their German parentage: "In 1869 I introduced the seminary method, bringing it from Germany, and putting my classes into the work of investigation. So far as I know this was about the first . . . historical seminary in the United States."[23] "Farmer

20. Herbert B. Adams, "Is History Past Politics?" *JHUS*, 13th ser. (1894), pp. 77–78.

21. An excellent study of both aspects of Ranke's thought can be found in Georg G. Iggers, "The Image of Ranke in American and German Historical Thought," *History and Theory* 2 (1962): 18 and 30.

22. For a continuation of that discussion, see Georg G. Iggers, "The Dissolution of German Historicism," in *Ideas in History: Essays Presented to Louis Gottschalk by His Former Students*, ed. Richard Herr and Harold T. Parker (Durham, N.C.: Duke University Press, 1965), pp. 288–90.

23. Letter from Charles K. Adams to Herbert B. Adams, 9 February 1886, in W. Stull Holt, ed., "Historical Scholarship in the United States, 1876–1901: As Revealed in the Correspondence of Herbert B. Adams," *JHUS*, 56th ser. (1938), p. 79. For corroborative chronology see Charles Adams's presidential address,

Adams" quietly began a movement that would demonstrate its scholarly value to most places of higher learning. He instituted a special class for studying topics in English constitutional history, ranging from the Saxon Witenagemot to the Reform Bill of 1832. Students in the senior class, attending the seminar in addition to a full load of regular courses, investigated primary sources and compared them to interpretations offered by previously accepted authorities in the field. Each seminar participant was required to prepare a weekly assignment consisting of an extensive essay and a written critique of another student's term paper.[24]

In 1879 Moses Coit Tyler followed the example of his colleague, Charles K. Adams, and began Michigan's second seminar.[25] His procedure also seems to have been limited to reading primary sources rather than predigested interpretations because he thought such a method of instruction could prove to be a better means of acquainting students with literary masterpieces. In 1881 he introduced the seminar technique to Cornell, changed the focus of his interests from literary to historical analysis and while at Ithaca directed investigations in American history for almost twenty years.

If the earliest history seminar in the United States was conducted by Charles K. Adams in 1869, then Henry Adams's seminar at Harvard in 1874 was the first based on independent work for graduate students. Though he had begun undergraduate seminars as early as 1871, by 1874 students like Edward Channing, J. L. Laughlin, and Henry Cabot Lodge had congregated around Adams, and together they began reading documents with the avowed purpose of producing original work in medieval history. One of those graduate students

"Recent Historical Work in the Colleges and Universities of Europe and America," *Papers of the American Historical Association* 4 (1890): 45–46 (hereafter cited as *Papers of the AHA*). Adams was correct in thinking that his seminar was the first offered *in history;* the first seminar of any kind was given at Harvard in 1831 by Charles Beck, a German-born classicist. His plans were well-considered, but ill-timed for American education. See Richard J. Storr, *The Beginnings of Graduate Education in America* (Chicago: University of Chicago Press, 1953), pp. 25–28.

24. Charles F. Smith, *Charles Kendall Adams: A Life-Sketch* (Madison: University of Wisconsin Press, 1924), pp. 14–15.

25. Howard M. Jones, *The Life of Moses Coit Tyler* (Ann Arbor: University of Michigan Press, 1933), p. 327. This particular piece of evidence derives from an unpublished dissertation written by T. E. Casady, a work that contributes substantially to Jones's finished product. The work is relevant here because Casady used one of Tyler's commonplace books and directly contradicted accepted notions about Tyler's work at Michigan.

described an evening at the Adams house: "We searched the early German codes of the Visigoths, Burgundians, and Salian Franks for the first glimmerings of the institutions which through the Normans and Anglo-Saxons formed the basis of English, and . . . American legal development. . . . We read and searched many times the whole collection of Anglo-Saxon laws, and plowed through twenty-five thousand pages of charters and capitularies in mediaeval Latin."[26] In 1876 the best products of that research were compiled in a volume entitled *Essays in Anglo-Saxon Law.* As the first publication based directly on graduate historical investigations, it proved that American professors and students could utilize the seminar method and produce valuable historical writing.

Three men at Michigan, Cornell, and Harvard had introduced seminars to students of history in this country, but Herbert Baxter Adams was unquestionably the most influential figure who promulgated the ideals of scientific historical method in late nineteenth-century America.[27] In 1876 he completed a two-year course of study at the University of Heidelberg and received a Ph.D. degree from the faculty of political science; that same year he received a fellowship in history at the Johns Hopkins University. His valuable training in seminars conducted by Johann K. Bluntschli influenced the composition and objectives of his seminars at Johns Hopkins and consequently much of the advanced historical study pursued in American universities. Even before he came to Baltimore, Adams had made it clear he would emphasize original work and strive to establish a new school for research in American archives: "It is my aim to pursue historical researches and to contribute something to Political Science. I would like to write the History of American Political Literature and to help organize the Sources of American History."[28] During the ensuing twenty-five years Adams assumed command of

26. J. L. Laughlin, "Some Recollections of Henry Adams," *Scribner's Magazine* 69 (May 1921): 580.

27. See for example letters to Adams from J. K. Hosmer (1888) and C. K. Adams (1891) acknowledging him as the "director and superintendent of historical work," in Holt, "Historical Scholarship," pp. 110, 147. Another accurate appraisal can be found in James A. Woodburn, "Promotion of Historical Study in America following the Civil War," *Journal of the Illinois State Historical Society* 15 (April–July 1922): 452.

28. Letter from H. B. Adams to President Gilman, dated Heidelberg, 21 May 1876, in Holt, "Historical Scholarship," pp. 31–32.

the department, developed its curriculum, issued (beginning in 1882) the *Johns Hopkins University Studies in Historical and Political Science,* and helped to organize the American Historical Association in 1884; as its secretary, he worked to obtain its national charter in 1889. He was even more influential in his personal contacts with students; more than any other historian of his day Adams was concerned with training students in the new methods of historical investigation and imbuing them with the ideas and characteristics requisite for producing scientific history.[29] After his men had become sufficiently grounded in scientific method, Adams used his influence to place them in important educational centers. His policy of extending what he called a Johns Hopkins "colonial system"[30] through the major universities is another indication of Adams's zeal for propagating the new historical science. In his pedagogical capacity, his writings on the science of history, and his editorial work in the two largest historical periodicals, Herbert Adams helped define and publicize current thinking about scientific history.

The seminar was an integral factor in the emergence of scientific history, but it did not, of itself, embody a specific definition of "science." Seminars were the chief means of stressing independent research and critical use of documentary evidence, but ideas regarding the way in which one actually conducted a scientific study of history were brought to seminars by the professors themselves. The seminar atmosphere was used by professors to instill what they considered a properly scientific attitude in their students; after seminar training they could be expected to proceed with their own analyses of source materials. Adams expressed the new viewpoint in these words: "Historically speaking, the seminary was a nursery of theology and a training school for seminary priests. . . . The seminary is still a training-school for doctors of philosophy, but it has evolved from a nursery of dogma into a laboratory of scientific truth."[31] The univer-

29. Adams confided to a friend that he chose the life of an educator and administrator rather than a more austere and scholarly one because he thought he could be more useful in the former capacity. See John F. Jameson, "The American Historical Association, 1884–1909," *American Historical Review* 15 (October 1909) : 5.

30. The phrase was coined by Adams himself and can be found in his bulletin, "The College of William and Mary," *Circulars of Information of the Bureau of Education,* no. 1 (1887), p. 74.

31. Herbert B. Adams, "New Methods of Study in History," *JHUS,* 2d ser. 1–2 (January–February 1884) : 64. See also Laurence R. Veysey, *The Emergence of*

sity emphasis on research and seminar methods provided a setting that promoted the growth of scientific history, but they did not fundamentally affect its origination or specify its content. The origin of those specific ideas can be viewed as personal achievements which the professional historians, who were mostly recipients of European training, were able to synthesize within themselves. The similar ideological content and combined impact are discernible as a distinctive pattern of thought, and present historians can construct a comprehensive discussion of their general attitudes and controlling assumptions. The following discussion, then, affords a composite description of ideas which hold intrinsic interest. At the same time it outlines a group of ideas and attitudes which seriously threatened and eventually conquered theological ideas prevalent in the writing of church history at that time.

THE ATTITUDES AND IDEAS OF SCIENTIFIC HISTORY

The ideas which men have attached to the general concept of "scientific truth" have varied and will continue to change because of epistemological innovations. During the latter half of the nineteenth century many Americans shared a common conviction that scientific accuracy was based on the direct observation of concrete evidence and on an impersonal process of inductive reasoning from that data. In describing how scientific evidence had outstripped earlier speculation about the natural world, Daniel C. Gilman reflected equally well the pride his generation felt in its high intellectual standards and the clarity it brought to man's problems: "It seems as if the human race, after years of groping, had at length, in these modern days, arrived at the right method of investigating the laws of nature. Abandoning authority as decisive respecting the material world, and resorting to observation, experiment, and mathematical investigation . . . [we] have been interpreting the laws of the Creator by methods which will endure, and thus [we] have come upon results of highest value to mankind."[32] In an era when scientific

---

the American University (Chicago: University of Chicago Press, 1965), pp. 153–56, for another mention of early seminars and a curious interpretation of Herbert Adams.

32. Gilman's speech was made at the dedication of Sibley Hall, a science building at Cornell; see W. P. Rogers, Andrew D. White and the Modern University (Ithaca: Cornell University Press, 1942), p. 79.

knowledge was becoming increasingly normative in both society and universities, it is not unnatural that a number of American historians became convinced that the criteria of scientific truth ought to apply to their research and writing. They adopted scientific attitudes and implemented them in graduate seminars, convinced that they were laying a sure foundation for their craft. Such strong convictions upheld their insistence that it was "of as much consequence to teach a young person *how* to study history as to teach him history itself."[33] With their method safely grounded in what they considered to be unimpeachable standards of accuracy and reliability, they took upon themselves the imposing task of winnowing the false from the true in previous historical narratives. The seminar method would, they hoped, serve to train up a generation of scientific historians and thus place serious thinkers on a new level of historical understanding.

Of all the conceptions individual historians held regarding their work, there were three paradigms that distinguished them from earlier investigative patterns and which permit us to think of them as comprising a distinctive consensus regarding historical research. That aggregation of scholars shared in a general way three values: an iconoclastic attitude, an emphasis on objective empiricism, and a naturalistic bias. The holders of those ideals, both intellectual and temperamental predilections, began with a determination to write the whole of history over again, accepting nothing on the mere authority of past interpreters. As one observer has described the unforgiving zeal of iconoclasts, those historians wanted to "throw overboard the sanctions of authority, ancient prejudices and the hallowed rationalizations of a priori philosophy, and to embrace the method of science."[34] In rewriting history they tried to be guided by empirical evidence alone, and that self-imposed stricture isolated a second common characteristic. They thought of scientific knowledge as restricted to the direct observation of concrete phenomena, and since their activity fell within that category, they were confident of transferring empirical procedures to the seminar table. Third, this mode of thinking was similar to other sciences in that it incorporated a naturalistic

33. Herbert B. Adams, "Special Methods of Historical Study," *JHUS*, 2d ser. 1–2 (January–February 1884): 12.

34. Sidney Ratner, "Evolution and the Rise of the Scientific Spirit in America," *Philosophy of Science* 3 (January 1936): 105.

bias. Scientific historians thought of facts as specimens, of investigation as a type of dissection and of libraries as their laboratories. The corollary to such a conception of evidence was a confidence that observable phenomena yielded an adequate explanation of historical questions. Also implicit in that viewpoint was the assumption that there are no unseen causes, no metaphysical entities to be considered, no intangible or mysterious forces at work in history. One recent analysis of the ideas shared by those men has recognized that the scientific historian avoided all entangling alliances with philosophy: "He scorned metaphysics and regarded the problem of historical knowledge as no problem at all. His goal was simply 'applying to the history of Man those methods of investigation which have been found successful in other branches of knowledge'—that is, in the natural sciences."[35] Those three ideals characterized the thinking of every man who considered himself a scientific historian, and they profoundly affected the standards set for writing history in the last quarter of the nineteenth century in the United States, particularly in the field of church history.

Men who viewed history as a scientific endeavor saw their first task as one of revising earlier writings because, from their vantage point, such tomes appeared to be riddled with romantic legend, error, and pious falsehoods. Charles K. Adams expressed the new mood in kindly words when he said, "It is a pity to have to say it, but it is nevertheless true, that many a good historical story, when subjected to the scrutiny of modern criticism, turns out to be little else than a venerable and beloved fiction."[36] Stating the revisionist's position more openly, he said, "This is sometimes called an age of iconoclasm. But rather it is an age in which, for the first time, there has been some general approach to an application of the rules of evidence to

35. H. Stuart Hughes, *History as Art and as Science* (New York: Harper & Row, 1964), pp. 8–9. The quote is taken from Henry T. Buckle, *History of Civilization in England* (London, 1891), 1:227. Jurgen Herbst, *German Historical School*, p. 102, described the attitude in these words: "The 'true' historians had reason to doubt whether 'a new messenger from the Infinite Spirit' could have been deduced from some speculative philosophical system, since they themselves had seen no incontestable evidence of either a guiding Providence or a spiritual messenger."

36. Charles K. Adams, *A Manual of Historical Literature, Comprising Brief Descriptions of the Most Important Histories in England, France and Germany: Together with Practical Suggestions as to Methods and Courses of Historical Study* (New York: Harper & Brothers, 1882), p. 13 (hereafter cited as *Manual*).

the methods of historical research. . . . In short, we question its character, its motive, and the basis on which it rests."[37] Moses C. Tyler gave a more elaborate defense of his determination to conduct independent research, but he embodied the iconoclasm of the new breed of historian in declaring that "every fact of American history for the last century has to be re-examined."[38] In trying to enunciate his group's sense of deliberate independence, Tyler was struck by the similarity between scientific historians and the attitude articulated by Descartes. The old Cartesian maxim still evinced a freshness and defiance that was particularly appealing to this new breed anxious to break away from the dead hand of past procedures. Descartes had said: "When I set forth in the pursuit of truth, I found that the best way was to reject everything I had hitherto conceived, and pluck out all my old opinions, in order that I might lay the foundations fresh."[39]

The year 1892, the four hundredth anniversary of Christopher Columbus's voyage, offered a case in point when several historians of a scientific temper tried to rewrite the history of that fateful journey. Most of the leading spokesmen in the new school produced volumes based on original sources, interpreted "in the spirit of modern criticism." Charles K. Adams made iconoclasm a salient part of his approach, serving notice that "the reader will not go far . . . without perceiving that I have endeavored to emancipate myself from the thraldom of that uncritical admiration in which it has been fashionable to hold the Discoverer, ever since Washington Irving threw over the subject the romantic and bewitching charm of his literary skill. . . . Irving's was not the spirit of modern scholarship. We should seek the truth at whatever hazard."[40] In contrast to uncritical romantic tales, the new historians utilized critically-tested information to get at such questions as the financing of the first voyage, the actual site of the first landing, and the real reasons for Columbus's ignominious return to Granada.[41] Another representative who attempted a critical

37. Ibid.

38. Moses C. Tyler's report in *Christian Union*, 12 March 1873; see also Jones, *Life of Moses Coit Tyler*, p. 153.

39. In Jessica T. Austen, *Moses Coit Tyler, 1835–1900: Selections from His Letters and Diaries* (Garden City: Doubleday, Page and Co., 1911), p. 67.

40. Charles K. Adams, *Christopher Columbus: His Life and Work* (New York: Dodd, Mead & Co., 1892), pp. viii–ix; pages 35, 67, and 85–87 are examples of his sorting legend from fact.

41. Justin Winsor, *Christopher Columbus and How He Received and Imparted the Spirit of Discovery* (Boston: Houghton Mifflin Co., 1892), pp. 214–16.

rewriting of history was Justin Winsor, librarian at Harvard and editor of the *Narrative and Critical History of America,* who was as avowed an iconoclast as the rest and willing to defend his viewpoint against all comers. Winsor said that he intended to "strip off the later accretions" in historical writing which stemmed from "ignorance and sentiment" in order to get at the real men and events. He thought he could write authentic history only if he succeeded in clearing away the "over-soiling" of legend and got down to "hard pan," the fundamental knowledge of historical reality.[42]

It must be emphasized, however, that scientific historians did not aim at a wanton destruction of all earlier research and writing. They sought rather to eliminate unsupported speculation, to clear the air of biased theories and finally to get at the real facts of each case. Their attitude of Cartesian iconoclasm was simply a preliminary step to new constructions. The new breed of historian felt that only his procedures were capable of producing a solid history grounded in hard facts, and so destructive criticism of previous writing was an unfortunate necessity. Those who pursued the science of history seemed interested not in building on earlier work but in new achievements based on their apparently unerring methodology and on their ability to, in Tyler's ambitious and naïve phrase, "write the whole absolute truth of history."[43]

History seminars, with their demanding labor based on first-hand knowledge of primary sources, were instrumental in propagating a second and more important ideal: objective empiricism. The new generation of historians paid strict deference to inductive principles of reasoning and tried to exclude all the a priori opinions or metaphysical considerations which they thought marred earlier historical explanations. In order to avoid the interpolations found in that era of more genteel historiography, they confined themselves to original sources of information: statutes, diplomatic correspondence, records of debates, log-books, political tracts, sermons, memoirs, private diaries, letters, newspapers, broadsides and account books, to name a few. One popularizer of the new approach, in attempting to explain its reliance on evidence, said that "the historian has not found the true path until he has learned to ransack . . . records of the past

42. Letter from J. Winsor to H. B. Adams, 21 January 1892, in Holt, "Historical Scholarship," p. 176.
43. Jones, *Life of Moses Coit Tyler,* p. 154.

with the same untiring zeal that animates a detective . . . in seeking the . . . evidences of a crime."[44] One modern student of historiography, John Higham, has described this concern for objectivity and empirical verification as one element in a general nineteenth century trend from romanticism toward realism. He characterized the "realist" as one who adopted a more impersonal stance than his predecessor, hoping to obviate the errors implicit in subjective judgments. In elucidating the contrast Higham could have had scientific historians in mind as he said: "The realist avoided identifying himself with his subject. He stood apart from it, observing it from the outside. He did not submerge himself in the mood and feeling that a situation suggested."[45]

Herbert Adams tried to illustrate the strictures of the new empiricism in history by means of a story about a young biologist. When the new instructor arrived on campus, the patriarchal college president asked him if the biology class would begin with a study of great and fundamental principles. The young scientist replied that, far from beginning with a set of a priori principles, the class would start work by dissecting a bushel of clams. Adams used that anecdote to point up the reliance on empirical investigation and inductive reasoning germane to both historical and natural science. "If there is any guiding principle in the study of historical . . . science," he said, "it is 'the way to that which is general is through that which is special.' For beginners in history concrete facts are quite as essential as clams or earthworms for beginners in biology."[46] Moses C. Tyler had begun relying on the same procedure in 1875, a year before Adams arrived at Johns Hopkins. He wrote George Putnam, his publisher, "I mean to do in this life no more hack-work, and no more second-hand work of any sort. Alas I have done eno' already. If I do this work [a projected history of literature in colonial America] I must do it thoroughly and artistically, from knowledge of my own in every case, from a direct study of the *quellen*."[47] He announced in the preface of his *Literary History of the American Revolution* that his work

44. John Fiske, "Old and New Ways of Treating History," in his *Essays: Historical and Literary* (New York: Macmillan Co., 1902), pp. 6–7.
45. Higham et al., *History*, p. 93.
46. Herbert B. Adams, "New Methods of Study in History," *Journal of Social Science* 18 (May 1884): 213.
47. Letter dated 9 August 1875, in Jones, *Life of Moses Coit Tyler*, p. 176.

was the product of a new method because, though some facts in the history of the revolution had been recounted often enough, Tyler understood himself for the first time to be looking at them from a strictly empirical perspective. He was one of "a new breed of American scholars" who avoided all sentiment, especially the well-worn and transparently anti-British bias common to American authors. Thus Tyler was one of the many who began serving notice on superficial and scholarly readers alike that his work had been "freshly rewritten in the light of larger evidence, and under the direction of a more disinterested and a more judicial spirit."[48]

The new breed of American historian was enthusiastic about objectivity and empiricism because he, like most other citizens in the new industrial state, had singular respect for scientific knowledge as the basis for improved social and intellectual standards. Since observable facts were the most accurate and productive avenue to understanding natural events and human activity, historians thought they could contribute to the sciences by keeping their own views to themselves, stifling presuppositions, and concentrating on the facts alone. In contrast to fables and legend on one hand or biased polemics on the other, scientific historians tried self-consciously to limit their writing to the evidence. The goal in theirs as in every other branch of science was dispassionate knowledge, objectively derived and inductively assimilated. Under the influence of that ideal, historians of the scientific frame of mind tried to produce nonpartisan reports by eliminating their own prejudices and avoiding the biases of previous schools of thought. A single example can be used to sum up this attitude about objective empiricism: "History . . . is fast ceasing to be a picture colored to please the eye of the too often partisan writer, and is becoming a mirror which reflects the opinions and acts of its makers, leaving each reader to draw therefrom his own conclusions."[49]

Up to this point the objective empiricism of scientific historians merely reaffirmed the same ideal which had been championed by the archivists, a group from which Adams and his confreres tried to distinguish themselves. The crucial additional factor here is that the

48. Moses C. Tyler, *The Literary History of the American Revolution, 1763–1783*, reprint ed. (New York: Barnes and Noble, 1941), 1:vii.
49. Paul L. Ford, "Bibliography of the American Historical Association," *Papers of the AHA* 4 (1890): 425.

archivists had been more consistent in producing volumes within
the strict rubrics of their methodological approach, while scientific
historians, professing the same standards, tried to bring new questions to empirical data and use them as the basis for a more complex
and realistic historical understanding. In their view, archivists had
been too pedestrian and impervious to the valid interpretations allow-
able by the evidence. Thus in their attempt to bring fresh questions to
old data, objectivity remained a goal imperfectly achieved by the best
of scientific historians. The most obvious flaw in the scientific historian's mixture of theory and practice is that men like Herbert Adams
did in fact have preconceptions, and they read them into the evidence. The most famous example was the "germ theory" which said,
sometimes with evidence to the contrary, that English and then American political customs derived from Germanic and Greek prototypes.
The Teutonic germ, or seed of liberty, found new life in New England soil.[50] The most incisive criticism of that preconception was made
by Charles McLean Andrews who showed, after basing his doctoral
dissertation on a careful study of the early settlements along the
Connecticut River, that the Teutonic theorists relied at every critical
point on superficial similarities for evidence rather than on demonstrable, genetic connections.[51]

Another criticism voiced was that the goal of complete objectivity
was itself a bias which the historian brought to the material. The
more thoughtful practicing historians were less caustic and recognized
that the nature of their activities debarred them from strict equation
with laboratory accuracy. Charles K. Adams sounded a sobering note:

Another limitation of history is in the fact that it cannot have the cer-
tainties of an exact science. . . . This assertion would seem to be too
obvious for demonstration, but for the ingenious theories of writers like
Comte, Buckle, and Spencer.
Historical facts are almost always, perhaps invariably, the result of
heterogeneous causes. Some of these causes are susceptible of examination and analysis; others are not.
Besides the uncertain element of individuality, there is another diffi-

50. Herbert B. Adams, "The Germanic Origin of New England Towns," *JHUS*
1 (1883): 45–78.
51. Charles M. Andrews, "The Theory of the Village Community," *Papers of
the AHA* 4 (1890): 47–61.

culty, often the impossibility, of securing trustworthy and conclusive evidence.

The difficulties in the way of learning the exact truth in regard to the simple affairs of every-day life are often quite insurmountable. Still more inaccessible is the truth in respect to events remote in point of distance or in point of time.[52]

Another characteristic, though not a unique one, of the many historians who appropriated the name of "scientist" was their narrow conception of what constituted proper subjects for historical investigation. Borrowing a phrase from British historian E. A. Freeman[53] (others say from the German scholar J. G. Droysen),[54] Herbert Adams defined the scope of legitimate interests: "History is Past Politics and Politics is Present History." Adams spoke for a circle of scholars wider than the confines of the Johns Hopkins seminar when he observed that "Man is the first postulate of history. He is the beginning and the end of it. Man in the State, Man as a Social Animal, Man living and moving in institutional groups,—this historical conception . . . we of the Johns Hopkins Historical Seminary regard as truly scientific and as practically modern."[55] In almost identical phrasing John W. Burgess of Columbia indicated that his seminars rested on the presupposition that the only historical questions worth considering centered on political activities.[56]

Although the ideal of objective empiricism was imperfectly realized, the fact that it remained a primary goal in the minds of most historians leads to a third common characteristic. Empiricism was attractive because historians thought data obtained by that method gave all the information about a given subject. That frame of reference was based on "naturalistic" values, and there was no room at all for considering the intangible forces of Bancroft's usage or the supernatural agents to which church historians frequently referred. Concrete phenomena—be they earthworms, chemicals or historical

52. C. K. Adams, *Manual*, pp. 4 and 7.
53. H. B. Adams, "Is History Past Politics?," pp. 77–78.
54. Herbst, *German Historical School*, pp. 111–12.
55. H. B. Adams, "Is History Past Politics?," p. 72.
56. John W. Burgess, "Political Science and History," *American Historical Review* 2 (April 1897): 403. For a balanced study of his thought in this regard, see Bert J. Loewenberg, "John William Burgess, the Scientific Method, and the Hegelian Philosophy of History," *Mississippi Valley Historical Review* 42 (December 1955): 490–509.

documents—were accepted as the only reliable sources of information. By 1876 a naturalistic disposition had begun spreading generally throughout the historical discipline, and an almost universal admiration for objective facts had reduced the avenues to truth to that single mode of investigation and discovery perfected by the natural scientists. Since all facts were considered open to the same type of scrutiny and since they alone afforded reliable information, some scientific historians went so far as to assert that it was possible to "reason about life, the soul, and truth, as though one were reasoning about phosphates and square roots."[57] Herbert Adams's graphic description of a scholarly paper illustrates the degree to which such a naturalistic bias could affect the basic pattern of language: "The second paper read at Cambridge was no less characteristic of the economic and biological methods which are influencing some of our younger historians. . . . Dr. Hart traced the course of the late River and Harbor Bill as a biologist would study the life-history of a chick, or a tadpole, or of yellow-fever germs."[58]

Herbert Adams was the epitome of scientific historiography in his own writing and more importantly in his efforts to produce a generation of scientific-minded scholars. He met weekly with graduate students and reviewed documents in European history or the archives of local American institutions. In the process of that training he announced that, "before a student has advanced very far in carrying on his investigations, he will almost inevitably arrive at the conclusion that the historical seminary is to the study of history, what the laboratory is to the study of the natural sciences."[59] Adams communicated to his students convictions regarding not only the nature of "solid facts," but also the reliability of primary sources as the single basis for scientific history. His description of Baltimore seminars as "laboratories where books are treated like mineralogical specimens, passed about from hand to hand, examined and tested," suggests a thoroughgoing naturalism.[60] Historians like Adams thought

57. In E. Samuels, *The Young Henry Adams* (Cambridge, Mass.: Harvard University Press, 1948), p. 211.
58. Herbert B. Adams, "The American Historical Association," *Independent*, 2 June 1887, p. 5.
59. Herbert B. Adams, "On Methods of Teaching History," in *Methods of Teaching History*, ed. G. Stanley Hall (Boston: Ginn, Heath and Co., 1885), p. 176.
60. H. B. Adams, "New Methods of Study in History," *JHUS*, 2d ser. 1–2 (1884): 103. For a similar statement made by another leader of the early AHA,

of themselves as colleagues with chemists and biologists, all sharing
the common task of pushing back the frontiers of knowledge with
the same tools. When the Johns Hopkins seminar inherited a suite of
rooms from the biology department, the latent symbolism was not
lost on Adams:

The influence of the newly acquired environment had, perhaps, some
effect upon the development of the seminary. It began to cultivate . . .
the laboratory method of work and to treat its book collections as materials for laboratory uses. The old tables which had once been used for the
dissection of cats and turtles were planed down, covered with green
baize, and converted into desks for the dissection of government documents and other materials for American institutional history.[61]

Scientific history thus became the goal of Adams and his generation
because they hoped it would furnish information as incontestable as a
naturalist's fossil and as accurate as chemical analysis.

These historians shared a feeling of compatibility or assumed a
psychological fraternity with other scientists, with regard to evidence
defined in a way congruent with scientific investigation and a definition of history coterminous with the study of political and legislative
changes.[62] Since scientific historians favored inductive reasoning and
scorned the metaphysical intonations of earlier writers, one can
readily understand their impatience with contemporary church historians who referred to providential acts in their narratives. At least by
implication they denied the validity of speaking about God in history
on the grounds that they could not see him or identify his actions.
Justin Winsor rejected the prophetic role in no uncertain terms:
"God in history . . . appears to be a noble phrase, but the ways of
Providence are no less inscrutable to the historian than laws of the
natural world that are not understood. What seems providential in
history is but the reflex of the mind that contemplates it, and depends
upon the training and sympathies of that mind. . . ."[63]

---

see C. K. Adams's letter to M. C. Tyler dated 9 June 1883, in C. F. Smith,
Charles Kendall Adams, p. 16.
    61. H. B. Adams, "Seminary Libraries and University Extension," p. 455.
    62. C. K. Adams, *Manual*, p. 16; see also Herbert B. Adams, "The Study and
Teaching of History." *Chautauqua Assembly Herald*, 10 August 1897.
    63. Justin Winsor, "The Perils of Historical Narrative," *Atlantic Monthly* 66
(September 1890): 294.

For some years Herbert Adams taught a course in church history at Johns Hopkins, and some evidence remains allowing us to see how he treated scientifically a subject "usually monopolized by theological seminaries." Instead of speaking about the truth of doctrines or discerning the traces of God's agency, Adams viewed the church as "the institutional exponent of Christian civilization," a human phenomenon which all men could scrutinize and understand.[64] The general skepticism regarding ecclesiastical claims was best expressed by Andrew D. White who quipped, "If the Divine guidance of the Church is such a sham that it can be dragged into a professional squabble, and the pope made the tool of a faction in bringing about a most disastrous condemnation of a proven truth, how does the Church differ from any human organization sunk into decrepitude, managed by simpletons and controlled by schemers?"[65]

Adams's treatment of church history was probably not grounded in an irreverence of that magnitude, but a list of his study topics shows how true he was to his fundamental conception of history as politics. Questions covered in his course included the influence of Jewish ceremonial on the Christian Church, the influence of Roman institutions on church structure, the clergy and laymen, the office of patriarch, metropolitan centers of church life, origin of the papacy, growth of ecclesiastical constitutions, extension of church authority into England, conversion of the Germans, the international position of the Holy Roman Empire, points of conflict between empire and papacy, and the great councils of the fifteenth century.[66] One of Adams's students reported that he used the Bible in the course not to determine what one should believe, but only as a source for investigating the laws, manners, and customs of a Mediterranean society during the first Christian century.[67] A rare set of notes taken in one of Adams's lecture sessions shows that he made everyone aware of the difference between his interests as a detached, scientific observer

---

64. Herbert B. Adams, "The Teaching of History," *Annual Report of the American Historical Association for the Year 1897* (Washington, D.C.: Government Printing Office, 1898), 1:251.

65. A. D. White, *A History of the Warfare of Science with Theology in Christendom* (New York: D. Appleton and Co., 1876), p. 57.

66. In *JHUS,* 2d ser. 1–2 (1884): 46–47.

67. F. L. Riley, "Study of Church History at the Johns Hopkins University," *Baptist Record,* 19 April 1894.

and those of theologians or theologically oriented church historians.[68] Except for minimal indications, there is no possibility of direct comparison between scientific and theological studies made of the same body of material. Contrasts must be made, therefore, by viewing both schools at work within their respective fields of interest.

The scientific historians, with their iconoclasm, their alleged reliance on objective empiricism and their materialistic or naturalistic bias, set the tone for respectable historiography in the last quarter of the nineteenth century. In subsequent chapters we shall study various ideas regarding the study of church history and view the ways in which they responded to the overpowering emphasis on science and its strictures. Before we move to those students of ecclesiastical history, some attention to the role of historical societies is in order to help understand how scientific historiography came into national prominence.

THE FOUNDATION OF THE AMERICAN HISTORICAL ASSOCIATION

By the early 1880s individual historians began to admit the impossibility of analyzing a vast range of source materials with the thoroughness they had learned to expect and still write universal histories.

They were sure of their methodology and worked constantly to fill many of the "long gaps of frightful ignorance"[69] confronting them, but the problems were too manifold and the demands too rigorous to permit writing on an extensive scale. The issue was not a lack of material but lack of time to produce accurate and detailed studies of all the questions involved in a broad field of inquiry. It became necessary to divide tasks into more manageable sections and cooperate with colleagues in piecing together a composite survey; thus a greater degree of specialization and cooperation characterized the general approach to studies. Many felt the need for an association of historical scholars that could serve as a forum for discussing new projects and for reporting the outcome of projects already completed. Herbert Adams, one of the most important figures behind the founding of the American Historical Association, gave the rationale for a new his-

68. "Modern Politics," pp. 8, 12, 31, 54, 57, and "Political Reformers," pp. 1, 8, 33–34, 35–36, 41, J. C. C. Newton Papers, Duke University, Durham, N.C.
69. In Samuels, *Young Henry Adams*, p. 249.

torical organization: "Fellowship in Science will always afford the individual greater strength than he can acquire alone. A connection with learned societies, special libraries, special journals, is highly advantageous. . . . The organization of scientific results are [*sic*] very important for American students, who wish to advance the cause of special education in this country, and thereby the cause of American Science."[70] Adams joined with men like Charles K. Adams, Moses C. Tyler, and Justin Winsor to found an association for scientific historians that would "afford a vantage-ground for the upbuilding of Science, [work] for the extension of new methods in America, [and] for the local establishment of new ideas."[71] That association promised to be not only a forum in which the latest projects could be discussed and results published; it could also be utilized to advertise the virtues of the new scientific methodology and encourage others to adopt its precepts.

The American Historical Association was officially organized on September 9, 1884, becoming the first historical society to be both imaginative in outlook and professional in scope. The first historical organization of any kind, the Massachusetts Historical Society, had been founded in 1791 for quite a different reason: to preserve "books, pamphlets, manuscripts and records" in order to rescue "the true history of this country from the ravages of time and the effects of ignorance and neglect."[72] More than sixty local and state historical societies were formed before the Civil War, but all of them had essentially the same antiquarian interest in preserving documents for their own sake. Only one large association could claim to be a true predecessor of the AHA. In 1836 an "American Historical Society" was formed in Washington, D.C., and informal meetings were occasionally held in the House of Representatives. Under the guidance of John Quincy Adams, its first president, and Peter Force, its most active member, materials on colonial history were collected to serve as the nucleus of an "American Archives."[73] The society wished to

70. Herbert B. Adams, "Co-operation in University Work," *JHUS* 1 (1883): 97; see also his "New Methods of Study in History," p. 222.

71. H. B. Adams, "Co-operation in University Work," p. 87.

72. Taken from the constitution of the Massachusetts Historical Society; in John F. Jameson, *The History of Historical Societies* (Savannah, Georgia: Morning News Print, 1914), p. 16.

73. H. B. Adams's discussion of this earlier group can be found in *Papers of the AHA* 1 (1885): 34–35.

believe it was a national organization, but it had never been more than a local club with great intentions; the AHA was justified in considering itself the first society that received support across state and sectional lines. The AHA was an innovation also in the sense that it actively supported the production of original essays and the application of new insights to familiar bodies of material. And though they did not discourage the compilation and maintenance of archives, the interests and emphases of scientific historians in the AHA were sufficiently different to make archivists feel outmoded.[74]

Justin Winsor, spokesman at the preliminary business meeting, greeted those who had convened at Saratoga, New York, to found a new professional society. His words left few doubts as to the controlling historiographical ideas which his audience shared: "We have come, gentlemen, to organize a new society, and fill a new field. . . . We are drawn together because we believe there is a new spirit of research abroad,—a spirit which emulates the laboratory work of the naturalists, using that word in its broadest sense. This spirit requires for its sustenance mutual recognition and suggestion among its devotees."[75] Those devotees had assembled in answer to a circular letter summoning all "professors, teachers, specialists, and others interested in the advancement of history in this country," to found an organization designed to facilitate "the exchange of ideas and the . . . discussion of methods and original papers."[76]

It is almost a truism to state that the AHA stimulated greater effort in historical studies. Its annual reports and volumes of documents were a boon to further research, and its successful work in preserving manuscripts throughout the nation articulated a growing interest in historical studies in the United States. The AHA came into being because Americans had begun showing a preference for the even-tempered judgments of historical understanding, and the association furthered that interest through its efforts. Herbert Adams, secretary of the national organization for its first fifteen years, was proud of its success because he considered the influence of its wide membership another means of realizing the "present possibilities for

74. See "A New Historical Movement," *Nation*, 18 September 1884, p. 240. No author is indicated, but the language and general tone of the article suggest that it was Herbert Adams.
75. Winsor's speech can be found in *Papers of the AHA* I (1885): 11.
76. Ibid., pp. 5–6.

the real progress of historic and economic science . . . and . . . [promoting] the development of a generation of economists and practical historians. . . ."[77] The AHA was far and away the largest and most vigorous historical organization in the country, and the standards it publicized and practiced had significant effect on historians in every field of inquiry.

Thus the general attitudes and ideas of the scientific historians set the standards for acceptable historical workmanship during this era. Against that background the following study concentrates on church historians of the period. An analysis of the major interests and ideas of the next two individuals indicate how theologically minded historians subscribed to methodological philosophies and interpretational patterns that differed markedly from the scientific stamp of mind outlined above. But as the nineteenth century drew to a close, the conviction grew among professional historians that history sensitive to theological implications contrasted unfavorably with history based on the model of scientific analysis. And the remaining five chapters consider the ideas of men who can best be understood within the context provided by a spectrum ranging from the scientific history of Herbert Adams to the pietistic church history of Philip Schaff.

77. H. B. Adams, "Co-operation in University Work," p. 89.

2 ✴CHURCH HISTORY AS A THEOLOGICAL DISCIPLINE

Beginning in 1844 the modest efforts Americans had expended in the area of church historiography received great impetus through the work of a single man, Philip Schaff. He brought new ideas about the church and its historical importance to the United States and gave fresh encouragement to studies of earlier ecclesiastical periods. Schaff's new ideas alienated many church officials at first, but through the 1850s and 1860s his emphasis on the intellectual value and practical usefulness of church history gradually found a positive reception among a number of the younger intelligentsia. During the last two decades of his life Schaff was able to publish in finished form much of his extensive research. Favorable response on both sides of the Atlantic was such that American church historiography was acknowledged as having emerged as a serious discipline, and its chief spokesman as a leader among the world's scholars.

In 1843 the American branch of the German Reformed Church had sent two of its clergymen to Berlin on a serious mission. The delegates from Pennsylvania wished to secure the services of a professor whose German ideas and ethnic loyalties would forge a strong link in the chain binding their churches to the fatherland. But the individual whom they eventually retained to teach at Mercersburg was not especially suited to achieve those objectives. Their original intention had been to secure the services of some eloquent court preacher or a famous theologian.[1] Failing in that, however, the emissaries consulted the opinions of several leading professors, and enthusiastic recommendations from all sides led them to approach a young *privat-dozent* who had a promising future in theological studies. So in that same year Philip Schaff accepted the professorship of church history and biblical literature at a relatively obscure institu-

---

1. For a good discussion of the background of Schaff's call to the United States, see H. M. Klein, *A Century of Education at Mercersburg* (Lancaster, Pa.: Lancaster Press, 1936), pp. 182–83.

tion in the new world. He was chosen because of his "sincere piety—his soundness in the fundamental principles of the gospel as they are held by the Reformed Church—his Theological Learning and his aptness to teach, as well in the pulpit as in the professional chair. . . ."[2] Schaff was invited by Americans, and encouraged to accept by Germans, who urged him to carry the "German national spirit" to his adopted land and to "assist in restoring to new life a German population whose national character [had been] half destroyed . . . [and] to rescue it to the consciousness of its original dignity. . . ."[3] But despite that conservative charge which included both cultural and theological components, Schaff spent a great part of his life urging American churches to develop their own ecclesiastical and intellectual distinctiveness. He called for a new church system and a broader theological consensus to improve the old vine of Christianity that it might bear new and better fruit in the unique setting of American culture. In retrospect Schaff was bound to disappoint many of those who originally supported his call to Mercersburg Seminary, and that disappointment was not long in finding an outlet.

THE UNHISTORICAL SPIRIT OF AMERICAN RELIGION

Philip Schaff was educated in a country where the serious study of history had been held in esteem for over fifty years, but in the United States he confronted two attitudes that compounded his adjustment problems. The most pervasive and lethargic obstruction was a prejudice against any kind of historical knowledge, but the one most difficult to reverse was that which distorted history for sectarian purposes. An example of the latter type appeared among leaders of the German Reformed Church who used a certain view of history to legitimize their denomination's particularities and defend its self-sufficiency. The first controversy over ideas concerning churches and their historical development followed Schaff's inaugural address in which he broached an innovative interpretation of the Protestant

2. The action of the synod is cited in George W. Richards, *History of the Theological Seminary of the Reformed Church in the United States, 1825–1934: Evangelical and Reformed Church, 1934–1952* (Lancaster, Pa.: Rudisill and Co., 1952), pp. 554–55.
    3. David S. Schaff, *The Life of Philip Schaff: In Part Autobiographical* (New York: Charles Scribner's Sons, 1897), p. 79. The words cited are those of F. W. Krummacher, main preacher at Schaff's ordination service.

Reformation. In the course of his address he contradicted a view dear to many Americans, not the least of whom was Joseph F. Berg, pastor of the First German Reformed Church of Philadelphia, president of the Synod and editor of the *Protestant Banner*. Eight days prior to Schaff's lecture, Berg had preached before the convened synod a sermon embodying the popular conceptions held by denominational conservatives about their church and its history. On October 25, 1844, Schaff contradicted those ideas and unwittingly earned the enmity of a vindictive faction in the German Reformed communion.

Berg's sermon had concentrated on the best means of "promoting the welfare of the Redeemer's kingdom" in the United States. As a staunch conservative he urged the repudiation of novel doctrines or "new measures" and called for a return to "the landmarks which the ancients [had] set." To support the wisdom of such a recommendation, Berg reminded his audience that "it is altogether a mistaken idea to suppose that religion and divine truth constitute a science which may be improved. The gospel system has long since developed its principles. Revelation is not a science which is progressive in character. It is complete and perfect. There are no correct views . . . which were not offered by the inspired teachings of God's book to our fathers before us."[4]

In Berg's opinion religious truth was timeless and unalterable; any change necessarily involved a movement away from the deposit of faith. He was convinced that "the truth, like its author, is the same yesterday—to-day and forever. Pure and undefiled religion is as unchanging as the holiness of God from whom it emanates."[5] In a more extended statement of his views the synod's president defined Christianity as a system of divinely revealed truths and Protestantism, the best embodiment of that system, as having derived all its doctrines and practices from the Apostolic Church. He was able to trace a concrete historical connection with earlier institutions by reference to a small band of twelfth-century dissenters, the Waldenses.[6] In terms of historical judgment, Berg's fundamental motivation seems to have

4. J. F. Berg, "A Sermon," *Weekly Messenger*, 20 November 1844, p. 1.
5. Ibid.
6. For an analysis of the debate, see James H. Nichols, *Romanticism in American Theology: Nevin and Schaff at Mercersburg* (Chicago: University of Chicago Press, 1961), pp. 108–9.

been a desire to assert that Protestantism had no historic relation to the superstition and wickedness found in the medieval papacy. Schaff asserted by contrast that Protestantism was organically connected to the papacy.

The ensuing controversy between Schaff and Berg raged ostensibly over the proper grounding of authority in doctrine. It resurrected the old Reformation debate over Scripture and tradition and included smear tactics that raised a furor over Schaff's alleged Roman sympathies, but from our perspective it seems clear that the real point of contention centered on the nature and importance of historical change in the life of contemporary churches. Berg argued that scriptural literalism and traditional theology provided a sufficient foundation for both doctrine and church polity; history added nothing to transcendental truth. Schaff's fundamental notion of the close relationship between sequential events was incompatible with a view that claimed a thousand years of Christian activity had no significance. But on theological grounds it was an even worse mistake to assert that the Waldenses had been the only faithful recipients of the Holy Spirit during that long period. Thus for both reasons he stressed an organic view that relied on strong historical ties linking Protestantism with the piety of medieval Christianity.[7] The statement which most angered Berg and other isolationist Protestants was Schaff's contention that Protestantism was more than the legitimate offspring of the Catholic Church: it was its greatest and fullest expression.[8] In answer to Berg's total reliance on Scripture, Schaff suggested a more balanced view that would allow history to supplement the Bible by illustrating in various circumstances ways in which biblical doctrines might be interpreted. But the basic element in his standpoint, which unhistorical Americans could not assimilate, was his

7. Nichols, *Romanticism in American Theology*, p. 108, has pointed out the valuable fact that Schaff printed these ideas earlier in the *Literarische Zeitung;* thus they may be taken as representative of his thinking and not as incidental points in a brief address.

8. Philip Schaff, *The Principle of Protestantism: As related to the Present State of the Church* (Chambersburg, Pa., 1845). This elaboration of an inaugural address was Schaff's first book in English, and it served its purpose in the debate. It is not, however, as valuable as later works for understanding his ideas. For a modern edition, see the Lancaster Series on the Mercersburg Theology, vol. 1 (Philadelphia: United Church Press, 1964), Bard Thompson and George H. Bricker, editors. All references are to the later edition.

claim that they could learn a great deal about Christianity and providential guidance by studying the collective experience of earlier ecclesiastical life.

Schaff must have been as perplexed by the unhistorical spirit pervading his new homeland as by the issues he was forced to argue. His European experience led him to expect debates in which particular denominations were defended against Roman Catholic claims of exclusive validity. But in the United States he suddenly found himself among Protestants whose sense of identity apparently did not extend to considering their institution in relation to others. Not many Protestant thinkers, and no group as a whole, spoke of themselves in the context of other contemporary religious patterns, and even fewer considered themselves as part of a continuous succession of ecclesiastical forms. When they did, most were content to claim apostolic derivation by means of an easy-going theory of doctrinal compatibility with precedents set in New Testament times rather than claim actual historical ties with ancient churches. Thus Schaff's carefully bolstered argument that Roman and Protestant churches were branches of the same historical trunk[9] had little appeal in an American audience because he caused others to fear he was destroying the fundamental basis of Protestantism. The real issue of historical development was so foreign to Berg that he never really grasped it. Berg's attack never had much force in the controversy because it argued a point Schaff did not raise.[10] The resulting confusion, bitterness, and factionalism did not settle the dispute,[11] but it served to point up the strong resistance to an appreciation of history Schaff found in the United States.

The Berg incident was symptomatic of a prevalent state of mind

9. P. Schaff, *The Principle of Protestantism*, p. 105.

10. The best account of the issues and personalities involved in the controversy can be found in George H. Shriver, "Philip Schaff: Heresy at Mercersburg," in *American Religious Heretics: Formal and Informal Trials*, ed. George H. Shriver (Nashville: Abingdon Press, 1966), pp. 30–40.

11. Berg drew up a list of charges "for review," but all parties knew them to be accusations of heresy. The synod found Schaff innocent after much litigation, and Berg withdrew from the German Reformed Church in 1851, entering the Dutch Reformed communion. Also as a result of Schaff's acquittal, one of Berg's colleagues, J. Helffenstein, and his entire congregation became members of the New School Presbyterian Church. There were many other examples of hard feelings against Schaff and Mercersburg Seminary (Richards, *History of the Theological Seminary*, p. 257).

in which the force, the meaning, the compelling sense of actually *being in* history was generally lacking among the American people. There were some religious leaders who applied themselves to serious study, but most were as skeptical about deriving any lasting value from historical studies as their parishioners. In most educational centers theological studies were prized as a worthy accomplishment, indeed Schaff had been transported to further ends within that system, but theological education was rather narrowly defined to emphasize linguistic facility that promoted the independent study of Scripture and secondarily to provide a mastery in various manuals of systematic theology. There was virtually no place for studying church history. A survey of the marginal role assigned to the area of church history in early seminary curricula may indicate the indifference citizens of the new nation showed to their historical predecessors and the depth of the unhistorical spirit of American religion.

The oldest theological seminary in the United States was founded at Andover, Massachusetts, in 1807 by a conservative wing of New England Congregationalists.[12] The constitution and early curriculum of Andover Seminary included ecclesiastical history,[13] but actual instruction in the subject did not receive the attention originally promised. As an indication of what ends church history should serve, the professor of the course was advised to review significant ecclesiastical events quickly and use the remaining class time to concentrate on more important issues where he might "pass over the ground of Theology, especially Polemic Theology."[14] In 1823 the curriculum was revised to provide young ministers with a more comprehensive and relevant plan of study. Though everyone still agreed that the study of Scripture and exegetical rules should receive most attention, there was still no accord on a place for church history. History was

---

12. It would be more realistic to say that Andover was the first permanently located faculty of theological studies. The Dutch Reformed Church appointed John Henry Livingston as professor of theology in 1784, but he had no connection with any college; some take this chair as the first American seminary. See C. E. Olmstead, *History of Religion in the United States* (Englewood Cliffs, N.J.: Prentice-Hall, 1960), p. 285. Good background material for Andover can be found in Henry K. Rowe, *History of Andover Theological Seminary* (Newton, Mass.: Thomas Todd Co., 1933), pp. 10–11.

13. The constitution can be found in Leonard Woods, *History of the Andover Theological Seminary* (Boston: J. R. Osgood, 1885), pp. 234–36.

14. Ibid., p. 192.

considered by most of the Andover architects to be simply a survey of "various clashing opinions and unauthorized practices." But even so, the fascinating diversity of its topics caused many to regard it as a dangerous and unsettling field of inquiry. As such it was considered safe only for members of the senior class whose mature minds, it was hoped, were firmly settled in their convictions, at least settled enough to remain unshaken by a survey of clashing opinions.[15] Thus historical studies were made an appendage to the program of the final year at Andover, a niche where presumably they would have the least effect. In that manner Congregationalist educators paid some deference to history and a well-rounded curriculum, but at the same time they protected impressionable minds from the incongruities and "unorthodox practices" it disclosed.

The Presbyterians founded their first seminary at Princeton, New Jersey, in 1812 and from the beginning placed a relatively strong emphasis on historical learning.[16] The Reverend Samuel Miller became professor of ecclesiastical history and church government in 1813. That post was the first established in the United States, but Miller was not able to concentrate all of his attention on historical study because his time was spent in more pressing matters like chapel oratory and classes in sermon composition. Miller used the Bible as a textbook in history lectures because he began his narrative with the act of Creation and defined his subject as the entire family of man under various dispensations of providential guidance. On theological grounds he considered it untenable to begin the development of the Christian church with any historical figure later than Adam himself.[17] Church history courses at Princeton Seminary, though made more substantially a part of ministerial education than at Andover, were nevertheless intended to familiarize students with material that only supplemented Bible study. Miller's lectures on the postbiblical epochs consisted of brief sketches of a few major events in ecclesiastical

---

15. Ibid., pp. 188–89.
16. Princeton Seminary catalogs from 1828 to 1862 list a required course in biblical history in the beginning year and another course in ecclesiastical history for middlers. A third course was added in 1861.
17. See a letter sent by Miller to a Professor Cogswell in 1843 describing his courses, in Samuel Miller, *The Life of Samuel Miller, D.D., LL.D., Second Professor in the Theological Seminary of the Presbyterian Church, at Princeton, New Jersey* (Philadelphia: Claxton, Remsen & Haffelfinger, 1869), 2:405.

annals, concluding with a statistical analysis of denominational align-
ments in his own century.[18] His extant manuscript notes are characterized by a sketchy, manual-like quality that must have assured
superficial knowledge and a rote system of questions and answers that
probably afforded little more than a shallow understanding of events.
Inadequate as they might seem, Miller's courses at Princeton were an
exception to the general dearth of interest in the history of the church;
but even among Presbyterians history lagged far behind biblical
studies, theology, and sermon composition as an absorbing or reward-
ing field of inquiry. Evidence of this prejudice can be seen in the fact
that no more than one-third of Miller's time was spent in historical
instruction. Even in 1861, when J. C. Moffat first occupied the newly
endowed Helena professorship of church history, the subject was not
deemed important enough to engage his full attention.

Yale began an academic program specifically intended for ministers in 1822, but it did not include church history in the curriculum
at any time during the next four decades. In the years following the
American Revolution Ezra Stiles is reported to have taught something
entitled "Church History" in the college, but the subject was allowed
to fade after his death and remain dormant until 1861. Library
records of the interim period show that some enterprising students
checked out and apparently read standard textbooks such as the old
standby written by Mosheim, but there is no indication that any
official emphasis was placed on history.[19]

In 1819 Harvard created a distinct administrative unit called the
"Faculty of Theology," consisting of the president and four professors
who concentrated on theology, languages, and the interpretation of
Scripture. At the same time the Board of Overseers approved other
professorships, including one in church history, but no funds could be
allocated to support any more positions. Ecclesiastical history was
considered the "orphan child" at Harvard Divinity School as it was
everywhere else and did not receive adequate attention in the early

18. Miller's handwritten and carefully sewn notebooks are housed in Speer
Library, Princeton Theological Seminary.
19. Roland H. Bainton, *Yale and the Ministry: A History of Education for the
Christian Ministry at Yale from the Founding in 1701* (New York: Harper &
Brothers, 1957), p. 186.

years.[20] The situation did not vary significantly between 1840 and 1880.[21]

In 1836 New School Presbyterians began self-consciously to depart from established practices when they founded Union Theological Seminary in New York City. Older seminaries in this country had been created under the direct control and surveillance of denominations which supplied the personnel and vocational outlets for graduates bent on institutional service. Union promised to be different because it had been founded by men who designed it as a rallying point for "all men of moderate views and feelings, who desire to live free from party strife, and to stand aloof from all extremes of doctrinal speculation . . . and ecclesiastical domination. . . ."[22] The founders of Union Seminary were not interested in buttressing denominational loyalty as much as they were intent upon furnishing "the means of a full and thorough education in all the subjects taught in the best [continental or American?] Theological Seminaries."[23] But the main difference in Union's curriculum was a wider sampling of theological opinion; a distinctively wider and richer selection of course topics did not emerge, and the study of church history was slighted there almost as much as everywhere else. There was no chair of church history until 1850, before which time the subject was sporadically treated "by a Professor Extraordinary, or by a temporary instructor."[24] Thus at Union as well as the other major seminaries, the unhistorical spirit of American religious interests kept historical studies in the background throughout the first half of the nineteenth century. There were isolated individuals at every institution who occasionally made strong pleas that historical studies should play a more important part in advanced education, but indifference usually held the upper hand. Whether this lack of interest was manifested by

20. C. Wright, "The Early Period (1811–40)," in *The Harvard Divinity School: Its Place in Harvard University and in American Culture*, ed. George H. Williams (Boston: Beacon Press, 1954), p. 53.
21. S. E. Ahlstrom, "The Middle Period (1840–80)," in Williams, *Harvard Divinity School*, p. 88.
22. George L. Prentiss, *The Theological Seminary of the City of New York: Historical and Biographical Sketches of its First Fifty Years* (New York: Anson D. F. Randolph and Co., 1889), p. 8.
23. Ibid., p. 44.
24. Ibid., p. 49.

the fact that funds were never found to support professorships or ex-pressed in subtler ways by loading the professor with other duties, the fact remains that church history maintained a precarious position in theological education.

Historical perspective was not given much serious attention in any aspect of American society. This fact was attested by contemporary observers such as Alexis de Tocqueville[25] and Michael Chevalier[26] as well as later analysts of American culture like Henry Adams.[27] It is not surprising, therefore, that the general tone of religious life shared the same unhistorical disposition that predominated in most other national attitudes. But in addition to being just another expression of a conventional preoccupation with mundane affairs, church history was discredited in the United States for more specific reasons. One basic cause was the conviction, perhaps anti-intellectual at bottom, that Bible study supplied ministers all they really needed for effective communication with the common man. As one spokesman from Andover put it:

The Bible itself is our sufficient and only guide and standard, thus our first business is, to learn what doctrines are taught in that sacred volume taken as a whole. And this can be done most successfully by pursuing the study of the Bible itself, without being embarrassed by an inquiry respecting the opinions of earlier or later uninspired writers. For what can the mere *opinions* of fallible men do towards determining the sense of the inspired volume?[28]

A widespread disposition to conceive of religion primarily in terms of doctrine, Bible-based and systematically arranged for ex-planation and defense, allowed historical studies little place in de-nominational self-consciousness or ministerial education. Most col-leges and seminaries at that time were not founded to pursue learning for its own sake as much as they were explicitly designed to serve the

25. Alexis de Tocqueville, *Democracy in America,* ed. P. Bradley (New York: Random House, Vintage Books, 1958), 2:42.
26. Michael Chevalier, *Society, Manners and Politics in the United States: Let-ters on North America,* ed. J. W. Ward (Garden City: Doubleday & Co., 1961), p. 262.
27. Henry Adams, *History of the United States during the Administration of Thomas Jefferson* (New York: Charles Scribner's Sons, 1931), 1:73–74, 108.
28. Woods, *History of the Andover Theological Seminary,* p. 89.

interests of a specific religious denomination.[29] If church history could be taken at all seriously in those circumstances, the greatest part of a student's information was constructed to serve as an apologia for his denomination's position on polity, doctrine, or liturgy.[30] But there was another reason for the poor showing church history made in American seminaries, a reason more in keeping with the cultural needs of the early national period. The prominent rise of revival techniques in almost every major religious group after the 1820s displaced historical consciousness as a means of religious nurture and caused it to decline even further. One pamphleteer for the Second Great Awakening captured the spirit of the campaign for souls by characterizing local colleges as Christianity's "magazine, the depot of its troops, its arsenal and its fortress."[31] The chief objective to the newly vitalized clerical army was, in the words of Albert Barnes, *"to save souls,* and to labour for revivals of religion."[32] Since personally appropriated salvation was the goal uppermost in the minds of both preacher and his congregation, historical reflection could be easily passed over because it promised no immediate returns in redeemed souls and contributed very little to the charisma of a revival setting. Scholarly theologians, parish ministers, and itinerant preachers treated church history as an unwanted, orphan child.

The spirit of individualism in religion, as in secular areas of the American mind, precluded a sustained attempt to understand the present by means of the past. People nourished on a diet of revivals saw little benefit in studying the lives of their predecessors, however saintly their example or profound their opinions, because knowledge of the past could not promise to bring salvation any closer. A modern observer of the period, noting the blend of revivalistic spontaneity and denominational allegiance, states that "religion was generally

29. See a perceptive statement by F. A. P. Barnard, in Donald G. Tewksbury, *The Founding of American Colleges and Universities before the Civil War: With particular Reference to the Religious Influences Bearing upon the College Movement* (New York: Teacher's College, Columbia University, 1932), pp. 4–5.

30. For example, Miller's course on church government at Princeton was structured to defend Presbyterian polity. See his manuscript notes in Speer Library, Princeton Theological Seminary.

31. An 1856 pamphlet by R. S. Storrs, in Tewksbury, *Founding of American Colleges,* p. 20.

32. S. E. Mead, "The Rise of the Evangelical Conception of the Ministry in America: 1607–1850," in *The Ministry in Historical Perspectives,* ed. Helmut R. Niebuhr and Daniel D. Williams (New York: Harper & Brothers, 1956), p. 238.

defined in the terms of traditional dogmatic theology seen through the somewhat foggy sentiments of American revivalistic evangelicalism." And through that fog and shifting double focus educationists "fumbled for a . . . program that would be both intellectually respectable and dogmatically sound."[33] But without the realism provided by a study of concrete historical events, their attempts at intellectual respectability were rather one-sided, placing disproportionate attention on the defense of confessional idiosyncracies. It was largely due to the eloquence, erudition, and stamina of Philip Schaff that some leaders in American religious circles slowly came to recognize the legitimate place of historical knowledge in theological education. His long list of publications and influential position in the educational structure, strategically placed at Union Seminary for almost three decades after the Civil War, afforded him opportunity to emphasize the relevance of church history. Eventually his conceptions came to be widely supported, and those ideas acted as a much needed corrective in the education of clergymen and their contemporaries.

SCHAFF'S CONCEPTION OF CHURCH HISTORY

It was one of Schaff's fundamental convictions that knowledge of developments comprising the history of Christianity was essential to the further progress of religion. After having studied at Tübingen, Halle, and Berlin, and after absorbing the ideas of Ferdinand C. Baur and August Neander, two giants in German church historiography, Schaff was disappointed by the shallow pragmatism of his adopted country with its preference for "look[ing] selfishly to the present and weigh[ing] all things by the standard of immediate utility."[34] On one level he expressed his criticism in terms of worldly wisdom, observing that "the man who undertakes to work for the future without knowledge of the past and constant regard for it, will build . . . a castle in the air," then adding a remark not calculated to appease sectarians, "as many striking examples in our American Church life serve clearly to show."[35] There was a more basic reason

33. Ibid., p. 242.
34. Schaff's first major statement on the value and proper methods of church history was entitled *What Is Church History? A Vindication of the Idea of Historical Development* (Philadelphia: J. B. Lippincott and Co., 1846); the citation is on p. 25.
35. Ibid.

for Schaff's emphasis on church history, more fundamental to his thinking and more shrewdly directed at the practical utility so prized by his new countrymen. He argued that historical understanding was the key to ecclesiastical progress because through it the great forces at work in previous epochs could be identified and possibly exploited for further development. If men could determine the direction in which earlier movements of Christianity had been tending, they might be able to align themselves with those historical forces and derive some additional impetus from the vast power of historical momentum. It was that conviction about the almost irresistible force of historical trends that lay behind Schaff's esteem for church history: "How shall we labour with any effect to build up the Church, if we have no thorough knowledge of her history, or fail to apprehend it from the proper point of observation? History is, and must ever continue to be, next to God's word, the richest foundation of wisdom, and the surest guide to all successful practical activity."[36]

Recent scholars have classified as "romantic" any philosophical position which insisted on comprehending all the earlier stages of an intellectual movement or national culture as the means of perceiving its overall tendency or defining one's present location on a historical continuum.[37] In the light of that single definition it is not unfair to say that Schaff, coming from Germany, the seat of such philosophical speculation, embodied a romantic attempt to understand church history. Romanticism has also been associated with a literary style that chose situations to be described with a dramatic flair. Schaff possessed the gift of poetic expression and was always able to brighten the

---

36. Ibid., p. 5.
37. The philosophical content of "romanticism" is elusive and has different connotations for different students, many of which are contradictory. One basic idea has been discussed by Arthur O. Lovejoy that is suited to Schaff's viewpoint, viz., "the idea of the Whole," a concept emerging initially in the 1780s. Whereas most eighteenth-century thinkers conceived of the individual as primary, a possessor of intrinsic rights, later thinkers began a new trend with the innovations of Immanuel Kant. In his *Kritik der Urteilskraft* Kant stated that every part of an organism depended for its existence on all the other parts; further, each part existed *for* all the other parts. Thus primacy was placed, not on the individual component, but on the whole, *das Ganze,* which sometimes took precedence over individual whims. Thus ideas contained in the organism, the biological or political entity as a whole, determined the future development of every segment comprising it. See A. O. Lovejoy, "The Meaning of Romanticism for the Historian of Ideas," *Journal of the History of Ideas* 2 (June 1941): 272–73.

pages of his books with vivid descriptions and arresting metaphors.[38]
Some of his prose would rank among the best example of romantic
historical narrative, but Schaff's methodological ideas should be
analyzed as products of a philosophical conception of events. His
approach to the field of religious studies reveals him as one viewing
"Church and History . . . so closely united, that respect and love
towards the first, may be said to be essentially the same with a
proper sense of what is comprised in the other."[39]

Schaff's initial stress on the importance of historical knowledge, its
solidity as a body of hard facts and its utility as a guide for prudent
institutional advance, was supplemented and qualified by what he
called the "proper point of observation." By that he meant primarily
a proper conception of the Christian church, a fundamental viewpoint based on a confession of faith which determined to a considerable degree his ideas about the church's development and the legitimate tasks open to a church historian. The implications involved in
that "proper point of observation" are relevant to the study of every
church historian both then and now. Schaff was more forthright than
any of the six other church historians included in this study because
he admitted the profound influence theological preconceptions have
on historical methodology, and he was more consistent than the rest in
following his line of thinking to logical conclusions.[40] In emphasizing
the importance of one's theological definition of the subject, Schaff
posited as a fundamental axiom that "a right conception of the
Church [was] . . . the conducting genius of the Church historian."[41]
For his own part, his particular definition raised church history to a
level on which the church could not be understood in human terms
alone. Common methods of investigation could not yield adequate
explanations unless they were supplemented by references to divine

38. George H. Shriver, "Philip Schaff's Concept of Organic Historiography:
Interpreted in Relation to the Realization of an 'Evangelical Catholicism' within
the Christian Community," (Ph.D. diss., Duke University, 1960), p. 4.
39. P. Schaff, What Is Church History?, p. 9.
40. It was particularly in this area of thought that Schaff revealed the richness
and sophistication of his historical awareness. True to his German mentors, he
predicated a fundamental difference between natural occurrences and historic events.
Most Americans who claimed to be following German historicism did not make
any such distinction. See Georg G. Iggers, The German Conception of History:
The National Tradition of Historical Thought from Herder to the Present (Middletown, Conn.: Wesleyan University Press, 1968), pp. 3–7, 58–61, 63–65, 76–80.
41. P. Schaff, What Is Church History?, p. 37.

intervention. Though Schaff's distinctive accomplishments in the area of interpretation and synthesis have been criticized by some as too uncritical in an age of science and skepticism, that should not alter the fact that his self-conscious approach to the rudiments of historical study was essentially correct. Basic definitions of the nature of the Christian church are a vital factor in analyzing the research methods and interpretive schemes of every church historian.

There was another element in Schaff's thinking that made preliminary definitions necessary, and it had to do with the essential nature of a phenomenon, its "idea," or "life force." He thought that the essence of an institution or a historical movement caused successive events in that subject's experience to develop organically, along lines intelligible to historians who had identified the basic nature of a phenomenon at an early stage of investigation. The logic of that train of thought tended to raise Schaff's evaluation of church history to a level on which the church, because of its essential nature, was not entirely a human institution nor one to be adequately interpreted in naturalistic terms. The type of development he had in mind was analogous to the growth of a plant: all essential components were present in the seed, and subsequent change was simply the natural extension of a single entity destined to flourish. His conception of historical change depended on a process that was both "regular and organic; since it follows with necessity an inward life force, proceeds with . . . order, and continues always true to the original nature . . . till in the end it has brought the whole fulness of it into view."[42] For Schaff all Christian churches were seen as sharing a common "life force." Though there had been several manifestations of Christian life over the centuries, he was able to discern a common origin and purpose which unfolded itself historically from within "by the necessity of its own nature." The many branches remained true to that nature throughout the exigencies of historical change just as a fir tree was able to keep its greenness through climatic changes.[43]

Schaff thought of historical development as an endless chain of events, a single framework of human activity that could not be seg-

42. Ibid., p. 84.
43. Ibid., pp. 5, 84, 91. For corroborative analysis, see Klaus Penzel, "Church History and the Ecumenical Quest: A Study of the German Background and Thought of Philip Schaff" (Th.D. diss., Union Seminary, New York, 1962), pp. 222, 264.

mented without doing violence to the whole. In his view, those who claimed they were the only group to maintain New Testament teachings in their original purity made a patchwork of the historical process. He pointed out that those groups were unable to trace any rich heritage of their own, and, moreover, they denied any value to medieval church history, thus obscuring hundreds of years in which providential activity could be discerned. Their self-righteous isolation violated Schaff's fundamental conviction that history "is a living organism, whose parts have an inward, vital connection, each requiring and completing the rest." He hoped to show them how the "living organism" of church history progressed according to "an eternal, unchangeable plan of infinite wisdom, and tends, therefore, as by an irresistible necessity, to a definite end."[44] As far as a general description of his approach is concerned, Schaff went beyond the romantic dictum that objects could best be understood in terms of their essential nature and subsequent interaction with their environment. He emphasized the importance of the church's historical experience, but he was primarily concerned to identify its essence, its divine reason-for-being that could be illuminated throughout the bewildering reversals of succeeding centuries and displayed before thoughtful readers. Thus Schaff's theological definition of the church enabled him to divorce secular and theological interpretations of church history and made it possible to speak about the religious significance of events without reference to scientific verification.[45]

Schaff began with the theological postulate that the Christian church was the earthly manifestation of the Body of Christ, the con-

44. Philip Schaff, *History of the Apostolic Church: With a General Introduction to Church History*, trans. Edward D. Yeomans (New York: Charles Scribner's Sons, 1853), p. 3 (hereafter cited as *HAC*).
45. It is interesting to see that Schaff and Adams resembled each other in that they shared variations of the "germ" theory. But, whereas Schaff began with the initial stages (and those theologically defined) and traced historical developments to the present, Adams was primarily interested in beginning with the present situation and going back into history to uncover antecedents. In Schaff's own terminology, the difference between "secular" and "sacred" history was that the latter category concerned biblical times, when special revelations guided men's actions. All post-biblical history was "secular" in that it occurred under a single dispensation of grace (Shriver, "Concept of Organic Historiography," p. 74). But Schaff's discussion of the unique origin and experience of the Christian church warrants our thinking he made a distinction between the history of Christianity and of, say, politics.

crete embodiment of God's promise to dwell with his people.[46] Of course, the earthly experiences of a divine institution necessarily involved a mixture of human frailties along with providential designs. But despite the effect of alien influences from extraneous sources or temporary malpractices within it, Schaff persisted in believing that the true church retained an essentially holy nature. In one of his early publications he described that pivotal assumption which informed his subsequent thoughts as a practicing church historian, a category so congenial to his major objectives that he made only slight changes throughout his long career: "In the Church, Christ carries forward . . . his divine human life, . . . gives believers his atoning flesh and blood . . . speaks by his work . . . repeats also his glorious resurrection and ascension, and continues evermore to visit his little flock, assembled with one accord for prayer, with the fulness of light and life by his Holy Spirit."[47]

Whenever it became necessary to distinguish between the ideal sanctity of Christ's church and the actual corruption found too often among Christians, Schaff employed a double standard of identification. The eternal truth of God's will and word was declared to be "objectively present" in Christ and in the Scriptures. This same truth was only "subjectively present" in the consciousness of the earthly church, a tentative presence that was often more promise than fact, subject to varying degrees of actualization, and vulnerable to occasional reversals or outright violation. Thus Schaff could admit that charlatans and self-seekers had from time to time succeeded under the cloak of clerical innocence, while simultaneously he could sustain his view that the true, holy church had been a vibrant force in the lives of men during every historical period.[48]

46. Schaff often alluded to Schleiermacher as the source of his ideas about the church (see *What Is Church History?*, p. 78). It might have been simply the fashionable thing to do, but Schleiermacher did include in his theology concepts of the church as a holy community centered in Christ. See H. R. Mackintosh's translation of F. D. E. Schleiermacher, *The Christian Faith* (Edinburgh: T. & T. Clark, 1948), pp. 565–66, 579–80. See also Shriver, "Concept of Organic Historiography," pp. 101–2. Of course the writings of Neander must have influenced Schaff even more directly than the general suggestions stemming from Schleiermacher. One selection of Neander's views which is strikingly similar to Schaff's later expressions can be found in his *General History of the Christian Religion and Church*, trans. Joseph Torrey (Boston: Crocker and Brewster, 1872), 3:1.

47. P. Schaff, *What Is Church History?*, p. 37.

48. Ibid., pp. 81–82.

After beginning his studies with an exalted view of the church, and having rooted them in the organic nature of historical change, Schaff was able to define church history as "the evolution of God's plan of redemption, proceeding according to [internally] rational and necessary laws."[49] Church history was, for him, a prophetic account of Christ's actually participating in historical events through the church as his chosen instrument for ministering to the nations. His favorite phrase characterizing the proper role of church historians (probably borrowed from Friedrich von Schlegel) was to say that they functioned as "retrospective prophets," discerning the activity of Christ in past events. The church's mission included both geographical expansion and an infusion of humanitarian ideals into the societies it encountered. A standard literary usage was to describe those internal and external themes as an extended commentary on two parables: the mustard seed growing to remarkable proportions and leaven permeating a lump of dough. Thus from the outset Schaff began with an idea of church history that called for a perspective extending it beyond the unimaginative process of collecting and arranging naturalistic data. In addition to employing the research methods common to all empirical investigation, he placed his own topic on a slightly different level by stating that religious insight should be included as a means of interpreting it. Adequate understanding in his craft followed upon proper theological orientation: "A right conception of the Church is indispensable for a living apprehension and satisfactory exhibition of its history. . . . The relation here is one of reciprocal light and confirmation. Only the art which has wrought . . . Church history furnishes at the same time the key for understanding it. Without its guidance, we see . . . but we cannot understand."[50]

Schaff's conception of church history allowed it to become a theater of action where human and divine agents could act independ-

---

49. Ibid., p. 115. One of Schaff's contemporaries in the United States echoed his ideas in these words: ". . . this history is invested with a solemn, a sublime interest, when it is viewed as the record of a divine economy, established in an apostate world, centering in the incarnation of the Son of God, and having for its object the redemption of the race. . . . He who explores the revelations of God in his new and spiritual creation [must] feel the constant need of that divine illumination which can alone enable him to distinguish what is from God and what is from man. . . ." See Henry B. Smith, "Nature and Worth of the Science of Church History: An Inaugural Address" (Andover: Warren F. Draper, 1851).
50. P. Schaff, *What Is Church History?*, p. 37.

ently or in concert. He believed in a "divine progress and government in the world" which assured him of certain tendencies history was likely to follow.[51] God might interpose directly in the stream of events, or, more commonly, act through the offices of his church, but either case afforded sufficient evidence to reaffirm the doctrine that God was omnipotent and dealt purposefully with his creatures. That conviction lay behind Schaff's declaration that he was able to see "uninterrupted progress in the history of the church." As a retrospective prophet he could see that "God has proposed for his kingdom upon earth a definite end [and thus] all history must . . . move [that] way."[52] So church history was to be written in faith and hope with an eye toward God's redemptive purpose through the ecclesiastical office. Anyone who tried to approach such a study without the requisite faith in that "definite end" would be able to understand only external matters. The fundamental structure of Schaff's ideas led inexorably to the conclusion that objective, completely empirical investigators lacked insight into the essential nature of the church and that they could never hope to comprehend the full meaning of events they described.

Despite the increasing popularity of scientific ideals, Schaff defended the necessity of a theological orientation by arguing that sympathetic union with the subject was essential to true understanding. Just as a man without poetic feeling could not be expected to interpret poetry, so one could not rightly comprehend the history of Christianity "without the spirit that animat[ed] and control[led] it." He persisted in the belief that, if an author based his interpretation of Christianity on naturalistic evidence alone, such "an unbeliever could produce only a repulsive caricature or at best a lifeless statue."[53] But once privy to the mysteries of faith, Schaff claimed that "scientific church historians" could be impartial and open-minded. He

51. Ibid., p. 107. In 1846 Schaff criticized several historians whom he called "rationalists" in words singularly appropriate for scientific historians: "Thus was God excluded from history altogether; which was . . . to thrust out its eyes and tear the living heart from its bosom. . . . The theatre of the kingdom of God in the world, was degraded into a wild arena of base, unholy passions."
52. Ibid., p. 107. See also HAC, pp. 3, 12.
53. Philip Schaff, Theological Propaedeutic: A General Introduction to the Study of Theology, Exegetical, Historical, Systematic, and Practical, Including Encyclopedia, Methodology and Bibliography (New York: Christian Literature Co., 1892), pp. 257–58. See also HAC, p. 3.

assured his readers that proper church history would "no longer be handled in [an] apologetic style, that requir[ed] it to lend itself . . . to the service of an established system."[54] Given the battles Schaff wished to fight on the basis of church history, it is not surprising to see him insist that a historian's theological viewpoint was a key factor in the insights he could gain, nor was it unnatural for him to defend the "scientific" nature of those judgments made in church history. Logical corollaries in his thought were unassimilable, however, with the new strictures placed by the American scientific historians against interpolation of any kind.

Historians who identified with the AHA and Schaff's ideal church historian shared a common duty to be faithful to the record. They agreed that history was no longer to be based on hearsay, opinion, vested interests, or legend. As Schaff put it, "The historian must first make himself master of the sources. This is a well-nigh endless task, but no one should attempt to write history without some knowledge of the primary sources of information."[55] All agreed that the first thing a historian did was to select the source materials for a particular topic or period and then scrutinize their integrity according to generally accepted laws of textual and literary criticism. In that tested manner he could measure the credibility of his witnesses and sift facts from fiction. Their common emphasis on primary sources and critical treatment served as a connecting link between Schaff and more secular-minded historians. Schaff even considered his methodology to be "scientific" and confused matters by using that term quite often when describing his distinctive type of activity. But historians within the AHA wanted to pattern their investigations after laboratory procedures, and Schaff thought a "scientific historian" was simply one who traced a historical phenomenon back to its origins, the better to understand its essence or "life force," and then chronicled its subsequent development. Though he did not embody the kind of objectivity they cherished, Schaff agreed with the iconoclasts that human comment could be kept to a minimum. The real point of historical investigation was to get

back to the most remote and scarcely perceptible beginnings of the object contemplated; which is then allowed to unfold itself from within

54. P. Schaff, *What Is Church History?*, p. 25.
55. P. Schaff, *Theological Propaedeutic*, p. 255.

according to the law of its own nature and constitution. . . . And what is thus made to pass before our eyes, is not the play of unmeaning blind forces. All is conducted by a higher spirit, which urges forward the wheel of history, . . . and through all events bears the world on continually towards the glorious and established for it in the eternal counsel of God.[56]

In his own conception of his discipline, "Church history as a science commenc[ed] where the Church [came] to reflect upon herself," where the historian brought "his own judgment into his work . . . so as to put life into it spiritually."[57] A cursory glance at the two points of view would find little disagreement, since both used the word "scientific" with full approval, but it is clear on more fundamental analysis that scientific and theological approaches to history had little in common. And the force of circumstances in late nineteenth-century American thought made it increasingly difficult for the older and more vulnerable perspective to defend itself and retain adherents.

Schaff contradicted a cardinal rule of scientific historiography by saying that the church historian's interpretation of events had to be based on a priori conception of the essential nature of the church. He was primarily concerned with tracing the "footprints of Christ" in the paths of history and in that way illuminating the "abundant manifestations of His Spirit which marked a sure progress toward the ideal church."[58] Naturalistic historians denied supernatural considerations a place in historical narratives, and they dismissed interpretations committed to preconceived patterns, especially those based on a confession of faith. But Schaff's conception of his discipline did not follow an epistemology patterned after the natural sciences; he thought of his work as a sacred science, "based on a divine revelation and concerned with the eternal interests of man." Not even Bancroft had confronted Adams with that formidable an alternative. Church history, or historical theology, as Schaff preferred to classify it, was a sacred task, one to be studied "spiritually as well as intellectually, devoutly as well as thoughtfully, on the knees as well as behind the

56. P. Schaff, *What Is Church History?*, p. 27.
57. Ibid., p. 41. This definition might also indicate some dependence on Schleiermacher; see his *Christian Faith*, pp. 26–30.
58. Philip Schaff, *Reunion of Christendom* (New York, 1893), p. 34. See also D. Schaff, *Life of Philip Schaff*, pp. 455–56.

desk."[59] In his interpretation of carefully researched primary sources Schaff was determined to include a belief in God's pervasive control of historical events. The significance of Schaff's side of the debate with scientific historians is not that he opposed naturalism with an equally one-sided supernaturalism, but that he persisted in blending elements of an empirical approach with discussions about God in the natural world.[60] From a theological definition of the discipline, any historian who excluded, for theological or methodological reasons, such a blend of human and divine activity was bound to derive nothing more than a shallow appreciation of unimportant details in the drama of human experience.

One of the more striking issues separating Schaff from thinkers of the scientific age centered on his insistence that sensitivity to providential intervention remain part of the "proper viewpoint" for practicing historians. His working maxims included one that said, "The recognition of God in history is the first principle of all sound philosophy of history. . . . He who denies the hand of Providence in the affairs of the world and the church is intellectually or spiritually blind."[61] Scientific historians who strove to meet the facts of each case with open minds made a point of denying all claims to a priori considerations, whereas Schaff tried to maintain a balance between empirical study and religious commitment, generally expressed as a belief in God's overarching control of historical events. A sense of deep, personal piety lay behind that attempt to recognize God in history and to balance religious views with scientific endeavor. It has been noted that in his younger days many influences worked together to encourage an attitude of devotional warmth in the future church historian.[62] This pietistic orientation urged him to make a confession of faith through his scholarly activity in hopes of

59. Philip Schaff, "The Theology of Our Age and Country," *Christ and Christianity* (London: J. Nisbet and Co., 1885), p. 7. Schaff's terminological preference indicates that he thought of church history as a subcategory of theological concerns, not an area of inquiry free to investigate and conclude what was found compelling. See *What Is Church History?*, p. 28, for an early statement to this effect.

60. Two late examples are in Schaff's *History of the Christian Church*, 6 vols. [vols. 1, 2, 3, 4, 6, 7] (New York: Charles Scribner's Sons, 1882-92), 6:2, 105 (hereafter cited as *HCC*).

61. P. Schaff, *Theological Propaedeutic*, p. 236.

62. Schriver, "Concept of Organic Historiography," pp. 3-4, 9-11, 79-80. See also D. Schaff, *Life of Philip Schaff*, pp. 11-16, 23-25.

eliciting similar responses from an audience or readers. Schaff's advice to future historians was to "remember that scholarship is but one end of your vocation. If you had all the wisdom and learning of the world, and were destitute of virtue and piety, they would profit you nothing. Cultivate your heart, as well as your head; look to your morals even more than to your attainments."[63] Such personal cultivation made a church historian receptive to the common spiritual experiences of man and made it possible to interpret history with an irenic and catholic spirit.

In this regard the influence of August Neander, Schaff's favorite historian at Berlin, comes through quite clearly. Since he arrived in Berlin with fairly mature views on many aspects of the church's past, it is to be expected that student and professor differed over specific points of interpretation. Schaff was able to criticize and dissociate himself from his mentor's views on theology and church orthodoxy, but in later life he acknowledged that he gained from Neander's works "more than from any other historian."[64] The most striking aspect of the older scholar, however, was his "moral purity and elevation" which confirmed much the same tendency in a young *privat-dozent* just beginning his work at the university. The empathy that existed between the two men becomes clear when Schaff wrote approvingly that church historical problems for Neander were "everywhere pervaded by a pious, at once earnest and yet gentle and deeply humble spirit. Neander . . . [viewed] theology, and consequently church history also, not as an exercise simply of the understanding, but as a practical business of the heart at the same time."[65] As far as moral sensitivity is concerned, Schaff might have been describing himself as well as the man he emulated, when he said: "The living centre and heart's blood of the science was for him faith in Jesus Christ, as the highest revelation of a holy and merciful God, as the fountain of all salvation and sanctifying grace for a ruined world. Whatever he found that was really great, noble, good and true in

63. From Schaff's "Autobiographical Scrapbook," in G. H. Shriver, "Philip Schaff as a Teacher of Church History," *Journal of Presbyterian History* 47 (March 1969): 74.
64. Philip Schaff, "Recollections of Neander," *Mercersburg Review* 3 (January 1851): 88–89.
65. Philip Schaff, "Neander as a Church Historian," *Mercersburg Review* 4 (November 1852): 566. See also his "Recollections of Neander," p. 77.

history, he referred directly or indirectly to the fact of the incarnation, in which he humbly adored the central sun of all history and the inmost sanctuary of the moral universe."[66]

Schaff's ideas gradually won a small following in the United States and held some promise of fostering a distinct school of church history. Another early practitioner was Henry B. Smith who also taught at Union Seminary and helped achieve greater prominence for church historical studies.[67] But the eminence of that group rested largely on Schaff's massive literary production; no other American scholar in Schaff's day conducted a more extensive plan of research, wrote on a wider range of topics, or pursued them with such mastery of primary source materials. In that latter capacity he was virtually indistinguishable from historians of the scientific school, and some of his work is still considered definitive.[68] But in the late decades of the nineteenth century it was increasingly difficult for him to find sympathetic professional response. Schaff formed his ideas about the nature of the church and its history early in life, and throughout his career he maintained the following position, grounded in faith and to his mind confirmed by observation:

The history of the church is [the story of] the rise and progress of the kingdom of heaven upon earth, for the glory of God and the salvation of the world. . . . Its proper starting point is the incarnation of the Eternal Word. . . . In his person lies all the fulness of the Godhead and of renewed humanity, the whole plan of redemption, and the key of all history. . . . considered as a theological science and art, church history is the faithful and life-like description of the origin and progress of the heavenly kingdom.[69]

By 1882, the year in which that statement was made, naturalistic historians were coming more and more to deny that such spiritual considerations had any legitimate place in historical narratives be-

66. Philip Schaff, *Germany: Its Universities, Theology and Religion, With Sketches of Distinguished Divines of the Age* (Philadelphia: Lindsay and Blakiston, 1857), pp. 273–74.
67. W. K. Stoever, "Henry Boynton Smith and the German Theology of History," *Union Seminary Quarterly Review* 24 (Fall 1968): 83–86, gives the best examples of ideas congruent with those Schaff wished to encourage.
68. The best example is *Bibliotheca Symbolica Ecclesiae Universalis: The Creeds of Christendom with a History and Critical Notes*, 3 vols. (New York: Harper & Brothers, 1877) (hereafter cited as *Creeds of Christendom*).
69. P. Schaff, *HCC*, 1:3–4.

cause they could not verify them by empirical means. Schaff's perspective found verification in evidence of a different sort: scriptural models, creedal guidelines, and the insight of a profound personal faith.

Keeping in mind the proper subject of church history and the sacredness of the historian's task, it is not difficult to understand Schaff's conclusion that his field was the most important of all forms of historical study. He posited that Christ was the central goal of creation and that his church was the focal point of all history developing from the Savior's ministry. Christ's life had been "the greatest fact in the history of the world," a fact of such paramount significance that other historical categories could only cluster around the central Incarnation event in supplementary roles. The church historian based his sense of priorities as well as his historical judgment on the belief that "the Spirit of Christ . . . uninterruptedly present in the church, [was] the chief factor in history, to whose power all human factors . . . must be regarded as subordinate."[70] How different from Adams (and others in the AHA) who expressed the view, "In Germany, I first learned the true method . . . I first began to realize that government and law are the real forces which bind society and the world together."[71] Secular historians defined history as primarily the study of politics, legislation, or economic developments, but Schaff regarded those details as background material for the central task of bringing the epic of *Heilsgeschichte* down to the present day:

The idea of universal history presupposes the Christian idea of the unity of God, and the unity and common destiny of men. . . . The central current and ultimate aim of universal history is the KINGDOM OF GOD established by JESUS CHRIST. . . . All other institutions are made subservient to it, and in its interests the whole world is governed. . . . Secular history, far from controlling sacred history, is controlled by it, must directly or indirectly serve its ends, and can only be fully understood in the central light of Christian truth and the plan of salvation.[72]

Thus the secular history of men and institutions was seen to be without ultimate meaning apart from the reality of Christ, and historians

70. P. Schaff, *What Is Church History?*, p. 82.
71. Herbert B. Adams, *The Study and Teaching of History* (Richmond, 1898), p. 8; also cited in Eric Goldman, *John Bach McMaster: American Historian* (Philadelphia: University of Pennsylvania Press, 1943), p. 14.
72. P. Schaff, *HCC*, 1:2–3.

who concentrated, albeit scientifically, on secular matters erred in two ways. They allowed themselves to be distracted by relatively unimportant details in human history, and they failed to find in that mundane preoccupation the only worthy goal of scholarly research, viz., knowledge of God.

When Schaff formulated his ideas on church history, he was primarily interested in the theological consequences his work might have for contemporary church life. A basic concern was to affirm the Judaeo-Christian understanding of religion as grounded in historical reality and thereby to refute those who interpreted religion rationalistically as a series of transcendental propositions. Another of his apologetic motives was a wish to display the reality and daily relevance of God's providential care. He wanted to point out the universal benefits of Christian activity and at the same time prove the validity of Protestantism as a true branch of the living church. Yet probably the most important factor in his thinking, which will be discussed below, was a hope to further ecumenical activity by means of historical understanding. He thought that if different religious groups could be made aware of their common history, they might appreciate the virtues of others and perhaps be chastened by knowledge of their own failings. With those goals in mind Schaff did not notice the serious threats implicit in the new scientific style of historiography supported by most historians after 1876. One of the ironies of the situation is that Schaff, in his desire to use historical evidence as a foundation for stating theological and philosophical truths, closely resembled the German master whom American scientific historians held as their model. Herbert Adams and other leaders in the AHA lionized Leopold von Ranke as the greatest practitioner of objective empiricism, but, as we have already seen, the scientific school was selective in its appreciation of him and failed to notice the philosophical overview which always informed Ranke's thinking. Schaff remained more comprehensive in scope than any of the university historians in the United States, but his ideas had the ill fortune of being dismissed as unscientific in comparison to what was thought to be Ranke's "strict empiricism."

There were at least three aspects of Schaff's historiography which had become anomalous in the intellectual climate fostered by the emphasis on science in the United States. Whereas scientific historians assumed that valid research depended on unbiased objectivity, Schaff claimed that sound theology was essential to understanding the church's past. Henry Adams and others like him trusted empirical evidence and claimed that the plain facts could speak for themselves. Schaff insisted that prior commitment to a view of the church as essentially a form of divine activity ought to have great priority in the minds of church historians. Of course there were hidden preconceptions in the minds of scientific historians, but their ideal of complete objectivity was contradictory to Schaff's frank avowal of theological purpose. A third factor separating the two viewpoints lay in their concepts of utility or the different directions in which their scholarship tended: Adams concentrated on political and social history in hopes of producing a generation of well-informed leaders in the body politic, but Schaff's great purpose for writing history aimed at providing a basis for ecumenical action among American churches. From the years in which he first expressed his ideas through the last published results of his work in the 1880s, Schaff's fundamental categories seem to have undergone little substantial change.[73]

Late in life Schaff came to realize that the widely accepted scientific historiographical ideas could not easily be reconciled with his own. In one of his last published works he summarized the crucial point of what constituted a major difference between himself and the AHA: "Secular history is the progressive development of the idea of humanity, with its "struggle for existence and survival of the fittest;" ecclesiastical history is the progressive development of the idea of Christianity or the history of the origin, growth, and triumph of the kingdom of God."[74] Schaff began with the "great principles" of Adams's anecdote, while the other group pored over its bushel of clams. His description of the proper church historian as a retrospective prophet was singularly inappropriate in a seminar laboratory. In both their starting points and evaluation of their own activity the sacred and secular historians occupied different ground. Of course the deli-

73. Schaff's ideas in *What Is Church History?* were expanded and incorporated into an introduction for his *History of the Apostolic Church* (1853); statements similar to those discussed above can be found in *HAC* on pages ii–v, 2, 8, 10–11, 16–17, 34–35, 46–47. A later set of volumes, *History of the Christian Church* (1882–92), contains corresponding ideas in vol. 1, pp. vii–viii, 2–5, 20, 25–26. Finally, selections of his *Theological Propaedeutic* (1893) show that Schaff maintained a consistent viewpoint; see pp. 234–35, 239–41, 255, 259, 293, 305–6.

74. P. Schaff, *Theological Propaedeutic*, pp. 239–40.

cate problem of interpreting the meaning and significance of events would provide the best illustrations of their differing perspectives. There is hardly any common ground for comparing them in that area, however, and so the more basic procedural questions will have to serve in this study. There are no indications that Schaff and Adams argued over methodological preferences or that any bad feeling developed to separate them into opposing schools of thought. But in retrospect it is clear that church history viewed as a theological discipline contrasted significantly with history defined along the lines of modern science.

THE FOUNDATION OF THE AMERICAN SOCIETY OF CHURCH HISTORY

Just as the American Historical Association represented the emergence of ideas regarding scientific history, the American Society of Church History can also be seen as representing a distinctive conception of the discipline. Of course neither organization tried to force a particular methodology or interpretational standard on its members, but distinctive qualities pertained to early leaders of the AHA and the ASCH which were associated with their respective institutions. Herbert Adams and other founders of the AHA were joined by some six hundred new members during the first five years; the presidency changed annually, and committees used different personnel frequently. The ASCH had a much smaller membership, and the presidency was held for the first six years by the man who founded the organization. A large membership and frequent changes in leadership make it difficult to generalize about prominent ideas in the AHA after a small group of scientific historians organized it. But the ASCH was able to retain the ideas and goals of its founder for a longer period of time. Policies guiding the professional society for church historians were in large measure formulated and supervised by Philip Schaff. After having surveyed his fundamental ideas regarding the prerogatives of his field and seen how they differed from ideas expressed in the AHA, it is understandable that an element of competition existed between the two groups. But though it might be partially true that Schaff founded the ASCH to counteract the influence of the AHA, the most important reason was to facilitate ecumenical activity in the United States. The reunion of Christendom was the conception that dominated and gave purpose to almost every phase of his life, and traces of it are unmistakable in his work to provide a vehicle for American church historiography.

By the 1880s Schaff had become disturbed by what he called "the increase of rationalism" which he found prevalent in the new scientific America. Several of his letters indicate how deeply concerned he was about "the negative and destructive criticism" that characterized the new breed of iconoclastic intellectual,[75] a negation of the main aspects of his life's work. As early as 1871 his assessment of the general shift in values led him reluctantly to observe that "theology is no more the all-absorbing and all-controlling science, as it was from the fourth down to the seventeenth century. Mathematics and the natural sciences . . . invite genius and talent into new channels. The morbid passion for sudden wealth and power, for extravagance and vain show, is . . . a serious check upon those ideal tendencies and pursuits which, after all, constitute the true nobility and abiding glory of man."[76] After almost fifty years' dedication to an amalgam of religious life and learning Schaff conceded that a generation was growing up around him which did not seem interested in perpetuating his ideals.[77] Casting back over his career in the United States, he drew a parallel between himself and Neander, the old champion of pietism and providential church history in Germany. A revealing analysis of Neander's activity in the face of similar criticism brought him to the conclusion that their objectives in different settings had been the same: to "resist the flood of rationalism and later the destructive

75. Letters from Schaff to an old friend, Frederic Godet, dated 1890 and 1892, in D. Schaff, Life of Philip Schaff, pp. 422, 443.
76. This particular passage is taken from Schaff's inaugural address at Union Seminary, "The Theology of Our Age and Country," p. 12. Schaff might have been led to make some remarks on this subject after having attended the Ely Lectures delivered at Union Seminary in 1871. James McCosh, president of the College of New Jersey, tried to derive what benefit he could from materialism and positivistic science, while at the same time holding out for higher laws, innate spiritual capacities in man, and a providential guidance in the natural world. Schaff might have been impressed by McCosh's attempt, but not enough to feel safe about the future. See James McCosh, Christianity and Positivism: A Series of Lectures to the Times on Natural Theology and Apologetics (New York: Robert Carter and Brothers, 1871), pp. 158–66, 175–78, 338–41, 346–48.
77. Letter in D. Schaff, Life of Philip Schaff, p. 413.

criticism of Baur and his school" in an effort to protect the divine truth in Christian history.[78] With such thoughts in mind, one would expect to see Schaff gather men around him in the ASCH in an effort to spread his own ideas about the church and the sacred science of chronicling God's redemptive activity. Though there never was any explicit antagonism between theological and scientific historians, the fact remains that Schaff founded the ASCH to be independent of the AHA.[79]

Taking the long view of his life and thought, one can begin to see how Schaff's hopes for denominational cooperation as a factor in the creation of an "Evangelical Catholicism" was the most important factor behind his founding the ASCH.[80] He had always considered denominational jealousy to be a major deterrent to cooperation and saw that it stemmed from misunderstandings between groups as well as from a mutual ignorance of their common Christian tradition. So he brought historians together in hopes of eliminating some of the grounds for bigotry and mistrust, replacing that poor foundation with a solid one of cordiality among various ecclesiastical bodies. Charter members of the ASCH were aware of the ecumenical thrust behind the

78. Philip Schaff, *Saint Augustine, Melanchthon, Neander* (New York: Funk & Wagnalls, 1886), pp. 142, 153–54. See also D. Schaff, *Life of Philip Schaff*, p. 410.

79. There was some mention of merging the ASCH with the AHA from the very start, but Schaff gained control of the committee which was to look into the matter. In a letter dated 4 May 1889 (Herbert Baxter Adams Papers, Johns Hopkins University, Baltimore, Md.), Schaff wrote Adams suggesting two societies be allowed to stand independently:

> My dear Professor Adams:
> I take pleasure in sending to you today a complimentary copy of the Papers of the Church History Society.
> They will enable you to judge wether [*sic*] a consolidation or confederation of the two Societies is practicable or desirable. You are on the Committee of Conference, and I shall be ready for a meeting or correspondence at any time in May or June.
> I wish you to understand that the Church History Society never thought of any other connection than such an one as will be advantageous to *both* Societies. Being a life member of both & founder of one, I could of course have no other object in view.

80. The wording indicates something of Schaff's eclecticism. He conceived of the new church as a compound of the best elements of Protestantism (evangelical piety) and Catholicism (wide applicability and concern for institutions). The New Church would embody old principles which had been *aufgehoben* to a higher level of existence; Protestantism as it stood was merely an interim stage to the highest realization of Christian witness. See Penzel, "Church History and the Ecumenical Quest," pp. 201–3, 314–15.

new society because Schaff made his concern explicit at the first meeting. Published reports, which do not record all that transpired but serve as a skeletal and all too cryptic report, state that "Dr. Schaff spoke upon the desirability and prospective usefulness of an American society of Church History on a catholic and irenical basis in the development of a taste and talent for historical theology by special researches, and by bringing into personal contact the workers in this department, and thus indirectly aiding the cause of Christian union."[81] Since an understanding of church history was indispensable to effective reunion, Schaff hoped to promote mutual understanding and historical self-awareness by means of the ASCH and thereby aid the churches' progress. The primary reason for founding the ASCH was to "prepare the way for the healing of the divisions of Chistendom and to unite all the worshippers of Christ," for historical knowledge might help them realize that "no one of them was perfect, but that they were mutually necessary to the other."[82] Thus the study of church history and the founding of the ASCH were important steps to nurture the development of an American theology. Schaff looked forward to the day when the new church in America would produce its vibrant theology because he thought it was essential to serve as "a wall to keep off the wolves, but not a fence to divide the sheep."[83] The foundation of the ASCH was part of his effort to raise such a protective wall and speed theological synthesis.

In Schaff's ecumenical vision, all periods of Christian history were viewed as transitional stages to improved conditions which eliminated previous failings and tried to reach a higher realization of the truth. The simple process by which historical epochs emerged in succession could be explained by analyzing the nuances of a German verb, *aufheben*. Every period of historical development was admitted to have some defect that made change desirable. The first step, then, was to abolish those debilitating aspects, or "diseases;" secondly, it was important to preserve all that had been good in the old order for continued use amid new circumstances. The final part of the move-

81. *Papers of the American Society of Church History* 1 (1889): vi–vii (hereafter cited as *Papers of the ASCH*).
82. Schaff made that statement in a book-review essay in the *Independent*, 28 March 1889; see also *What Is Church History?*, p. 127.
83. P. Schaff, "The Consensus of the Reformed Confessions, as Related to the Present State of Evangelical Theology," *Christ and Christianity*.

ment tried to synthesize those new variables, innately beneficial elements purged of their previous corruption, into a better manifestation of the movement's original purpose.[84] For example, the Protestant Reformation abandoned the corruption of the medieval papacy, retained its essentially holy ministry and transcended it to a new level of religious intensity. In that manner it stood heir to the New Testament, *aufgehoben* to a higher plane and able to continue its witness in northern Europe. But even Protestantism represented a temporary level of religious accomplishment that would eventually yield to greater expressions of insight and devotion. Further developments rooted in the historical process would be able to build on that foundation and move beyond Protestantism and Catholicism to achieve "the blending of the truth and virtues of both, without their corresponding errors and defects, in the ideal church of the future, . . . forming not a *new* church, but the final perfect product of that of the present and the past."[85] Schaff believed that the new world would furnish the site for that emerging level of Christian life.

The Washburn Professor of Church History viewed America as the land of promise, a virgin land where the best of the old world might be improved and new ways of life could be tested. Schaff conceived of the United States as "the theatre of the last decisive conflict between faith and infidelity, . . . of the greatest collision between the various Christian nations and confessions and also of their final reconciliation."[86] Just as America took European immigrants and formed them into a single nation, so Schaff believed that the various forms of American churches would eventually be brought to the point of creating a single religious perspective from their creeds and ecclesiastical positions. As early as 1846 he prophesied that an "American church" would "soon come to the consciousness of . . . her great calling; subordinate her sectarian activities to the general interest that lies far beyond that of any single existing denomination; and assume in this struggle towards a better future, the genuine his-

84. Shriver, "Concept of Organic Historiography," pp. 91–92, 101–110.

85. P. Schaff, *HAC*, p. 678.

86. Philip Schaff, *America: A Sketch of the Political, Social and Religious Character of the United States of North America* (New York: Charles Scribner's Sons, 1855), p. 272. Another edition, more recent but not used in this study, has been edited by Perry Miller (Cambridge, Mass.: Harvard University Press, Belknap Press, 1961).

torical standpoint."[87] His learned optimism about the progress ensured by that "genuine historical standpoint" fed on the contagion
that held America surety for every immigrant's hopes. But after a
decade of more realistic experience in his adopted land, faith in the
future remained undiminished. In 1857 he reaffirmed the conviction
that America was destined to witness the rise of a new Reformation, a
union of the best strains of each denomination and the creation of
a distinctive theology:

America will no doubt produce . . . a classical theology of its own, that
shall rise superior to the sectional and denominational schools, which so
far have mostly prevailed amongst us, and be truly catholic in spirit, and
influence. That theology . . . will not be simply a continuation of either
the English, or the German alone, but the result of the combined action
and reaction of both, as applied to the peculiar wants and condition of
American Christianity and society.[88]

There is no clear indication as to exactly what Schaff had in mind for
the future of institutionalized Christianity, but at times he spoke of
the final stage as a union of the best aspects of previous creeds and
polities, the creation of a new church where Christian beliefs and
practices would "come together, consolidate, concentrate itself, and
out of the phoenix-ashes of all Christian denominations and sects, rise
glorified, as the truly universal, evangelical Catholic Bride of the
Lord, adorned with the fairest flowers of the church-history of all
centuries."[89]
       The new world held promise to actualize the latest developments
as history slowly moved upward; so the task for forward-looking
men was to aid historical progress and help foster the developing
American church. Schaff conceived of his function as churchman and
as historian—offices which cannot be separated in his thought—to
be one of aiding the further development of ecumenism. In his
research he utilized a providential, Christological interpretation of

87. P. Schaff, *What Is Church History?*, p. 114. Penzel, in his careful study of
the origins of Schaff's thought ("Church History and the Ecumenical Quest,"
pp. 219, 311), points out that Schaff drew heavily upon Schelling in his hopes for
the future of Christianity. His unique contribution lay in allowing Germany first
place in developing ideas, while making America the scene of the most accomplished
application of the faith.
88. P. Schaff, *Germany*, pp. 8–9.
89. P. Schaff, *America*, p. 263; see also p. 97.

history that contained a strong eschatological element to emphasize those events which he thought contributed to the final goal.[90] At annual meetings of the ASCH he again took the opportunity to lecture on the proper methods and ultimate goals of those calling themselves church historians.[91] Most of his publications were intended to "promote better understanding among the Churches of Christ." They sought to exhibit (one of his favorite verbs) the presence of Christ throughout the ages and enrich the reader's understanding of ways in which that presence could solve theological and ecclesiastical problems.[92] Of course the writing of historical treatises would not in themselves be enough to effect reunion. History could provide the necessary mutual understanding, but human endeavor alone would not suffice. As one modern observer accurately put it, "Schaff knew that sharing separate traditions and the common past would not bring reunion automatically. Here emerged the significance of Schaff's Christocentric piety. He believed that as Christians drew nearer to the Christological center, the greater would be their eagerness to manifest their oneness in the body of Christ in their common faith and life."[93] Activities of the ASCH supplemented the general task of church historiography; all efforts served the ultimate purpose of service to God in his plan for touching the lives of his people.

Perhaps the most valuable literary achievement in an ecumenical vein was the American Church History Series, thirteen volumes summarizing the history and pertinent data of major American denominations to the end of the nineteenth century. Sometime before 1890 Albert Henry Newman, professor of church history and comparative religion at Baptist College, Toronto, began urging a plan for a series of denominational histories because he thought some publication should continue the story where Schaff's *History of the Christian Church* ended.[94] Schaff had terminated his historical survey at the

90. Shriver, "Concept of Organic Historiography," p. 144.

91. These speeches are mentioned from time to time as having been made, but unfortunately no manuscripts or copies seem to have survived. They would have been invaluable as a source for understanding Schaff's thought and the plans he held for the ASCH.

92. P. Schaff, *Creeds of Christendom*, i:vi.

93. James H. Smylie, "Philip Schaff Ecumenist: The Reunion of Protestantism and Roman Catholicism," *Encounter* 28 (1967): 16.

94. A. H. Newman, "Report on a Proposed Series of Denominational Histories to be Published under the Auspices of the American Society of Church History," *Papers of the ASCH* 3 (1891): 209.

middle of the seventeenth century for two reasons: he claimed to be distracted by lecturing responsibilities and too old to continue the rigors of first-hand research; he also thought the complexity of recent developments made generalized studies such as his too superficial to do them justice.[95] He had made attempts to initiate a denominational series as early as 1886, before he became involved with editing the Nicene, Post-Nicene Library, but he was unable to interest a publisher in the project. Thus when Newman arrived at similar ideas about a set of historical volumes, Schaff responded favorably and offered his earlier format as a working guideline. The two men, with the help of the organized society of church historians, inaugurated the project and saw it through to complete publication. Newman's ideas about the series were congruent with Schaff's, and together they influenced both the selection of authors and the execution of their tasks. Though Schaff had a six-man editorial board to help him, it is probably not an overstatement for his biographer to state that "Dr. Schaff originated the plan, selected the contributors and arranged for the publication."[96] The announced goals of the series indicate how thoroughly it was a Schaffian enterprise:

While each writer would have every inducement to exhibit his denomination in the most favorable light that the facts of history would warrant, it would be impossible for him to write in complete disregard of the rights of other denominations to favorable consideration. Thus the character of the readers addressed would minister to fairness of treatment in matters of controversy and could scarcely fail to secure the production of works decidedly irenical in spirit.

As the circumstances under which such a series should be prepared would be favorable to the production of peculiarly valuable works, so also might large irenical results be expected in the readers. . . . A wide reading of histories of all the denominations, prepared, according to the plan suggested, by the members of each, could not fail to be promotive, in a high degree, of truth and peace.[97]

Philip Schaff, founder and guiding light of the ASCH, thought of church history as a fundamental category of theological knowledge.

95. Ibid., p. 211.
96. D. Schaff, *Life of Philip Schaff*, p. 518.
97. Newman, "Report," p. 210. Schaff's written statement about the viewpoint desirable in writers included this description: "The histories are to be written by representative historians of the respective denominations, who combine loyalty to their own Church with comprehensive culture and a liberal, catholic spirit."

Several members of the early society agreed with him and joined in efforts to extend those interests in the United States. Schaff's immense personal prestige helped the organization maintain its dominant ideas and activities with some degree of success, but even in its first years the ASCH was large enough to include historians of different persuasions. Throughout its history the organization has been considered the meeting place for all American church historians, a forum for discussing ideas about their craft and a medium in which their work could be critically reviewed.

After Schaff died in 1893, the presidency went to men who shared the founder's conception of blending the roles of prophet and scholar, but the issue of methodological implications of science versus theology became increasingly pronounced. John Fletcher Hurst and George Park Fisher reflected familiar theological ideas about church history in their publications, but they failed to guide the ASCH with the vision and energy the original president had provided.[98] The years immediately following Schaff's death were ones of more debate occasioned by the inroads of scientific historiography. It became apparent to many in the society that institutionalized efforts to perpetuate Schaff's theological and ecumenical ideas about church history were difficult to maintain. Perhaps even those who held disparate ideas about their craft had common doubts about the practicability of a separate organization for church historians. By 1896 the more secular

98. Hurst gained early fame with a book entitled *History of Rationalism* (New York: Charles Scribner and Co., 1865). He won Schaff's admiration and was chosen to succeed him as president of the ASCH. There are only two works which can be called his own: *Short History of the Church in the United States, 1492–1890* (New York: Chautauqua Press, 1890) and *Short History of the Christian Church* (New York: Harper & Brothers, 1893). Two other products bearing his name, *History of the Christian Church* (New York: Eaton and Mains, 1900) and *History of Methodism* (New York: Eaton and Mains, 1902–4), show that much of the work was done by research assistants. Aside from any really sustained efforts toward scholarship, Hurst's narrative is marked by historical oversights and inaccuracies which place it in the second rank of literature produced in his day. G. P. Fisher presents a problem of another sort because he treated the history of biblical religion with Schaffian circumspection and dealt with later developments by means of the best critical, historical tools available. The best volume illustrating how these compartments could be juxtaposed is his *Discussions in History and Theology* (New York: Charles Scribner's Sons, 1880). A publication based on a confessional approach is *Essays on the Supernatural Origin of Christianity: With Special Reference to the Theories of Renan, Strauss, and the Tübingen School* (New York: Charles Scribner and Co., 1865). Then, on the other hand, see *The Reformation* (New York: Charles Scribner and Co., 1873).

and scientifically oriented historians gained control of the ASCH and brought an end to its independent existence.

Among the reasons given to explain the move for dissolution, the most important one concerned methodology and struck directly at one of Schaff's fundamental ideas. Denying any uniqueness to the historical church or any special consideration to a study of its history, the final resolution stated that, since "Church History is only a part of general history, its students should ally themselves with the students of the general subject."[99] Throughout the list of resolutions and supporting arguments there was no mention of ecumenism or the formation of an American theology as goals for serious church historians. One is left with the impression that framers of the manifesto thought such goals were not central to the task of scholarly research. But the official pronouncement and subsequent action should not lead to the conclusion that they were accepted unanimously. There were probably many members still loyal to Schaff's point of view who were forced to acquiesce by the chronic difficulties of the decade. They might have wished to defend the original conception of churchly history planted in the ASCH, but they must have recognized the impossibility of continuing an institution with minimal support.

Nine years after it began, the ASCH was dissolved and made a section of the AHA. The original format of the ASCH which attempted to foster a distinct set of ideas about proper church historiography had become outmoded during the last decades of the nineteenth century because of prevailing scientific standards. The climate of opinion which had been gaining ascendancy since the 1870s made it increasingly difficult to write a serious narrative that emphasized spiritual agents or the theological significance of ecclesiastical activity. By the 1890s it had become virtually impossible to base church history on a confession of faith and still command respect in the scholarly world. Termination of the society marked a turning in American intellectual history because it was a significant indication that secularists had replaced religious spokesmen in a domain which the latter had occupied for centuries.

It would be a mistake to interpret the dissolution of the ASCH as a

99. Four reasons are listed in the *Papers of the ASCH* 8 (1897): xxviii–xxix.

clearcut victory of scientism over religious-minded history. A more accurate reading of the materials would indicate that Adams and the AHA belong on one side of a spectrum, Schaff and the ASCH on the other, but each set of ideas had goals, presuppositions, methodological priorities, a legitimacy all its own. The juxtaposition of theological and scientific historiographies serves to display the options available to church historians in the last quarter of the nineteenth century. Now that these limits have been discussed, studies of the following scholars may be more easily understood within that context. Men in some of the following chapters tried to further the idea, in theory and in practice, that church histories based on theological presuppositions were suspect in the scholarly community. But it cannot be said that the influence of science on some church historians, as strong as that was, stifled all attempts to write history from a balanced appreciation of scientific fact and religious conviction. By 1896 men with fresh theologies had begun developing interesting perspectives that produced compelling studies of church history. Those innovators tried to retain the advances science had brought to historiography and integrate them with their own views as to how church history should be written. Such men were educated at a time when science and theology were in tension, and their historiographical ideas may be studied in terms of that fruitful interchange.

3 ♂CATHOLIC HISTORIOGRAPHY

It is almost universally recognized that John Gilmary Shea has written the classic historical survey of American Catholicism and deserves the title, "Father of American Catholic History."[1] Though he also won recognition in such ancillary fields as philology, geography, ethnology, and bibliography, Shea's lasting fame rests on accomplishments in historical narrative, and he adds to our knowledge of the complex ideas related to scientific procedure and the historian's craft. His concern to speak to both secular and Catholic readers, his concept of history written both as impersonally recorded data and still as an act of faith, was an interesting combination of ideas in the age when critical scholarship began to flourish in the United States. Thus his intellectual career, pursued during a period which some critics judge to have been stifling of real achievement among members of a minority,[2] affords insight into the beginnings of historical scholarship among American Catholics. Apart from his intrinsic interest, Shea presents another perspective from which the student can analyze theological interpretations of church history in this country. John Shea was Philip Schaff's ideological and chronological contemporary. Though the two men held significant differences of opinion about the nature and location of the true church, though they were far apart on the

1. Peter Guilday, *John Gilmary Shea: Father of American Catholic History, 1824–1892* (New York: United States Catholic Historical Society, 1926), pp. 146–47; John T. Ellis, *A Select Bibliography of the History of the Catholic Church in the United States* (New York: Declan X. McMullen Co., 1947), pp. 16, 103, and his *A Guide to American Catholic History* (Milwaukee: Bruce Publishing Co., 1959), p. 19; E. R. Vollmar, *The Catholic Church in America: An Historical Bibliography* (New Brunswick, N.J.: Scarecrow Press, 1956), p. xiv; see also Adrian T. English, "The Historiography of American Catholic History (1785–1884)," *Catholic Historical Review*, n.s. 5 (January 1926): 563; and J. Dolan, "Church History in England and America in the Nineteenth and Twentieth Centuries," in H. Jedin and J. Dolan, *Handbook of Church History* (London: Burns and Oates, 1956), 1:56

2. English, "Historiography of American Catholic History," pp. 564–65; see also John P. Cadden, *The Historiography of the American Catholic Church: 1785–1943* (Washington, D.C.: Catholic University of America Press, 1944), pp. 2–3.

restrictions placed on the historian in constructing his narrative, their views were similar on several fundamental matters. Both scholars formed ideas about scientific method before the middle of the century, thus inevitably placing themselves in contrast to members of the AHA who shared attitudes fashioned in a different matrix. Both men acted on a second conviction that welded them together and vitiated their influence in the age of science: in the last analysis theological understanding was viewed as the ultimate goal, and historical research was thought to have meaning only when it served that edifying end. This essential compatibility was never recognized in their own day, but it places them rather closely together on one side of the spectrum of historiographical thought, that side which experienced diminishing eminence in the age of science.

Shea was a self-taught student of historical methods and was perhaps more sensitive than most to the standards for acceptable research. Thus he came to reflect current paradigms defining what sorts of questions could legitimately be asked, what research techniques would prove fruitful, and what types of explanation were considered satisfactory. Shea also articulated a body of ideas about the Church and the nation that enriches our comprehension of post–Civil War America and the travail of Catholics, so many of whom were classed as "immigrants." His simple ecclesiology is revealed in the way he discussed the hierarchy and emphasized the institutional growth of dioceses and provinces. Such general themes as the heroic piety of pioneer missionaries, the calumny of English Protestants, the patriotism of American Catholics in times of national peril, and the bitter irony of consequent ostracism and religious persecution—all lend distinctive color to his volumes. Those motifs reveal some of the major concerns faithful laymen held for the American Catholic church at that time, and they indicate the reaction of cultivated Catholics to a society which did not allow them a status commensurate with the respectability of their past. Shea's histories serve as documents for understanding the intellectual and religious milieu confronting Catholic spokesmen a century ago.

SHEA'S CONCEPTION OF HISTORY AS A SCIENCE

John Dawson Shea was born in New York City on July 22, 1824, and received early schooling in a grammar school connected with

Columbia College, of which his father was principal. Inexplicably, he did not enroll at Columbia but rather entered the employ of a Spanish merchant and, once he had mastered the language, filled a useful post for six years. In 1844 Shea, following the example of his brother, began reading law and was admitted to the bar two years later. As in his merchant days, Shea continued to be absorbed in historical studies and devoted more time to them than to his profession. He was admitted to the New-York Historical Society in 1846. On June 7, 1847, he entered the Society of Jesus,[3] changed his middle name to Gilmary (servant of Mary), and considered himself at last settled in a vocation. His studies at Saint John's, Fordham, in New York, and at Saint Mary's in Montreal allowed him ample time to pursue historical research. But poor health brought what appears to have been a happy novitiate to a premature close, and in 1852 John Gilmary Shea was forced once more to seek a new livelihood. Having acquired some literary facility, he eventually assumed a career as editor of the Frank Leslie popular magazines. For over twenty years he executed his daily duties at the publishing house, while his real life lay in the hours he could salvage for studying Catholic activities in American history. His remarkable list of publications attests to the success of that double life.

In 1852, when Shea inaugurated his career as a practicing historian with a slim volume of eyewitness reports on early exploration in the Mississippi Valley, historians were loosely grouped into two general categories, the romanticists and the archivists. The basic approach of both groups has already been discussed above, and here it merely needs to be added that Shea's ideas regarding historical methodology followed the general strictures laid down by archivists, although he had a few discernible romantic traits. The best indication of his position is to be found in his activity as a compiler of documents, but once in 1854 Shea made an exception to his usual reticence about personal views and stated his position openly: "In writing [I have] indeavored to be just to all men, to avoid all partiality, to take no part in the rivalries which have existed and still exist, all tending to overshadow the truth, and give theories or party views for a real pic-

---

3. Guilday, *John Gilmary Shea,* p. 19, has the date 1848, but that must be a typographical error, of which there are many in the book.

ture of the historical facts."[4] In avoiding the influence of biased theories or "party views," Shea tried to limit his writing to a bare introduction to the documents he had collected. His approach went beyond a simple fair-mindedness common to almost every historian and aimed at subjugating personal narrative to the dominance of original texts. A more thorough explanation of the rigor with which such historians regarded their function was made by one of Shea's contemporaries, Orestes Brownson:

History is not a speculative science; it deals exclusively with facts and is simply a record of events which have succeeded one another in time. [If one theorizes about data,] this theory must be historical, not speculative; that is, it must be a theory for the explanation of the purely historical, not the metaphysical . . . meaning of facts, and, like all inductive theories, a mere generalization or classification of facts in their own order.[5]

Once the method Shea chose becomes clear, a coherent pattern emerges from his diffuse literary activities. Insofar as his major historical works are concerned, the early volumes on discovering the Mississippi (1852), Catholic missions (1854), translations of historical surveys (DeCourcy, 1856 and 1879; Charlevoix, 1866–72), and the printing of unrelated Jesuit records (the twenty-six volume Cramoisy Series, 1857–66) all serve as preliminaries for the major opus of 1886–92. Viewed as parts of a single process, those works indicate how Shea labored to bring together enough materials to supply a connected history of the Roman Catholic church in the United States from its earliest stages. Such a procedure of remaining strictly within the confines of original documents always includes the hazard of occasionally sketchy explanation due to insufficient evidence, but Shea tried to meet that problem by collecting more and more material. By the 1880s some estimate his library to have contained over 20,000 books, pamphlets, and manuscripts, many of

4. John G. Shea, *History of Catholic Missions among the Indian Tribes of the United States, 1529–1854* (New York: Edward Dunigan and Brother, 1855), p. 17. For a good example of such impartiality, see Shea, *A History of the Catholic Church within the Limits of the United States: From the First Attempted Colonization to the Present Time,* 4 vols. (New York: John Gilmary Shea, 1886–92), 1:639–40 (hereafter cited as *History*).
5. In Thomas McAvoy, "Orestes A. Brownson and American History," *Catholic Historical Review* 40 (October 1954): 258.

which are the only copies known still to exist.[6] His first two books on Catholic missionaries were popular because they were a double revelation: they furnished a great mass of factual information about the work brave and durable priests accomplished in converting native tribes; then on a different level, they disclosed the simple fact that such detailed information about precolonial America was available.[7] The initial success of those volumes confirmed Shea's ideas about the proper course of historical research, and he followed them consistently throughout his life. That unpretentious method of "tracing" (a favorite verb) the church's annals gave his four-volume *History of the Catholic Church within the Limits of the United States, from the First Attempted Colonization to the Present Time* both the authority that massive documentation commands and an inevitably uneven narrative.[8]

A reputation for producing volumes based on primary source materials won Shea the honorific invitation to be a writer in Justin Winsor's *Narrative and Critical History of America,* a post which might lead some to say that Shea qualified as a scientific historian. His work certainly deserved to be included in a series intended to "set forth a bibliographical and critical record of all the sources of the history of the American continent down to the middle of the [nineteenth] century."[9] His articles on "The Jesuits, Recollects and the Indians" (volume 4) and "Ancient Florida" (volume 2)[10] are good examples of the careful verification and painstaking analysis of sources which Winsor's edition contained. That he was chosen by

6. Cadden, *Historiography of the American Catholic Church,* p. 29. This estimate seems too large and does not agree with Shea's own statement contained in the text. The American Antiquarian Society possesses a copy of entries in Shea's library, and that list includes approximately 2,763 volumes, with some duplicate titles.

7. See F. E. Tourscher, "Catholic Scholarship in the United States," *Catholic Historical Review,* n.s. 7 (October 1927): 476, for a full explanation of the significance of the *Relations* and Shea's part in publicizing them.

8. Some examples of uneven narrative due to spotty evidence are Shea, *History,* 1:375–76, 530, 535, 456, 2:192, 454–94, and most abrupt, 497; 3:57–70, 93–98, and 200.

9. In Horace Scudder, "Memoir of Justin Winsor, LL.D.," *Proceedings of the Massachusetts Historical Society,* 2d ser. 12 (February 1899): 478; see also Joseph Borome, "The Life and Letters of Justin Winsor" (Ph.D. diss., Columbia University, 1950), p. 411.

10. Winsor's series, dependent on many authors, had a curious publication sequence from 1884 to 1889, all published in Boston at Houghton Mifflin Co. Shea's articles in their order of appearance are found in 4:263–94 and 2:231–98.

Winsor substantiates the observation that Shea was recognized as a careful, thoughtful researcher by scientific historians. It also confirms the suggestion that the nonacademic practitioner had proven himself to be an exemplary archivist. From such an eminence Shea occasionally reviewed other historical works and further revealed his methodological norms by the criticisms offered. One of the most indicative pieces was a review of Alzog's treatment of American Catholic history which Shea criticized for its numerous inaccuracies and poorly researched topics. His final judgment was that any work depicting Junipero Serra as an Italian or stating that the See of Quebec had been established in 1675 with the aid of Louis XIV, that American Catholics had been placed under the London Apostolic Vicariate during the Revolutionary War, or that New Orleans had been made a suffragan of Baltimore in 1808 was "scarcely pardonable for so sorry an account of the Church in this country."[11] In what was his clearest attempt to distinguish himself from those too irresponsible to be trusted as historians, Shea indicated how documentary evidence was the last word on any disputed question; the contrast was obvious when he remarked: "We shall endeavor to extract from his rambling and declamatory text various propositions and meet them by [sic] the fruit of thirty years' study and a collection of nearly two thousand books, pamphlets, and volumes of papers and periodicals bearing on the Catholic Church in the United States."[12] At the same time, this fundamental conviction about procedure notwithstanding, Shea admired the work of George Bancroft and even went so far as to call him the "first great philosophic historian" in the United States.[13] Shea's method and goals were not unmixed with a mild appreciation of romantic ideals, but as a rule, esteem for documents dominated his entire approach.

The exact origin of Shea's conceptions is difficult to determine. Apparently he always had a taste for collecting things, and very early

---

11. John G. Shea, "The Catholic Church in the United States in the Recent Translation of Alzog," *American Catholic Quarterly Review* 4 (January 1879): 139–42 (hereafter cited as *ACQR*).

12. John G. Shea, "Is Froude a Historian?," *ACQR* 5 (January 1880): 115; see also pp. 136–37.

13. John G. Shea, "Bancroft's History of the United States," *ACQR* 8 (October 1883): 672–74. The general tone of the article is critical of Bancroft's revising his earlier work, revisions Shea considered unjust to Catholics; see pp. 682–83.

accumulated valuable exhibits of flowers, coins, and minerals.[14] Those who spoke from personal knowledge of him told of an unwillingness to venture private opinions on controversial subjects; but once on a topic related to his life work, the comprehensiveness of his information was said to be "literally encyclopedic."[15] So with private inclinations showing an initial preference for compiling data and restricting personal views, it is easy to see how scholars could have helped mold those traits into a definite research procedure. The most genial of those men was Edmund Bailey O'Callaghan who achieved repute as a "patient, careful, and judicious investigator of documents,"[16] especially in his *History of New Netherland* (1846) and *The Documentary History of the State of New York* (1849–51). Many prominent scholars and statesmen noted his "avidity for antiquarian lore" and urged him to concentrate on the early records of New York in order to "rescue [them] from obscurity and oblivion in which they have . . . lain."[17] As one of the earliest historians to attain eminence by concentrating on manuscripts and as one of Shea's closest friends, the influence of O'Callaghan on the development of ideas in Shea must have been great.[18]

But the most important individual who influenced Shea's thoughts on historical method was Felix Martin, S.J., rector of Saint Mary's College in Montreal during the years Shea was a novice there. Martin's personal example as a practicing historian and archivist of early Jesuit activity in Canada was crucial in shaping the future American historian.[19] Father Martin earned distinction among historical scholars

14. Cadden, *Historiography of the American Catholic Church*, pp. 20–21.

15. See for example James J. Walsh, "John Gilmary Shea," *ACQR* 38 (April 1913): 185.

16. Guilday, *John Gilmary Shea*, p. 20.

17. From letters to O'Callaghan, in Francis S. Guy, *Edmund Bailey O'Callaghan: A Study in American Historiography, 1797–1880* (Washington, D.C.: Catholic University of America Press, 1934), pp. 41–42.

18. For a similar estimate, see James J. Walsh, "Edmund Bailey O'Callaghan of New York: Physician, Historian and Antiquarian, A.D. 1797–1880," *Records of the American Catholic Historical Society of Philadelphia* 16 (1905): 2–22.

19. Guilday, *John Gilmary Shea*, p. 20, is unclear in his discussion of the two men. It seems that O'Callaghan was the friend who sustained Shea during his labors, but Martin was the one who gave him something to sustain. See Shea's own statement to this effect in his translation of Felix Martin, *The Life of Father Isaac Jogues: Missionary Priest of the Society of Jesus* (New York: Benziger Brothers, 1885), p. 3; see also a general assessment in T. J. Campbell, *The Jesuits, 1534–1921: A History of the Society of Jesus from its Foundation to the Present Time* (New York: Encyclopedia Press, 1921), 2:873–74.

by collecting those documents about New France which eventually found their widest dissemination in R. G. Thwaites's seventy-three volume series. Shea had been a trusted aid in redacting the *Relations des Jesuites,* and as such he must have learned a great deal about careful and detached research procedures. Not only did his later activity follow much the same pattern, but he also seconded Father Martin's motive which was to allow the records to "refute all calumnies, and tell their own story in simple and unvarnished language, leaving it forever to the admiration of the world."[20] The records telling their own stories included reports about French North America from 1611 to 1672 (many derived from the archives of Paris and Rome) and erudite biographical sketches of Bressani, Chaumonot, and Jogues. Shea's later publications were obviously patterned, in style and content, after Martin's valuable studies. It is unfortunate that we know little about the sources of Martin's thought or about the general content of French Jesuit education in the early decades of the nineteenth century,[21] but the few scraps of available evidence support our general understanding of his approach to history. Father Martin indicated an interest in archaeology, and that significant interest helps explain his historical activity as a process of publishing collected specimens with critical notes.[22] Shea often referred to Martin

20. In A. T. Sadlier, "Father Felix Martin, S.J.," *Catholic World* 45 (April 1887): 112–13.

21. This is a significant question which could add to our knowledge of the influence of European historical thought on American scholars and open up another set of ideas to supplement the dominant German strain. There are, however, too many gaps in our knowledge about Jesuit intellectual development in France to support any concrete conclusions. Much more needs to be done in this area. For a survey of the general situation, see C. S. Philips, *The Church in France, 1789–1848: A Study in Revival* (London: A. R. Mowbray and Co., Ltd., 1929), pp. 180, 202; James MacCaffrey, *History of the Catholic Church in the Nineteenth Century, 1789–1908* (Dublin: M. H. Gill and Son, 1910), 1:56–58. For some idea of Jesuit education and the place of history and inductive sciences, see R. Schwickerath, *Jesuit Education: Its History and Principles Viewed in the Light of Modern Educational Problems* (St. Louis: B. Herder, 1903), pp. 125, 194–98; A. Thebaud, *Three-Quarters of a Century (1807–1882): A Retrospect Written from Documents and Memory in 1877–1882* (New York: United States Catholic Historical Society, 1912), pp. 187–88, 288–89. For works that touch Felix Martin specifically, see J. Burnichon, *La Compagnie de Jesus en France: Histoire d'un Siècle, 1814–1914:* (Paris: Gabriel Beauchesne, 1916), 2:299–300; F. Vignon, *Le Père Martin* (n.p., n.d.), pp. 2–3; and finally the excellent study by P. Desjardins, *Le Collège Sainte-Marie de Montréal: La Fondation, Le Fondateur* (Montreal: College Sainte-Marie, 1940), p. 179.

22. Desjardins, *Collège Sainte-Marie,* pp. 180–82, contains correspondence between Felix Martin and his brother Arthur on this topic; pages 218–19 are prime examples of his activity that served as a model for Shea's later work.

as the most stable factor in his haphazard education, and it seems that archaeology was in fact the methodological prototype both men tried to approximate.

A natural corollary to the activities of an archivist was participation in local historical societies because their emphasis lay in the preservation of original materials. Until the American Historical Association was founded in 1884 to foster a new rationale and format for individual research projects, all local and state historical societies had sought to "collect, preserve, and diffuse the materials for the history of the United States, or a section of it."[23] From the oldest such organizations, the Massachusetts Historical Society (1791) and the New-York Historical Society (1804), down to the youngest mid-western associations, all subscribed to the notion that the publication of dry records was considerably more useful than issuing opinionated historical essays. The volumes of material rescued from oblivion by such societies are generally indispensable to later students. The various *Proceedings* or ventures supported by the federal government such as Force's "American Archives" served as timely counterparts to the famous *Monumenta Germaniae Historica* (begun in 1826) and the *Documents inédits sur l'histoire de France* (begun in 1833). But Herbert Adams and other scientific historians, fresh from working with such massive volumes in European seminars, founded the AHA for more creative purposes. When compared with their views, Shea's compilation of material along the same old lines seems to have been insensitive to modern changes.

Shea belonged to several state historical societies, and when the Third Plenary Council (1884) added some titular support to the study of church history in this country, he utilized that pronouncement as a means of fostering the United States Catholic Historical Society in New York.[24] As early as the 1850s Shea had mentioned with dismay the rapid disappearance of Catholic historical materials and had tried, like Martin and O'Callaghan before him, to "preserve

23. Leslie W. Dunlap, *American Historical Societies, 1790–1860* (Madison, Wisconsin: Privately published, 1944), p. 17; see also John F. Jameson, *The History of Historical Societies* (Savannah, Georgia: Morning News Print, 1914), pp. 16–17; and E. B. Greene, "Our Pioneer Historical Societies," *Indiana Historical Society Publications* 10 (1931).

24. The bishops' support remained largely nominal, and Shea was forced time and again to petition aid in a more substantial form. For evidence to this effect, see John T. Ellis, ed., *Documents of American Catholic History* (Milwaukee, 1962), pp. 419, 423–28.

the documents . . . relating to the progress of Catholicity in the United States."[25] He hoped those local Catholic historical societies would perform such a task. He was also invited to help found the American Catholic Historical Society of Philadelphia, another organization which he viewed as a means to "save much precious knowledge from perishing," but he declined to make the effort. At times the impression is given that the New York and Philadelphia groups were competing with each other, as their names imply, for national status.[26] There was really no competition between the two, and Shea did not side with a New York faction in refusing to attend the Philadelphia society. He simply considered both, and in fact they were, local groups committed to preserving records in their respective areas. The stated purpose of Shea's society indicated its circumscribed objectives: "The discovery, collection, and presentation of historical materials, relating to the introduction, establishment, and progress of the Catholic Church and Faith in the United States . . . the publication of essays, documents and rare books, relating to the above, and the maintenance of an historical library and museum of historical relics."[27]

Few men have attained the knowledge, industry or ability to complete great enterprises, all of which John Shea possessed to a remarkable degree. When popular histories of the topics he studied have long been forgotten, his volumes will still be consulted because they contain a vast amount of factual material instead of a private interpretation of the data. Viewed as masterful compilations of documents then available, it is fair to call Shea's major historical works "the guide and . . . index to those who followed him."[28] As a self-trained scholar Shea overcame many obstacles and won singular honors in a task requiring "the most patient investigation and research . . . the collection of scattered documents of all kinds. . . . Once prepared, however, [his volumes became] almost invaluable for succeeding generations, and particularly for those who want to be sure of data."[29]

25. Guilday, *John Gilmary Shea*, pp. 31–32, 90–94.
26. Ibid., p. 92.
27. In Cadden, *Historiography of the American Catholic Church*, p. 42. Note how this corroborates the archaeological aspect of Shea's paradigmatic model.
28. Tourscher, "Catholic Scholarship," p. 475; Cadden, *Historiography of the American Catholic Church*, pp. 33–34.
29. Walsh, "John Gilmary Shea," p. 197.

One of the major difficulties inherent in Shea's historical method was that of organization. Since he was fastidious about the integrity of original sources and as unwilling to force them into arbitrary patterns, the documents fail to supply a sustained narrative line of their own and often follow none at all. Indeed, one critic has described the last two volumes of Shea's major *History* as "a mixture of information [involving] a lack of any unifying thought and a necessary loss or misapprehension on the part of the general reader of the movements common to many . . . dioceses."[30] Yet, while admitting that his work would have gained in strength and clarity had Shea followed a less rigorous method—an impossible change considering his fundamental ideas—the imperfect volumes remain a rich mine for those seeking basic information.

Another limitation was the severely restricted insight which Shea brought to the documentary evidence. One later student has suggested that Shea was endowed with "a critical faculty worthy to rank him as a leader in the modern school of genetic historiography."[31] Even Peter Guilday, his biographer and a historian of sound judgment, thought that if "once he had completed his great work of depicting . . . the story of Catholicism in the United States, the larger field would have found in him one of the most mature students of the time."[32] Both observations are based on a failure to see that Shea exhausted the possibilities afforded by his methodology. He was quite different from the genetic historians who criticized his kind of writing, and he was incapable of accomplishing anything in that "larger field" which Guilday wished him to enter.[33] Another way of

30. Edward P. Lilly, "A Major Problem for Catholic American Historians," *Catholic Historical Review* 24 (January 1939): 445; see also Vollmar, *Catholic Church in America*, pp. xiii–xiv. Shea was not unaware of the problem of arranging materials, as can be seen in his "Bancroft's History of the United States," pp. 680, 683, 688. Also his very well constructed *A Child's History of the United States* (New York: McMenamy, Hess and Co., 1872), shows that he could write an intriguing narrative when he wished. Thus the distinctive arrangement of materials and the narrative line in his last, best effort must have been executed that way purposely.

31. English, "Historiography of American Catholic History," p. 596.

32. Guilday, *John Gilmary Shea*, pp. 141–42.

33. Thomas T. McAvoy, *The Great Crisis in American Catholic History, 1895–1900* (Chicago: Henry Regnery Co., 1957), p. 9, calls Shea "the great chronicler of the Church in the United States" and notes that no one has continued his work beyond the Second Plenary Council. One ought to conclude as a result of this present study that no one can ever succeed Shea because no one "thinks history" that way any longer.

making the same judgment is to state that, however much Shea's writings preserve the vital statistics of churches, they did not describe the real life of the Catholic people.[34] Based on his convictions about proper method, his analysis could not rise above a description of the physical alterations in hierarchy and diocese. It was impervious to the broader aspects of Catholic development and to questions about its relation to American life such as the social and theological problems caused by immigration, the possible interaction between religion and environment in frontier settlement or crowded slums, the changes wrought by the American experiment in church-state relations, or by industrialization, including the centralization of financial and political power and the rise of organized labor. Shea had already settled on methodological paradigms long before the impact of scientific historiography or the emphasis on fresh interpretations of familiar material. When new viewpoints opened and new questions were broached by later scholars, he failed to appreciate their contribution to learning.

Thus Shea's methodological ideas placed him squarely among the "middle group" of American historians. When he wrote the *History of Catholic Missions,* his approach was fresh and commanding, but by the time his major *History* appeared thirty years later, the same plan and method were considered retrogressive by scholars of a later generation. Shea was bitterly disappointed at not being chosen professor of church history at the Catholic University of America, but considering his restricted and outdated historical tools, his exclusion seems natural.[35] By that time the climate of opinion was changing, marked by the rise of graduate seminars in history and by university scholars

34. For similar judgments, see McAvoy, *Great Crisis in American Catholic History,* p. 45; T. F. O'Connor, "Trends and Portends in American Catholic Historiography," *Catholic Historical Review* 33 (April 1947): 9; Lilly, "Major Problem," pp. 431–32; and Jedin and Dolan, *Handbook of Church History,* pp. 3–5.

35. Of course his non-clerical status, lack of formal education, old age and lack of familiarity with current European theology all tended to exclude him. See John T. Ellis, *The Formative Years of the Catholic University of America* (Washington, D.C.: American Catholic Historical Association, 1946), pp. 350, 358–60, 372–73; also P. H. Ahern, "The First Faculty of the Catholic University of America," *Catholic Historical Review* 33 (July 1947): 143, 149, 152. Both of these scholars indicate that John J. Keane had no intention of engaging Shea or any other American as the first church historian.

who insisted on bringing new questions to old evidence.[36] The new
approach went where Shea never dared and considered "the deeds of
men . . . *per se* [Shea's primary concern] of little consequence to
history unless . . . these isolated things are brought into vital connection with the progress and science of the world."[37] Catholic
scholarship did not reach that level until 1920 when it declared that
church history should "cease to be a mere chronicle of past events
and . . . become a living . . . reality."[38] Of course the ideals dear
to Shea were superseded as early as the 1880s in the broader circles
of historiographical activity, though several years went by before
implications worked themselves out. But there is still an austere dignity to the narrow task to which Shea limited himself, and one can
imagine that he had himself in mind when he eulogized Edmund B.
O'Callaghan: "As a historian he followed no philosophy of history,
marshalling and distorting facts to suit it, but he gave the facts in all
their truth, and from these facts formed his picture of the past. Full of
honesty himself, he bore impatiently to see ignorance or want of
fairness arrange historical data so as to sanction false views. This love
of truth . . . established the reputation which he . . . long enjoyed
among scholars."[39]

THEOLOGICAL MEANING BEHIND THE METHOD

It is unnecessary to belabor the fact that no historian has been sufficiently unassuming to work within the limits of a strictly "objective"

36. There is a great deal to be said for the view that the AHA flourished because
there were finally enough men of a scientific frame of mind to support it. It is
not clear that the ogranization succeeded in changing the methodological rubrics
of its members or in suppressing different ideas about the craft. There were some
creative, critical historians before 1876, and they accomplished work that pre-
figured the essays delivered at AHA meetings. Shea was editor of the *Historical
Magazine* from 1859 to 1866; Henry B. Dawson took over and pushed even harder
for good, critical work and solid documentation in the journal's pages. So even
though it was meager, there was a tradition of critical scholarship before the
scientific historians gave it greater impulse. See D. D. Van Tassel, *Recording
America's Past, 1607–1884* (Chicago: University of Chicago Press, 1960), pp.
131–32, 161–65.
37. Herbert B. Adams, "Co-operation in University Work," *JHUS* 1 (1883):
88–89; see also his "Special Methods of Historical Study," *JHUS*, 2d ser. (1884),
pp. 22–23.
38. Peter Guilday, "The American Catholic Historical Association," *Catholic
Mind* 18 (June 1920): 234–36.
39. John G. Shea, "Edmund Bailey O'Callaghan M.D., LL.D.: Historian of
New Netherland and New York," *Magazine of American History* 5 (July 1880):
80.

methodology. Since Adams failed to attain the ideal of working without bias or assumption, it should not be surprising to see that Shea also employed determinative preconceptions in his work. In addition to piecing together a factual chronicle of the Catholic church in the United States, Shea selected data according to a theological understanding of the nature of the church and, from that ecclesiological viewpoint, blended several significant motifs into his historical writing. His most positive theme was intended to bolster the self-respect of Catholics by informing them of their past, including the admirable piety of missionary priests and the stalwart patriotism of Catholic citizens, a past that contributed greatly to building the nation. A more negative but forceful goal was to provide definitive answers to Protestant slurs on Catholic life, whether those attacks applied to religious or civic activity. Shea intended to show once and for all that Catholics belonged in the United States and that their history proved them to have been a significant part of the nation's heritage. Finally, he conceived of the Catholic church as the only agent capable of welding divergent groups into a single people. Catholicism, rather than nationalism, was the principle that guided his understanding of America's past and his hopes for its future.

Various conceptions of the nature of the church have profoundly affected the research and writing of every distinctive church historian, and it is relatively easy to understand Shea's definition of the subject. Whereas Schaff and other notable Protestant historians of his day went to great lengths in discussing the relationship between earthly churches and a perfect, transcendental prototype, Shea did not engage in philosophic distinctions between appearance and reality. He viewed the church as coterminous with duly consecrated Roman Catholic hierarchy and the activities sanctioned by them: "The trials, the labors, the hopes and the consolations of the Spouse of Christ are distinctly and authoritatively expressed in the synods and councils which have been held in provinces and countries, or in world-gatherings by the bishops of the Church of God. This has been the case from the first Council of Jerusalem. . . ."[40] He obviated the Protestant

---

40. John G. Shea, "The Coming Plenary Council of Baltimore," *ACQR* 9 (April 1884): 340. Such a definition allowed Shea to contain a theological conception of the church within an institutional framework and concentrate on that exterior phenomenon. He could be deeply committed to theology and yet be considered "scientific" by his secular contemporaries.

difficulty of localizing the activities of the Holy Spirit by the same restrictive definition. In relating a segment of the history of that single, authorized church, Shea addressed himself to two separate audiences: the faithful and outsiders. On an external level he thought his work contained valuable information for those whom he called "the student and statesman," while for Catholics he intended the volumes to be something more profound, "a record full of the deepest interest and consolation, [ones] to which [they could] appeal with pride."[41] On those two levels, then, Shea attempted a chronological survey of American Catholicity," a word deliberately chosen to convey his notion that the true, unchanging faith cannot be reduced to one among a number of competing "isms." With such a canonically defined idea of the church, Shea very early chose a number of categories useful for understanding the practice of religion, or as he called them, "four enterprises essential to the religious prospects of the United States."[42] Those enterprises—education of the young, the formation of a national clergy, the erection of church buildings, and the foundation of communities of religious—provided a fundamental structure for evaluating the rate of ecclesiastical development in any particular period.

Shea viewed every phenomenon pertaining to church history through such concise preconceptions about valid authority and the scope of religious activity that he arrived at predictably uniform interpretations of the evidence. It was unthinkable in his view for Catholicity to alter its doctrine, rites, or educational structure to suit the occasional demands of nature or native. The alternatives he allowed "Catholicity in America" (never "American Catholicism") were either survival and expansion with valid forms and programs or retreat. Shea refused on theological grounds to believe in the possibility of internal change because he viewed them to be fatal compromises rather than enriching diversification. But any narrative as long as his, written on such a rigid pattern, was bound to become tedious. His biographical sketches of the clergy tended to be flat and repetitively hagiographical (especially of those persons in process of canonization);[43] he always sided with the hierarchy in reviewing

41. Shea, *History*, 1:10, 607; 2:279, 410-37.
42. Henry DeCourcy de Laroche-Heron, *The Catholic Church in the United States: Pages of Its History*, trans. and enlarged by John G. Shea, 2d ed. (New York: T. W. Strong, 1857), p. 64 (hereafter cited as DeCourcy-Shea).
43. Shea, *History*, 1:282, 305-9, 486-94, 526-28.

struggles with laymen, dismissing the latter as impious quasi-Protestants;[44] his conviction that no good would come from Protestant circles led him into distorted interpretations of their ideas and biased evaluations of their activity.[45] Yet the main areas of Shea's concern yielded a wealth of information about the physical development of Catholic churches in the United States, and he considered it an adequate summary to write:

When the centennial year of 1876 arrived, the Catholic body, so insignificant a hundred years before, without a bishop, with few priests, fewer churches, and no institutions, either of learning or mercy, had become one of 6 millions of faithful, under 11 archbishops, 56 bishops, and 5,074 priests. In more than 5,000 churches was the holy sacrifice offered . . . ; 63 colleges were training young men . . . and hundreds of thousands of children received in the parochial schools knowledge based on morality.[46]

He was not concerned with assessing the weight of factors to explain *why* the institutions had developed as they did; Shea was interested only in the fact *that* they had succeeded in quantifiable terms. He felt great pride in that success and at several places in the narrative took time to remind his readers that "in spite of every adverse event or combination of circumstances, the Church of the Living God seems to gather new courage and new strength from every battle and every defeat, and to advance like a giant to run its course."[47]

The reverence in which Shea held the hierarchical structure of the Catholic church and the controlling paradigms stemming from such an ecclesiology are relatively simple to understand; it is more difficult to uncover the origins of his lyrical, gratuitous statements about the

44. Shea, *History*, 3:200, 260; he came close to a critical analysis of Archbishop Marechal (pp. 98–99), but that exception proves the rule.
45. John G. Shea, "Vagaries of Protestant Religious Belief," *ACQR* 10 (July 1885): 432; Shea, "The Boston of Winthrop," *ACQR* 12 (April 1887): 197, 204, 209.
46. John G. Shea, "The Progress of the Church in the United States, from the First Provincial Council to the Third Plenary Council of Baltimore," *ACQR* 9 (July 1884): 495; see also Shea, *History*, 3:629; 4:715–16. T. T. McAvoy's better analysis in *Great Crisis in American Catholic History*, pp. 40–41, and "The American Catholic Minority in the Later Nineteenth Century," *Review of Politics* 15 (July 1953): 275–302, shows fundamental changes and tensions at work. Shea was insensitive to those changes.
47. John G. Shea, "Christopher Columbus: This Century's Estimates of His Life and Work," *ACQR* 12 (July 1887): 387. See also *History*, 2:25.

excellence of all things Catholic. In the last analysis the source was probably two-fold: they were based on a natural resentment of unfair Protestant discrimination as well as a genuine pride in the character of his faith and the conduct of the faithful. On the negative side Shea constantly chafed against the "iron wall of prejudice" which relegated Catholic activities to such isolation that they were "treated almost as if non-existent." With bitterness and yet with determination he observed that

many denominations act together for common ends, and always do so as against the Church. They believe . . . that they alone are Americans, and that Catholics have no claim to the title. . . . As the oldest, the most widespread, the most numerous organization in the country . . . doing good for religion and morality, for loyalty and devotion to country . . . the Catholic body has certainly some claims, and if properly and eloquently presented, they will be recognized by the great body of the American people.[48]

The roots of Shea's defensive attitude are embedded in both Catholicism and an Irish genealogy, a combination difficult to separate into neat categories.[49] But that religio-cultural background afforded Shea a perspective that counteracted much of the self-congratulatory attitudes held by Protestant Americans who had an interest in their history. He saw, for example, that pretensions to religious freedom and civil equality based on state constitutions of the 1780s had been empty ones, and he deflated any possible pride by listing several of them which had openly discriminated against Catholics, concluding

48. John G. Shea, "The Columbus Centenary of 1892," *ACQR* 14 (October 1889) : 700.
49. A good discussion of the way these viewpoints blended can be found in J. Shannon, "The Irish Catholic Immigration," in *Roman Catholicism and the American Way of Life*, ed. Thomas T. McAvoy (Notre Dame: University of Notre Dame Press, 1960), p. 206; see also Thomas N. Brown, "The Origins and Character of Irish-American Nationalism," *Review of Politics* 18 (July 1956) : 327–58. We know that Shea was proud of his Irish origin, as he was of the Catholic faith; see his letter to O'Callaghan in Guy, *Edmund Bailey O'Callaghan*, p. 53. In the DeCourcy-Shea volume, p. 120, he went so far as to state that "in the extension of Christianity, in the propagation of truth, the Celtic race has ever led the way."
For sound studies of nativism, see John Higham, *Strangers in the Land: Patterns of American Nativism, 1860–1925* (New Brunswick, N.J.: Rutgers University Press, 1955), p. 4; and his essay, "Another Look at Nativism," *Catholic Historical Review* 44 (July 1958): 151–52; and C. J. Barry, "Some Roots of American Nativism," *Catholic Historical Review* 44 (July 1958): 138–39, 143.

that "in 1800 toleration was regarded as much of an evil egg as it was a century and a half before."[50] In another place he quipped that such preferential laws in an enlightened and self-governing nation indicated how "the people and their leaders had not [yet] risen to the level of the Catholic Calvert."[51] As an Irishman, born in New York but an Irishman nevertheless, and as a Catholic, Shea had little good to say about Englishmen; he blamed them for almost every set-back Catholicity had suffered in the new world, ranging from pil-lage to trusteeism.[52] After reviewing an almost interminable list of such atrocities Shea penned one of his most withering observations: "How devoid of Christianity must be creeds which train their adher-ents to believe it lawful to deprive Catholics of life and property, and how damaging the fact that their religious literature contains not a volume to condemn the idea."[53] Throughout Shea's career events which included the Nativists' reaction to Archbishop Bedini's tour of the country in 1853 and the apparently anti-Catholic purge of Presi-dent Grant (both his proposed constitutional amendment about pub-lic schools and his Indian peace policy which delimited Catholic mis-sionary activity) confirmed Shea in his determination to use history as a means of informing the public about the true course of events and thus curtailing prejudice.[54] One is a bit overawed by his persistent faith in the power of reasoned argument.

Shea's rhetoric became almost grandiloquent whenever he de-scribed the pioneering activity of American Catholic churchmen in

50. DeCourcy-Shea, pp. 45–46; see also Shea, *History*, 2:160–61, 441.

51. Shea, *History*, 2:155.

52. Shea, *History of Catholic Missions*, pp. 119–20. Other examples are in Shea, *History*, 1:178–79, 222; 2:25–35, 90–91, 117, 134–39; 3:186, 232, 420; 4:503.

53. Shea, *History*, 4:510.

54. Those two events seem to have stimulated Shea to an increased literary out-put. Though his historical interests were perennial, there seems to be a correlation between anti-Catholic outbursts and his own responses. For the most thorough study of the first event, see J. F. Connely, *The Visit of Archbishop Gaetano Bedini to the United States of America, June, 1853–February, 1854* (Rome: Libreria Editrice dell' Universita Gregoriana, 1960), pp. 95–104, 131–35. For an adequate treatment of Grant's policies, see P. J. Rahill, *The Catholic Indian Missions and Grant's Peace Policy, 1870–1884* (Washington, D.C.: Catholic University of America Press, 1953); and Higham, *Strangers in the Land*, pp. 28–29. For Shea's version, see his "The Catholic in American History," *ACQR* 1 (January 1876): 165–66, 169; and "What Right Has the Federal Government to Mismanage the Indians?," *ACQR* 6 (July 1881): 520–41.

that joint effort of his to encourage his own coreligionists and convince Protestants that "many were men of eminent sanctity and devotedness and [that] America no less than Catholicity claims them as her heroes."[55] Traits of the romanticist's preference for flamboyant expression came to the surface as Shea painted scenes of overwhelming physical hardships and lonely trials amid terrifying and implacable enemies: "Picture to yourself a Jesuit four hundred leagues away in the woods, with no resource but the liberality of people who know not God, compelled . . . to pass whole years without receiving any tidings, with savages . . . among whom, instead of finding society or relief in sickness, he is daily exposed to perish and be massacred. This is done daily by these Fathers in Louisiana and Canada."[56]

At times one gets the impression that Shea absorbed the expansionist sentiments current in his day and spoke of the growth of churches in the imperialistic tones used to extol America's "manifest destiny." Standard phrases reveal his sense of power as he watched Catholicity "plant her standard" on these shores and "claim the land for Mary" in a laborious but triumphant "march of the Blessed Sacrament . . . across the continent."[57]

In addition to pointing up the grand progress of religion in the United States, Shea repeatedly emphasized the fact that Catholics had helped build the nation from earliest times. Catholics had discovered territories and rivers, they had been "the peers of those around them" and cleared land for the vanguard of civilization, they fought shoulder to shoulder with other Americans against common foes and constructed an environment to benefit future generations.[58] Still the most important agents had been the priests who toiled selflessly in the face of appalling odds. Shea chose John Carroll as a universal type, "the American priest," to symbolize a distillation of religious zeal and American patriotism. The same old patterns of institutional development were employed in studying the Maryland Jesuit, and the heroic character of Carroll's achievements were based on standard categories

55. Shea, *History of Catholic Missions*, p. 128.
56. David Levin, *History as Romantic Art: Bancroft, Prescott, Motley and Parkman* (Stanford: Stanford University Press, 1959), pp. 220–21; and Shea, *History*, 1:575. Yet even here Shea's language is based on the diary of a French naval officer.
57. Shea, *History of Catholic Missions*, p. 485; *History*, 1:12, 123.
58. Shea, *History*, 1:638; 3:264–65, 419–20.

in Shea's mind, but volume 2 of the *History* comprised such a master-ful treatment of those themes that it has remained the best piece of writing Shea ever accomplished.[59] But Carroll served only as a rep-resentative figure for hundreds of devoted priests and nuns who spent themselves in the cause of religion. Shea summed up his admiration for the first archbishop and all those "providentially raised up for the task":

The Catholic Church in this country does not begin her history after colonies were formed, and men had looked to their temporal well-being. Her priests were among the explorers of the coast, were pioneers of the vast interior; with Catholic settlers came the minister of God, and mass was said to hallow the land and draw down the blessing of heaven be-fore the first step was taken to rear a human habitation. The altar was older than the hearth.[60]

Next to the pioneering spirit of American Catholic forebears Shea emphasized their patriotism during the Revolutionary War to re-mind both statesman and communicant that Catholics had helped win the nation's independence. He concentrated heavily on colonial studies, probably because most historians of his day worked in that period, but during the centennial celebration he had a special goal in mind: to use historical records as an affidavit of Catholic citizenship. Shea disclosed that goal in such passages: "Surely Catholics are as ardent supporters of American liberty in 1875, as they were in 1775, when John Wesley and the Wesleyans denounced it, and the Ameri-can Catholics with their priests . . . supported it to a man; and stood by the cause sturdily when men like Arnold made their Protestantism a pretext for deserting the cause."[61] He became unequivocal and rather overweening in his eagerness to declare all Catholics unyielding patriots, to show that no missionaries had abandoned their posts for the safety of British protection, that John Carroll lent his personal and official influence to support the republican government, that the whole Catholic body was "unswervingly faithful" to the American cause.[62] He even went so far as to state categorically: "There were no

59. See ibid., 2:26, 330, 363, for key statements about the role of Carroll in the historian's thought.
60. Ibid., 1:10; a similar eulogy can be found on pp. 341–50.
61. Shea, "The Catholic Church in American History," pp. 149–50.
62. Shea, *History*, 2:81–83, 153, 185–86, 656.

Tories, no falterers and final deserters among them; none to shout for Congress, while they carefully carried a British protection for emergencies. The Catholics were to a man, with their clergy, staunch and and true, which can not be said of the other sects. . . ."[63] Using language reminiscent of George Bancroft in both its flair and unqualified praise for popular democratic ideals, Shea wrote: "Catholics spontaneously, universally and energetically gave their adhesion to the cause of America. . . . There was no faltering, no division. Every Catholic in the land was a Whig. In the lists of the Tories and Loyalists, in the volumes since written about them, you cannot find the name of a single Catholic. There were no Catholic Tories."[64]

The American Revolution loomed large in Shea's mind as the proving ground for Catholic citizenship; he barely mentioned the 1812–15 conflict and made only a minimal issue out of the Civil War. By the time his narrative reached the 1860s, Shea's patterns of explanation had long been determined. So once again he contrasted the stability of Catholic churches with Protestant denominations torn by sectional allegiance, noting how the neutrality of the national hierarchy and its efforts to maintain peace were more effective than the local sects which "furiously took one side or another." The calamities suffered in the South were like salt rubbed in a wound because "the Catholic Church had done nothing to cause the war; they did much to mitigate its horrors, and keep Christian lessons before the soldiers; [yet] they suffered great losses as their reward on earth."[65] In such discussions Shea underscored the role of Catholicity in two basic areas of national growth—initial settlement and continuing defense—to show all Americans that Catholics were legitimate citizens of the republic.

The final theme emerging from Shea's historical writings had

63. Shea, "The Catholic Church in American History," p. 154.
64. John G. Shea, "Catholics and Catholicity in the Days of the American Revolution," *Proceedings of the First Public Meeting Held by the United States Catholic Historical Society at the University Club Theatre, New York City, Thursday, May 14, 1885* (n.p., 1886), p. 20. For a corrective to that extreme viewpoint, see C. H. Metzger, "Some Catholic Tories in the American Revolution," *Catholic Historical Review* 36 (1950): 405–27. In his later book, *Catholics and the American Revolution: A Study in Religious Climate* (Chicago: Loyola University Press, 1962), Metzger cites Shea as a foil and proceeds, on pp. 243–50, to demonstrate that there were a few Catholic Tories.
65. Shea, *History*, 4:384–86, 431–33, 446–50, 633–35.

nothing to do with the experience of being the victim of discrimination. It rose above the tendentious, argumentative level of previous motifs and spoke only to those inside the Catholic communion. Yet even there one is able to see in Shea a distinctively American viewpoint, displaying his doctrine of the church against a background of confusing intellectual and social change. Since voluntarism made possible an almost unlimited number of sects in America, Catholics emphasized the stability of their doctrine and polity as the only alternative to despair or indifference. Shea was proud of his ecclesiastical heritage, and one of his ultimate historiographical goals was to instill in his readers some of that same veneration he held for "the Church one in her government, her doctrine, her sacrifice, everywhere [establishing] the same Christianity that she had planted among the Gaul, the Celt, the Saxon, the Teuton, the Iberian. Many as are the tongues of men, the Church has but one, that of unerring truth."[66]

The single, unchanging ecclesiastical form of God's abiding presence existed for all men to see; it was easily identified, and once materials about its past had been collected and arranged, its historical development in any land could be traced, and God's handiwork could be exhibited. Those with faith could see as much. With that theological intention supporting the use of an objective method, Shea carried his studies through a period of three and a half centuries, concluding with the view of an institution unaffected by extraneous factors but augmented to great power and influence. There are several places in which one might question the accuracy of his judgment or dissent from the necessity of his conclusions, but it is important to notice that Shea was expressing a belief, not a generalized interpretation based on accumulated data. He wanted to impart a feeling, not information, when he wrote, "New York was erected . . . 1851 [sic] into an archiepiscopal see. . . . Thus the Northern States, which of old proscribed Catholicity by public opinion and penal laws, became an ecclesiastical province, with all the liturgy, rites, and ceremonial of the Church that prevailed when the Catholic Northmen came or the Catholic Columbus sailed."[67]

66. Ibid., 1:638.
67. Ibid., 4:122; see also DeCourcy-Shea, pp. 534–35. The Archdiocese of New York was established in 1850, not 1851.

By the last decades of the nineteenth century immigrants had begun arriving in the United States from almost every European country, and the new world as yet had been unable to assimilate them. Shea posited Roman Catholicism as the solution to that series of problems as he had done in the area of theological disputes. He felt that the Irish on the seaboard, Germans in the Midwest, French in Louisiana, and Spanish in the Southwest were united by religious bonds that transcended ethnic incompatibilities; indeed, he even held the view that America would continue as a democratic state only if it became a Catholic nation. But whether he spoke from a conviction that the church was able to overcome all internal difficulties, or from the fear that a divided Catholic body was too vulnerable to Protestant influences, Shea reiterated his faith in the "wondrous things God has accomplished in this land where by his Providence men of all nations are in a few generations moulded into a homogenous people . . . itself a token of the union of spirit which should prevail among the faithful."[68]

Shea's intellectual development in absorbing current ideas about historical method and his record of publication, embodying both those ideas and a theological interpretive structure, must be viewed as an outstanding victory over discouraging obstacles. He experienced many incidents of both private and national scope which tended to convince him, against his will, that Catholics were perennially fated to second-class status in America. But by the end of his lifetime numerical growth led Shea to be optimistic about the future. Both his methodological view of what constituted historical progress and his faith in the superior character of the Catholic church led him to view the 1880s as a zenith of triumph and vindication. One culminating expression, placed prominently at the front of his great historical survey, can be allowed to epitomize that confident aspect of Shea's perspective and summarize his salient ideas:

The Catholic Church is the oldest organization in the United States, and the only one that has retained the same life and polity and forms through each succeeding age. Her history is interwoven in the whole fabric of

68. Shea, "The Coming Plenary Council," p. 356; "The Catholic Church in American History," pp. 172–73; and the most florid of all, "Progress to the Third Plenary Council," p. 481. .

the country's annals. . . . At this day she is the moral guide, the spiritual mother of ten millions of the inhabitants of the republic, people of
all races and kindreds, all tongues and all countries, blended in one
vast brotherhood of faith. In this she has no parallel. No other institution in the land can trace back an origin in all the nationalities that
once controlled the portions of North America. . . . All others are recent, local, and variable.[69]

A theological substratum undergirded the work of John Shea as
much as it did that of Philip Schaff. Though they differed as to the
identifiable locus of God's activity, both historians worked on the
principle that such a locus had to be considered by those attempting
to interpret churches, whether viewing their earthly roles or their
heavenly destination. Shea's theological concern was less outspoken,
though no less pervasive and consistent, than Schaff's, and this basic
substratum is rarely noticed in his work. Shea was able to concentrate
on the external, more factual, elements in the history of Catholicism
only because he had settled the prior question of spiritual agents by
conflating that category with the Roman hierarchy. After that, he
could limit his narrative to specific details, and historians of many dis-
positions could describe his work as "scientific." There is more accla-
mation than accuracy in that title because a theological meaning always remained beneath his apparently scientific methodology. Some
historians might have missed Shea's ultimate intentions and welcomed
him because of his apparent lack of theological preconceptions, but
those two aspects cannot be separated in viewing the total man as he
really was. Though some contemporaries might have mistaken Shea
as a supporter of new perspectives in historiographical thought and
judged him to be one of the new breed who supported the AHA
(an organization which he never joined), there was another issue
separating them. As an archivist who relied on the incontrovertible
weight of data and that alone to substantiate his case, Shea was unable to appreciate the breakthrough made in 1884. His methodology
and the goals which he hoped it would support were formed in an
age foreshortened by the advent of scientism. Philip Schaff and John
Shea are the most representative practitioners of historiographical

69. Shea, *History*, 1:9.

ideas on the other end of a continuum from the AHA, ideas which had clearly reached their fullest expression by the 1880s. New conceptions and new spokesmen superseded those giants in succeeding decades, and most of their new ideas bore the stamp of scientific approval.

4 &THEORY OF THE CHURCH AS A SOCIAL INSTITUTION

Two decades of debate over the ideals of scientific methodology versus the uniqueness of ecclesiastical materials disclosed a wide range of opinion among church historians. Several of those scholars tried to assimilate the values and ideas publicized by the American Historical Association, and in so doing they distinguished themselves from thinkers like Schaff and Shea. Their work was based on concepts which more nearly approximated scientific history than history with a theological substratum. Ephraim Emerton, church historian at Harvard Divinity School from 1882 to 1918, articulated perhaps better than anyone else the theory that church history ought to be placed on the same level as general history. His college experience under professor Henry Adams at Harvard (A.B. 1871) and his graduate work at Berlin and Leipzig (Ph.D. 1876) led to a natural acceptance of scientific ideals and seminar research methods. His personal achievement was to utilize those ideals and construct a distinctive, influential theory of church historiography, expressing that system of ideas with a clarity rarely attained in academic circles. But in addition to making a contribution in the area of historiographical theory, Emerton is valuable to the historian of ideas as evidence of the degree to which scientific ideology tended to break down the conventional separation of secular and religious categories in the historian's craft.

After completing his dissertation on "William Temple und die Triple-allianz vom Jahre 1668," Emerton returned to Harvard and began a teaching career that originally included German literature as well as European history. Because of his professional training, his continued use of seminar methods and his non-clerical status, Emerton was chosen in 1882 to fill the newly founded Winn Professorship of Church History, a chair established with the explicit intent that "the history of the Christian church [might be] treated not by a minister as a subject separate from 'Civil History' but by a trained layman as a part of the general history of mankind, [a broader treatment that] might be profitable to other than divinity students."[1] As a vigorous advocate of American participation in the scientific revolution (which he traced to Darwin but never explained how myriad changes resulted from the naturalist's influence), Emerton was convinced that his profession could be based on "a method as purely scientific as those of the contemporary sciences" and could produce church historical studies of comparable precision.[2] In terms of both ideology and methodology Emerton was suited to fill the new chair, and he even further gratified his colleagues by bringing "to the study and teaching of Church History the new methods used in studying . . . history in general."[3] In that office he became one of the earliest and most articulate proponents of a rational inquiry that regarded churches as social institutions and treated their history as part of a larger study, one comprising all groups which influenced events or shaped an era.

THE SCIENTIFIC CHARACTER OF EMERTON'S METHODOLOGY

Ephraim Emerton was determined to take his place among scientists and intellectuals who insisted that concrete evidence substantiate the truth of every generalization. His continued use of historical seminars and his conception of that research tool as equivalent to laboratory procedures placed him within the general area of thought exemplified by Herbert Baxter Adams. It is no small thing that Adams himself cited passages in Emerton's writing during the early stage of his methodological defense to assert that "it must be made clear that the claim of history to rank among the sciences is founded in fact—the fact that it has a scientific method."[4] Emerton did not depart from

1. Ephraim Emerton, "History," in *The Development of Harvard University: Since the Inauguration of President Eliot, 1869–1929*, ed. Samuel E. Morison (Cambridge, Mass.: Harvard University Press, 1930), pp. 158–59. Jonathan B. Winn made his bequest in 1877. The fact that it came independent of Emerton's influence shows that several individuals during this period were beginning to deny church history a special position in scholarly circles. Emerton has been chosen simply as an outstanding proponent of that point of view.

2. Ephraim Emerton, "The Practical Method in Higher Historical Instruction" in *Methods of Teaching History*, ed. G. Stanley Hall (Boston: Ginn, Heath and Co., 1885), p. 200.

3. The statement was made by President Eliot, cited by L. Reynolds, Jr., "The Later Years, 1880–1953," in *Harvard Divinity School: Its Place in Harvard University and in American Culture*, ed. George H. Williams (Boston: Beacon Press, 1954), p. 167.

4. In Herbert B. Adams, "New Methods of Study in History," *JHUS*, 2d ser. 1–2 (1884): 91.

that fundamental orientation when he took another step and made explicit the corollary that even historical knowledge about the church could be based on "material capable of precise definition and [analyzed by] a method as purely scientific as those of the contemporary sciences."[5] In addition to insisting on that basic definition of historical method, Emerton also embodied the three major attitudes shared by Adams and the new generation which constituted the AHA.

Behind every iconoclast there lies some degree of indignation that the situation befalling him is due to the ineffectual means employed by his predecessors and that earlier activity only compounded problems rather than helped to alleviate them. In the realm of historical writing, Emerton was able to reject a great deal of earlier work by saying simply that it had not observed the ground rules of trustworthy reporting:

Until our own century . . . history was written usually for a purpose. This historian had at heart to prove the divine right of kings. . . . Another would prove the right of a certain dynasty to its throne. . . . There was at bottom a certain volume of tradition handed down from one historian to another, and out of this each selected what suited his purpose, interpreting the record in his own fashion. The historian was not a searcher after truth so much as he was a man with a mission, and the world was inundated with a flood of such distorted pictures. . . .[6]

With the assurance of one who has already thrown off the mistakes of an earlier method, Emerton reviewed previous historical works to produce a favorable contrast with his own. When investigators like himself went to the sources rather than draw upon an interpretation in keeping with orthodox traditions, "they found, as they had suspected, that the picture had become distorted, because the original had been but imperfectly discerned. Men had taken too much upon the faith of others, and had been too willing to find their own views confirmed, without searching deeply enough for possible arguments against them."[7] Though he couched his revisionism in mild phrases because he knew historians could no longer hope to stand as an

5. Emerton, "History," p. 200.
6. Ephraim Emerton, "The Study of Church History," *Unitarian Review and Religious Magazine* 19 (January 1883): 3.
7. Ibid.

authority in any field for very long, Emerton held the view that modern methods outstripped those of the past, and he persistently called for fewer platitudes and more accurate investigation in the records of his chosen subject. Any student accustomed to treating books like mineralogical specimens would have understood his assertion that

the essential principle . . . is to lead the student back . . . to the original sources. . . . The charm which has heretofore surrounded the names of great historians vanishes. [The critical historian] learns to accept nothing on their word. He demands the proof of every assertion, or if . . . proof is impossible, he demands at least evidence as to the degree of probability.[8]

In his crusade to destroy the prevalence of second-hand authorship and replace shoddy work with original studies based on a mastery of the evidence, Emerton chafed at the intellectual timidity of those harboring what he called "the ancient dread of free inquiry." He urged his students to accept the liberation modern scientific methods gave them and from that rejuvenated perspective to write history over again, using as their single standard the "absoluteness of the law of evidence." Such an iconoclastic attitude toward earlier historical tomes entailed the destruction of many "precious illusions" and "hallowed traditions," but Emerton was convinced that the final product of critical and forthright historical inquiry would make any incidental unpleasantness worth the effort.[9]

The first Winn professor was more emphatic and at the same time more balanced in his conception of objectivity, the second characteristic of American scientific historians. Since he insisted that authenticated evidence was the single acceptable ground of historical knowledge, Emerton simply would not allow unsupported inferences to be derived from some source other than extant records. Any narrative extending beyond the circumspect generalizations yielded by inductive procedure served Emerton's axiom that "in this day a man who wrenches the plain records of history to prove anything overreaches

8. Emerton, "The Practical Method in Higher Historical Instruction," pp. 37-38.
9. Ephraim Emerton, "The Place in History in Theological Study," Learning and Living: Academic Essays (Cambridge, Mass.: Harvard University Press, 1921), pp. 318-19.

himself and fails of his purpose." Such tendentious exercises were not only bound to produce a disreputable history, but as a corollary they aroused "violent opponents, who . . . allowed themselves to strain the truth in the opposite direction." And each opposing camp with its own distorted version "fared no better" than the other.[10] Instead of favoring any approach which prejudiced the issue from the start, Emerton began work on the principle that objective historians should have no foregone conclusions, letting the records tell their own story as best they could:

The study of history must not be perverted to the service of any theories or causes whatever. Its record must be real and studied for itself; its evidence must be weighed on its merits, and its sequence of cause and effect must be established in accordance with the evidence. Nothing has contributed more effectively to the . . . success of modern historical science than this inflexible rule.[11]

But at the same time Emerton was ready to admit the possibility of error or a faulty interpretation of that empirical evidence. So he remained tentative in accepting conclusions because he thought the true scientific historian would "hold himself in readiness to change or to abandon his point of view . . . when the discovery of new truth . . . made his former position untenable."[12] The important element in his attitude was that the proper objectivist always came to fresh material without preconceived theories and maintained "an absolute impartiality in view of all records" throughout the investigation. By "absolute impartiality" Emerton actually had in mind an interpretive scheme more sophisticated than the mere accumulation of data because he knew that facts could not adequately speak for themselves or give a univocal account of past events. Emerton was close to the heart of the problem when he observed that "there is never a controverted point on any subject upon which a vast array of opposing facts cannot be summoned to the art. The decision must rest, not upon the number or weight in avoirdupois of these facts, but upon

10. Emerton, "The Study of Church History," p. 5.
11. Emerton, "The Place of History in Theological Study," pp. 323–24. In a devastating book review, Papers of the AHA 1 (1886): 442, he ridiculed theological historians who "rested on a 'higher law' . . . than that which admits . . . laws of evidence. . . . [those who] asked no higher sanction for their work than the 'imprimature' of some holy man."
12. Emerton, "The Study of Church History," p. 6.

the preponderance, one way or the other, of the whole body of evidence, rightly understood or interpreted."[13]

The ideal of impartiality did not necessarily mean that the historian's personality had to be suppressed at the same time, "for that very process of withdrawal is a piece of himself, and it brings into his work the very personal element he has been trying to suppress." Emerton never resolved the complex epistemological problems facing historians, but at the same time he did not unwittingly accept a type of objectivity which proved more shallow than earlier patterns that had slanted the record to support party views. Still, this honest complexity aside, the issue in church history in his day concerned the relative freedom of historical researchers to state whatever conclusions they reached. Emerton's position in debates about the proper approach to church history can be understood when one sees how he tested the integrity of a narrative in the light of verifiable public documents. As we shall see below, he aligned himself fairly closely with Adams and other scientific historians by endorsing a degree of objectivity that precluded the subjective procedures of theologically oriented writers.

Emerton's ideas about the nature of historical evidence further defined his compatibility with scientific standards, and although he avoided analogies that equated human records with natural phenomena, he subscribed to the viewpoint which we have chosen to term "naturalistic." In keeping with his conception of the historian's approach, he emphasized a confidence in the capacity of written records to afford the scholar a view approximating "absolute historic truth."[14] In the field of church history Emerton concentrated on the specific issue of whether empirical evidence would allow interpretations that included divine guidance, providential intervention, spiritual agents, and other intangible forces discernible to the man of faith. With that specific question in mind, he declared that only human records could be used as historical evidence and that they yielded knowledge about nothing other than human activity. His naturalism, then, was intended primarily as an excluding factor—to silence the pretensions of various retrospective prophets with their conflicting visions. But such an

13. Ephraim Emerton, untitled book review, *Papers of the AHA* 1 (1886): 443.
14. Emerton, "The Study of Church History," p. 4.

exclusive perspective did not claim to give the historian absolute certainty about past affairs. Emerton never thought that empirical evidence would be able to explain past events in exhaustive detail; he did insist that such evidence was all one could legitimately consult, however imperfect one's understanding remained. His distinctive treatment of his own narrow field of specialization illustrates more clearly the impact of scientific ideas and attitudes on the area of study once thought to have been a subcategory of theology. In that sustained discussion, rather than its practice because he never really accomplished much in actual production, Emerton can be seen as a significant theoretician. He gave expression to the ideas of many men who were committed to scientific standards and yet interested in church history as a legitimate field of inquiry.

EMERTON'S CONCEPTION OF CHURCH HISTORY

Ephraim Emerton began his career as an academic church historian in 1882 with an inaugural address defending the ideal of impartiality in the historical investigation of church matters. In that essay and subsequent publications he argued against theological historians who prefaced their studies with a conception of the church's divine origin, but he did not fail to appreciate the tremendous weight of tradition which caused many of his colleagues to work with such a premise. He appreciated (perhaps more than many of his secular contemporaries) the problems historians faced in understanding the church and did not introduce irresponsibly the ideal of impartiality in a field where few thought it possible to study without preconceptions. But he refused to admit that predetermined interpretations constituted sound scholarship. With his admiration of science it was disconcerting to recognize that a great many church historians had published works in which evidence had not been "judged not by the ordinary rules of human observation . . . but in the light of certain immovable and unchangeable preconceptions."[15] Wherever records were silent about the crucial factors involved in an important incident, Emerton was able to see how devout historians in earlier times had often been led to fill in details which only their faith made plausible. But the problem he found most difficult to solve was that a continuing reliance on such interpretations tended to perpetuate a supernaturalist habit of

15. Ibid., p. 6.

mind. The conclusions produced by that frame of mind could be handed down within a religious tradition and remain unaffected by improvements in historical method. Faith assumptions disguised as historical conclusions could go too far by demanding assent from those outside the circle of faith. Emerton observed that "the meagerness of the record of the early days of the Church" not surprisingly left "almost endless space for the working of the devout imagination;" there were so many questions and so few causal explanations that "it seem[ed] to many persons actually to demand the operation of supernatural . . . powers."[16] But as a historiographical theoretician committed to another standard Emerton refused to submit to that demand or to supplement chronicles with his own ideas.

On the specific issue of categorizing church history as a scientific or a theological discipline, Emerton denied that supernatural elements played any part in historical events or that they could figure in a historian's judgment. In his view of things, any system of thought, however venerable, which claimed to see an interaction of human and superhuman forces was "unhistorical." No amount of empirical evidence could possibly prove the existence of supernatural agents, and he discounted the work of those historians who had written as if history exhibited such forces because science had supplanted their conception of reality. In his own field Emerton attributed those outdated publications to the "almost wholly theological treatment which church history had [heretofore] received." He was able to grant that theology, although it rested on a number of basic principles derived from revelation and dealt almost exclusively with questions about the supernatural, was still relevant to some areas of men's lives. But he insisted that history, which included studies of the church, was not theology and that it dealt with matters of another kind, following epistemological guidelines of modern derivation. He considered theologically oriented history unacceptable because its conclusions were subordinated to serve predetermined ends in much the same way some political histories favored various factional interests.[17]

By and large scientific historians had little respect for most attempts in church history because they thought the work to be based on

16. Ibid., pp. 6–7. He even went so far as to say that theological commitment "affected the judgment" of church historians.
17. Ibid., pp. 7–8.

faulty procedure and served objectives irrelevant to objective inquiry. Emerton, resenting the injustice of having his area of study brushed aside so hastily, fought throughout his career to establish the legitimacy of including church history among the topics open to general historical study. In order to convince his colleagues in the American Historical Association of their error and to convert his fellow members of the American Society of Church History to what he considered a more viable methodology, he argued that all church historians should adopt scientific paradigms as their criteria. Between 1882 and 1921 he admonished a generation of church history students at Harvard to be rigorously empirical and nontheological in their research and writing. The fact that he was still arguing the basic point so late attests to the consistency with which Emerton maintained his ideas about historical method. It also comments on how unreceptive the majority of church historians had been to his advanced notions. Despite what must have appeared to be a deep-seated reluctance to change basic perspectives, he reminded his co-workers that scientific procedure had set the standard for acceptable studies of the past. That standard had affected every branch of the discipline and exerted pressure on "the organized representatives of this craft [the ASCH], set up and to observe standards of procedure no less exacting than those which govern our fellow craftsmen in other departments of historical study."[18] From Emerton's point of view, church history as a division of general history was a science interesting enough to be studied for its own sake, and he thought it should not be forced into an alliance with a different sphere of interest such as theology. He reserved special scorn for curricula where he found "Church History regularly [listed] as a part of 'Historical Theology,' as if history were no independent subject by itself, but only a form or mode of theological speculation."[19] Those instructional schemes too often led students to amalgamate theological and historical functions to an extent that produced a curious mixture known as "theological history," a historical narrative based on theological consideration as well as historical evidence. Many such historians were led, by their faith or theological objectives, to make statements which no amount of evidence

18. Ephraim Emerton, "A Definition of Church History," *Papers of the ASCH,* 2d ser. 7 (1923): 60.
19. Emerton, "The Study of Church History," p. 8.

could support. Emerton listed a series of such unhistorical statements to show how pious zeal could overbalance historical judgment and lead the writer into gratuitous inferences. The first two dealt with a definition of method and general approach:

The office of the historian of the Church is not to untie a tangled skein, but to follow the golden thread of the divine presence in all Christian ages.

To show when the divine force has controlled all human events, and made them subserve the steady progress of God's servants is the mission of him who treats the history of the Church.[20]

Another pair of citations illustrated the serene faith in a providential guidance which reduced such histories, in the estimate of scientific historians, to the level of fanciful and unverifiable claims:

When the hour came for the wrong to cease, the controlling hand intervened.

The Church has been saved from fatal error and downfall by divine interposition.[21]

   Emerton differed from theological historians primarily on methodological grounds, but that contrasting methodology was compatible with a conception of the church at variance with both church historians already discussed. Schaff and Shea had recognized the importance of ecclesiology and had made it more or less explicit in their distinctive selections of relevant data, their conclusions drawn, and the ends they wished historical narrative to serve. Emerton was less overt in making statements about the locus of religious vitality or its relation to institutional churches, but an ecclesiology was nonetheless there, and it contributed to his solution of historiographical problems. In Emerton's case questions of method received greater attention, and his theology acquiesced in those prior considerations. There was no

20. In Emerton, "A Definition of Church History," p. 57.
21. Ibid. It is interesting to note that the man Emerton singled out as typifying all the wrong attitudes plaguing church historiography was the man hand-picked by Schaff to succeed him as president of the ASCH, John Fletcher Hurst. This is even further evidence to point up the significant differences between men in the AHA and Schaff's organization, and it also shows to which side Emerton was inclined. The statements can be found in J. F. Hurst, *Short History of the Christian Church* (New York: Harper & Brothers, 1893), pp. 3–4. See also his *History of the Christian Church* (New York: Eaton and Mains, 1897), 1:17.

thought in his mind of allowing theology to have any effect on the procedure or the eventual outcome of historical investigation. He never indicated that an ecclesiology or religious orientation could be derived from a study of history, and he forcefully rejected the assertion that historical method should be influenced by theology or even work in harmony with it. With that caveat, then, the compatibility of Emerton's religious views, conception of churches, and his scientific inclination seems to have been fortuitous. If his ideals of empirical objectivity and naturalism are to be taken seriously, it is likely that the religion coinciding with them formed a workable, uncontrived congruence of ideas. Though the evidence is scant, Emerton apparently conceived of religion as a quiet, personal affair in the hearts of isolated individuals.[22] That type of pietistic atomism could have no necessary connection with ecclesiastical institutions, and thus the historian was free to treat churches as he would any other social group, viz., according to the canons of strict scientific inquiry.

Whereas Schaff's view of religion was connected to the vitality of ecclesiastical structures, Emerton's understanding of religion as private experience obviated the problems related to institutions altogether. Schaff would have criticized Emerton's history as destructive of the true meaning and historical significance of the church, but Emerton remained satisfied with that view because it left his ecclesiology untrammeled and corroborated his pursuit of another ideal, scholarly excellence in the scientific historical method. With questions about theological validity and the religious significance of historical churches neatly excluded, Emerton proceeded to argue that historians ought to be students of a strictly human past and not pretend to be "expounders of a miracle" or act as "high priests in the temple of knowledge." He dissociated himself from those who tried to retain theological goals in the interpretation of concrete historical evidence: "For my part I do not aspire to any such lofty mission. I cannot claim to know 'the golden thread of the divine presence' when I see it, and am sure that if I made any such claim there would be a dozen rival claimants to dispute it, and every one of these would differ from every other in his description of what the golden thread was like."[23] Since men could never speak about God with the same

22. Williams, *Harvard Divinity School,* p. 232
23. Emerton, "A Definition of Church History," pp. 57–58.

certainty that could be derived from a study of human history, Emerton was content to avoid the heights of theological speculation and restrict his labors to the more modest confines of empirical research and objective reporting.

Though he made only a few explicit references to the nature of his subject matter, enough emerges from Emerton's writing to see that he thought of "the Christian Church as a great human institution," part of "the record of human life."[24] As for the question of which institutions could legitimately claim to be part of the Christian religion and thus merit the attention of church historians, Emerton was latitudinarian enough to include all divergent forms, saying that "there can be no important difference among the many divisions into which the Church has fallen. The divisions have taken place according to that law of all human beings whereby men left to themselves will inevitably differ as to the best means of attaining a common end."[25] Similarly, the historical study of doctrinal change should not attempt to winnow the false from the true, but view the development of all doctrines simply as "a record of . . . honest attempts to understand and to express the ideas [contributing] to the world's religious thought."[26] For his own part, Emerton did not concern himself with the history of doctrine very much, preferring studies related to the growth of medieval institutions as his professional specialty. Herbert Adams once reported that the better topics in church history taught at Harvard concerned the relations between the papacy and German emperors, the origin of medieval social systems, the rise of French communes and problems of church and state in the eleventh century.[27]

Emerton saw the task of the church historian as one which undertook a study of ecclesiastical institutions, worship, or theology "with the same methods and the same materials that were employed in other branches of historical inquiry."[28] Church history was for him a historical science, not a theological exercise, one in which men could pursue research as fully as they scrutinized any other area of human

24. Emerton, "The Study of Church History," p. 16.
25. Ephraim Emerton, *Unitarian Thought* (New York: Macmillan Co., 1911), pp. 203-4.
26. Emerton, "Ministerial Education," *Learning and Living*, p. 297.
27. Herbert B. Adams, "New Methods of Study in History," *JHUS*, 2d ser. 1–2 (1884): 90–91.
28. Emerton, "The Study of Church History," p. 11.

affairs.[29] In discussing the type of documents to be used, he pointed out that "the church is . . . not standing over against the world but [is] an organic part of it. The human agents who at any time have it in their keeping are subject to the same laws of association that govern all other forms of associated human life. They write their record of human passions, of motives lofty and ignoble, precisely as do the trustees of other great human institutions."[30] Emerton was willing to grant the hypothetical possibility that churches might contain within themselves elements of supernatural power, but he insisted that historians should not speak to that issue because their scientific methods could neither verify nor disprove the presence of intangible qualities. He often reminded readers that his interests lay in understanding the mundane activities within a specific category of human life and thought, not in exhibiting or tracing the progress of divine truth.[31]

After making clear his position on the nature of the church and the proper task of church history, Emerton launched another attack on theological historians, further illustrating his dissatisfaction with earlier historiographical efforts and outlining some hopes for an amended future. In one essay he compared historical investigation to a court of law in which the historian served as judge. Whenever witnesses in that court asked the favor of special consideration, claiming to possess divinely inspired knowledge, Emerton maintained that the true historian should reject their plea. He considered such claims to be inadmissible because "historical evidence rests entirely upon human foundation. . . . No matter what the subject or the nature of the trial, the decisions of the judge depend wholly upon the testimony of human witnesses. Every document produced in the court is the work of human hands and represents human purpose."[32] Many theological historians had written narratives occasionally punctuated by references to divine intervention, basing them on their own faith assumptions or the piety of some earlier writer. But Emerton sternly held that "it [was] then the cruel function of the historian to recall

29. Emerton, "A Definition of Church History," pp. 55–56. One good statement was that "Church History is nothing more or less than one chapter in that continuous record of human affairs which we give the name of history in general."
30. Ibid., p. 58.
31. Another memorable phrase illustrating his nontheological orientation was: "The absolute truth of any given dogma is for our purposes comparatively unimportant" (Emerton, "The Study of Church History," p. 18).
32. Emerton, "The Place of History in Theological Study," p. 319.

[them] . . . to the order of the court whose jurisdiction they would both acknowledge, the court of sound science and sound reason."[33] Perhaps he thought the AHA could function as such a court, when he said proper historians would never admit revelation as a trustworthy source of knowledge.[34]

Emerton carried the debate a step further by anticipating an objection from theological historians. He saw that some like Schaff or Shea might refuse to stay within the strictures of scientific methodology because it yielded such meager knowledge about God and His church. The answer was simple and straightforward but hardly one calculated to comfort those in search of profound assurances: "So it is with the decisions of the historical student." As a scientific historian Emerton knew that historical writings were "fallible, as are all human things," but he resisted the temptation to let faith intervene and settle all remaining uncertainty. The cumulative progress of interdependent data implied that there always be unanswered questions, eliciting further work. And consistency demanded that such work follow similar lines as previous inquiry: "It was in the best interest of true science that [concrete evidence] shall be accepted until further evidence shall . . . correct their error."[35] Emerton defended the criteria and modest conclusions of scientific knowledge by declaring that history was tentative and always needed to be modified, but corrections and additions could be derived only from new empirical evidence. A truly scientific historian who chose the church as his subject would not admit evidence of any sort other than the plain human record: "Not miracles nor inspirations, nor revelations, nor the dictations of any authority whatsoever, but more documents and better authenticated ones are what we must have."[36] Such knowledge might seem tenuous, but its accuracy and reliability made it the best science had to offer.

Throughout his life Emerton reiterated his theory that theological considerations were to be kept apart from historical studies. The definitive clarity of his statements made in relatively obscure publica-

33. Ibid., p. 320.
34. Ibid.
35. Emerton, "The Place of History in Theological Study," p. 321. The best example of his using this principle in actual practice can be seen in his discussion of "The Chronology of the Erasmus Letters," *Annual Report of the American Historical Association for the Year 1901* (Washington, D.C.: Government Printing Office, 1902), 1:186.
36. Emerton, "The Place of History in Theological Study," p. 321.

tions encourages us to include further documentation here. He argued that

no glamor of antiquity, no weight of tradition, no presumption as to good intention can cover violation of those rules laid down by modern science as the unshakable foundations of historical certainty. . . . The method of theology has been applied to history, and the natural result has been loss of confidence, a suspicious distrust of conclusions on the part of those whose good opinion was of the highest value.[37]

How then could scientific historians deal with ecclesiastical materials and modify writings in that area to rectify such undeserved mistrust? In an attempt to establish working guidelines for sifting through church documents, Emerton distinguished between the hypothetical activity of the supernatural (which common men could never know with certitude) and human belief in the supernatural, a widespread phenomenon recorded in a variety of ways and open to empirical verification. His simple axiom, based on a mixture of methodological and theological assumptions, was that "the superhuman . . . is not a subject for historical record. The *belief* in the superhuman . . . because it is a fact of human experience, has its historical record and can be studied historically."[38] With that distinction in mind Emerton hoped a new phase of church historiography could be inaugurated. He looked forward to a mode of scholarship that would eradicate thoughts of intangible forces at work in the church's past, one to replace the old form of study, which the meddling of theologians had caused to be "vitiated . . . in the opinion of the learned world."[39]

Emerton explicated those types of statement which were unhistorical according to his guideline. For example he pointed out the error in making an uncritical declaration that God led the Israelites out of Egypt; "it [could] not be proved by reference to any record, for no record which we can read unveils the mystery of divine action."[40] Yet he had no hesitation in affirming that Israel's faith in divine assistance had been a powerful factor in producing national independence because that faith was a historical phenomenon, well supported by

37. Emerton, "A Definition of Church History," p. 59.
38. Ibid., p. 62.
39. Ibid., p. 61.
40. Ibid., p. 62.

the evidence. In a similar argument he used the example of Pentecost to make the point, saying, "I should consider myself trespassing beyond my own limits, if I should say that on a certain day the gift of tongues descended upon the disciples of Jesus. . . ."[41] Emerton limited himself not only to the written records but to a naturalistic understanding of what those records could disclose. On that basis he felt justified in saying that a band of men began preaching certain doctrines based on their experience with Jesus of Nazareth and that the zeal of those men, not legendary tongues of fire, had been the driving force behind the spread of Christianity. Then, in an aside which indicated how much he insisted that historians remain free from the blight of theological promptings, Emerton remarked, "If you desire to know whether these men received . . . a gift from God, marking them out as men specially detailed on a divine mission, you must inquire of a professed theologian, not of me."[42]

It is a fair assessment to say that Emerton tried to solve many historiographical problems by simply defining them out of existence, but it is not true that he deprived theologians of a proper sphere of activity or even that he failed to relate the areas of historical and theological information. His main concern was to differentiate between the standards and functions of distinct activities and to separate them for their mutual benefit. But he did not end his discussion of church history without suggesting its possible uses. As a historian who viewed data according to a single standard, Emerton admitted that his narratives were bound to lack theological content: "Historical evidence concerns only such things as are perceptible to human powers and can be recorded by human means. Miracles—*all* miracles—are to be excluded from the historian's function, because no human evidence can establish the fact of a miracle."[43] But that did not mean that the historian's task or his distinctive approach excluded the theologian's; it simply preceded it. The sternly critical standards of the historian's craft allowed him to do nothing more than study past ecclesiastical activity by the best scientific methods available, and it was his duty to narrate his understanding of those events with fastid-

41. Emerton, "The Study of Church History," p. 18.
42. Ibid.
43. Emerton, "A Definition of Church History," p. 63.

ious attention to documentary evidence. Such attention to methodological uniformity would provide all men, including theologians,
with a reliable account of the church's previous experiences.[44]

Emerton's view of the task of the historian was, to contradict the
one historian he singled out for criticism, that scholars *ought* to un-
tangle the skein of data and provide a cogent understanding of the
past. Then and only then theologians would have a sound basis on
which they could make claims about seeing "the golden thread of
the divine presence working through all the confusions and perplexities of an aged world."[45] Emerton tried to show how historians, with
their distinctly limited criteria and goals, could provide knowledge
and contribute modestly to theological advance. But it was always
clear that the relation could never be reciprocal. He even allowed for
historians' believing in the church as a divine institution, as long as
they restrained their faith inside a confessional sphere and kept it
out of their work as serious students. The best arrangement for a
scientific historian whose faith resembled Schaff's was a separation of
activities: public study with modern tools, private devotions with
undisclosed attitudes. Emerton thought such an arrangement would
work, and he never doubted the possibility that "if theology will cease
to bind history to its service, it will be found that the unwilling hand-
maid has yet become a servant in a better sense. Left to its own
methods and its own results history offers theology, as to every other
branch of human knowledge, an auxiliary of incalculable importance."[46]

Perhaps it would be instructive to take what few historical produc-
tions Emerton did make and see how he put his theory into practice, contrasting the judgments with those in Schaff's writings for
illustrative comparison. Emerton's discussions of the church are
marked by a strong interest in sociopolitical developments and the
bearing they had on changes in jurisprudence. Topics of that sort, as
well as methodological considerations, led him to exclude references
to supernatural agencies, an element which Schaff considered essential
to a satisfactory narrative. He also denied church history a special
place, opposing Schaff again, by claiming that it was not the key to

44. Emerton, "The Place of History in Theological Study," p. 324.
45. Emerton, "A Definition of Church History," p. 65.
46. Emerton, "The Study of Church History," p. 9.

all human history but only part of the general picture. Several selections from each man's respective works on medieval history will illustrate their different perspectives.

Philip Schaff had interpreted the period from 900 to 1073 as one of "shocking corruptions" in the papacy, and he thought it necessary to expose such black periods of church life to provide later generations with "wholesome lessons of humiliation and encouragement." As a member of the living church, Schaff was embarrassed by the fact that it could sink so low, but through it all he found enough evidence of good to assure his readers that "God [was] never absent from history, and [that] His overruling wisdom [brought] good out of evil."[47] His primary concern in discussing this period as a retrospective prophet was to show the need for church reform and thus provide a background for the emerging Protestant Reformation. He employed painstaking methods of critical investigation to show that the church had been "dragged through the quagmire of the darkest crimes, and would have perished in utter disgrace had not Providence saved it for better times."[48]

Whereas Schaff's interest in the church had been moral and theological, Emerton viewed the Roman institution as a political power, a ruler of Western Christendom, arbiter of kings and princes, wielder of two swords, wearer of the triple crown. His interpretation dealt largely with the struggle between popes and emperors over the rather mundane prizes of revenue and political power in western Europe.[49] A good example of Emerton's perspective is the fact that he considered Otto I important primarily because he succeeded in establishing a stable Holy Roman Empire.[50] Schaff thought his reign was significant because under him the papacy had been "morally saved."[51] In the year 1033 a ten-year-old boy with few spiritual inclinations, Benedict IX, ascended the papal throne to succeed his uncle, John XIX. Schaff interpreted the event as another sign of deterioration and paraphrased Isaiah to denounce the corruption: "Once more the Lord took from Jerusalem and Judah the stay and

47. Philip Schaff, *HCC*, 4:281.
48. Ibid., p. 283.
49. Ephraim Emerton, *Mediaeval Europe, 814–1300* (Boston: Ginn and Co., 1894), pp. 116–17.
50. Ibid., p. 145.
51. Schaff, *HCC*, 4:289.

the staff, and gave children to be princes, and babes to rule over them."[52] Emerton admitted that the young pope was degenerate, but found him hardly worth mentioning because of his impotence in areas that really mattered. For Emerton the important figure of that period was Conrad II who consolidated his power despite petty rebellions and who forced Rome to cooperate in his plans for empire.[53]

The German Reformation of the sixteenth century offers another area for an illuminating juxtaposition of the two perspectives. Schaff considered the Reformation to be the second greatest event in history, following closely behind the early years of Christianity in its importance for men in western Europe. Moreover, to his mind it had been a movement originating from purely religious motives, "ushered in by a providential concurrence of events and tendencies of thought."[54] Schaff lost no opportunity to point out that the Magisterial Reformers, like the apostles, "gave proof that God's spirit working through his chosen instruments [was] mightier than armies or navies."[55] Of course he also included a blend of many historical factors in the narrative, but he unerringly forced contemporaneous political and philosophical circumstances into a framework that supported his view of divine purpose behind the rise of Protestantism. The summation of his study was that "it was evidently the design of Providence to develop a new type of Christianity outside of the restraints of the papacy, and the history of three centuries [since 1517] is the best explanation and vindication of that design."[56] Emerton contended, on the other hand, that the Reformation period was too complex to be reduced to purely religious motives or any single interpretive theme.[57] He generally viewed the ecclesiastical function to be one of educating European peoples to higher standards of life and accomplishment, and so by that standard he placed his criticism on those churches of the late thirteenth century. By that time he said the clerical system had become a tyrant instead of a school-

52. Ibid., pp. 297–98. See Isaiah iii 1–4.
53. Emerton, *Mediaeval Europe*, p. 185.
54. Schaff, *HCC*, 6:1–2, 15.
55. Ibid., p. 105.
56. Ibid., p. 12.
57. Ephraim Emerton, *Desiderius Erasmus of Rotterdam* (New York: G. P. Putnam's Sons, 1899), p. 288.

master.[58] In earlier medieval times an occasional individual had rebelled, none too successfully, against the intellectual oppression of clergymen. But with a series of events beginning with the Italian Renaissance, great masses of men rose in force and achieved victory in both "individualism of taste" and "individualism of soul."[59] In the last analysis Emerton thought of the Reformation as a demonstration of human courage against an oppressive institution. The reformers drew upon a century-old precedent and grounded their faith "in what they conceived to be the pure sources of Christian thought and practice," not a providential directive. Emerton declined to say whether their conceptions were valid, concluding only that the Reformation succeeded in overthrowing papal tyranny because it drew strength from an irrepressible heritage of freedom common to all those within Graeco-Roman culture.[60] Schaff probably would have thought Emerton's treatment too reductionistic and short-sighted, but the Harvard historian was content to pursue his study as an exercise in scientific objectivity, congruent with the work of other historical craftsmen in seminar laboratories.

The small number of Emerton's publications indicates that he was more interested in historiographical theory than in the actual production of thorough historical studies. That latter achievement was provided by Williston Walker, a prolific writer who composed solid volumes in keeping with Emerton's theoretical position. The significance of Emerton's arguments is that they were the first real departure from Schaff's position to emerge from within the guild of church historians. As a scholar unashamed of choosing the church as his topic, Emerton defended the criteria and conclusions of scientific history by restricting its scope and providing for possible modifications in the light of new factual evidence. His insistence that careful historians of the church admit no evidence other than the plain human record tended to lessen the pretensions, and the dangers, of his craft while it freed research from the control of theological preconceptions. Knowledge based on those research techniques might always be tenuous, and it might be confined to human life rather than divine truth, but he thought it was the best science had to offer. Emerton

58. Emerton, *Unitarian Thought*, p. 208.
59. Emerton, *Desiderius Erasmus of Rotterdam*, p. 279.
60. Emerton, *Unitarian Thought*, pp. 208–9.

found such an irreducible form of learning to be sufficient for an inquiring mind. On that conviction he tried to lay a foundation for church historians to produce factual studies worthy of scientific esteem, and at the same time ones reliable enough to be of possible use for theologians. But, as much as theory provides an essential beginning, it is important to see how a scholar was able to carry out that theory in an extensive coverage of topics in church history.

5 &THE THEORY APPLIED

It remained for Williston Walker to carry out a sustained attempt to write objective church history, and his monumental literary achievements epitomized the ideas about which Emerton had theorized at length. Like many other influential historians of that period, he received part of his historical training in Germany, attending the lectures of prominent scholars at the University of Leipzig and surviving the rigors of independent research in seminars led by Arndt and Maurenbrecher.[1] As a result of that training he became an accomplished historical scholar who chose to investigate church matters using the same set of values and procedures on those materials which he had acquired pursuing a degree in French medieval history. Walker's emphasis on responsible scholarship and sober judgment has preserved his works from a fate common to most histories, allowing them to survive the generation in which they were written and causing them to be valued as classics in their field by secular historians and churchmen alike. The content and guiding principles of Walker's work followed guidelines best exemplified by scientific historians, and they remain impressive examples of the departure from theological church history that gained momentum in the 1880s.

GUIDELINES OF WALKER'S METHODOLOGY

Three distinguishing characteristics of those who considered history a scientific discipline have been singled out for the sake of convenient summary. For our purposes they have been classified under the gen-

---

1. From a "Biographical Sketch" printed on the inside cover of Walker's published dissertation, *On the Increase of Royal Power in France under Philip Augustus, 1179–1223* (Leipzig: Gressner and Schramm, 1888). At the beginning of our analysis of Walker's ideas, it would be helpful to remember that H. B. Adams said of Maurenbrecher: "While recognizing that there are other fields of historical inquiry . . . such as religion . . . he urged that history proper is political history. . . . History reaches its goal in politics and politics are always the resultant of history," Herbert B. Adams, "Is History Past Politics?," *JHUS*, 13th ser. 4 (1895): 78.

eral headings of iconoclasm, objectivity, and naturalism. It is difficult to analyze Walker's ideas on historiographical procedure because he rarely theorized about such matters. But no one reading his work can fail to recognize that the principles supporting his activity placed him much closer to the standards of scientific historiography than those practiced by Schaff or Shea. He was not stridently iconoclastic, but he insisted that the deficiencies of past historians be exposed to the light of more thorough investigation, to more comprehensive knowledge and, most important, to the critical scrutiny of unbiased research techniques. As far as methodological objectivity was concerned, Walker tried to avoid all bias and produce narratives of surpassing equanimity. He was so careful to excise contentious opinions that some of his factual chronicles leave the reader in the curious position of having no interpretive scheme at all upon which to arrange his data. But although the compilation of facts is usually dull and often bewilderingly complex, the finished product is always precise, compact, and reliable.

In the broader question of whether church history was a unique discipline that called for special insights and additional objectives to be determined by the faith of the writer, Walker took a secularist's view of things. His career as professor of several different historical fields as well as his writings in church history indicate that he saw no difference between the methods applicable to the field of ecclesiastical affairs and those appropriate to other historical subjects. Under the third heading, at least in terms of inferences from his works, it is certain that Walker never resorted to a discussion of supernatural influences in accounting for historical change. It is clear he was confident that any change in doctrine, polity, liturgy, or social program could be explained by reference to mundane factors. Apparently, he never felt any need to move beyond a controlled delineation of factual data and raise the question of theological significance or the ultimate meaning of history. His view of church history grew from and reflected an ethos in which men no longer cared to ask questions about the church's spiritual foundations or its providentially determined goals. The fact that Walker found professional support and public acceptance of his literary efforts indicated how prevalent his type of thinking was becoming.

Walker's writings fall naturally into two types. There are broad chronological surveys, comprehensive in scope and fastidious in detail, which of necessity relied on wide reading in secondary source material; and then on another level he wrote several penetrating studies of New England Congregationalism which were based on a mastery of primary sources in that area. Though he never undertook any writing with a casual knowledge of the materials of a given topic, some of Walker's histories were obviously intended for general reading and, as a consequence, were not based on exhaustive research in the original documents of each period. Publications of that sort did not pretend to be definitive works or scholarly contributions to a new perspective in the field of inquiry. Such writings were not sustained by Walker's accustomed documentation, but his judgments on source materials in selected areas can be used to illustrate some of his working guidelines. One of the more successful publications in which he relied largely on secondary sources but still sought to achieve a picture of true, almost photographic, clarity was a study of the career and significance of John Calvin, a topic on which Schaff had also expended a great deal of effort. In a preliminary discussion used for assessing earlier literature in the field, Walker mentioned and then summarily dismissed Schaff's work (volume 7 of the massive *History of the Christian Church*) with the cryptic observation that it was "marked by his well-known merits and limitations."[2] The only authors whom he found to be of real value were Doumergue and especially Roget, the latter a historian whose seven volumes Walker considered "remarkably impartial and essentially objective" in their use of Genevan archives.[3] One of the few American works Walker depended upon was a monograph printed under the auspices of the AHA; there is no reference to Schaff or the work of any other member of the ASCH in the entire volume.[4]

It would be a mistake to conclude that Schaff's and Walker's methodological differences generated a feeling of professional ani-

2. Williston Walker, *John Calvin: The Organizer of Reformed Protestantism, 1509–1564* (New York: G. P. Putnam's Sons, 1906), p. xvi.

3. Ibid., p. xv. Walker said (p. xvii) about Doumergue: "The most conspicuous criticism to be passed upon it is that it is everywhere a defence of its subject. Professor Doumergue is above all a worshipper of his hero, but a very painstaking worshipper. . . ."

4. Ibid., pp. 163–64, 171–72, 177–79, 181, 190. The American monograph was by H. D. Foster, "Geneva before Calvin (1387–1536): The Antecedents of a Puritan State," *American Historical Review* 8 (January 1903): 217–40.

mosity or personal incompatibility. They seem to have enjoyed friendly relations at ASCH meetings, and Schaff chose Walker to write the volume on Congregationalism in the American Church History Series. But that friendliness notwithstanding, Walker was critical of Schaff's work and did not utilize theological interpretations in his serious historical efforts. There was one instance, however, in which he recommended Schaff to readers, but in that specific publication he knew they wished to derive something more than historical information. His book was part of a religious education series that attempted to provide "a religious interpretation of all life processes whether of science, literature or social phenomena."[5] Apparently Walker thought all of Schaff's work belonged in that category, and readers interested in that field were urged to consult him.

Whether his projects resulted in scholarly monograph or general survey, Walker was always careful in his choice and use of source materials. In discussing those choices he usually broached the essential questions pertaining to diverse subjects, always taking care to represent fairly the alternative scholarly opinions, but with a detachment similar to Emerton's, he refused to take sides in any debate where the evidence was not conclusive. For example, after reviewing several interpretations of the way in which a distinctive type of polity developed in early Christian communities (an area in which many spokesmen have been eager to posit a normative interpretive pattern), Walker always remained tentative and open-minded. In the light of such scant information, his characteristic attitude was: "The utmost that can be done is to trace the scattered hints of the course of development and to confess ignorance regarding many stages . . . where the evidence is insufficient for a clear judgment."[6] In treating most of those well-worn arguments fostered by denominational zeal, he usually sought a middle path, avoiding the extremes that were produced by one faction or another, and restricting himself to

5. In Williston Walker, *Great Men of the Christian Church* (Chicago: University of Chicago Press, 1908), p. 379. The quotation is not from Walker's writing, but is a description of the series, taken from the back cover. His book constituted part of a series known as "Constructive Studies."
6. Williston Walker, "The Early Development of Church Officers," in *Approaches towards Church Unity*, ed. Newman Smyth and Williston Walker (New Haven: Yale University Press, 1919), p. 11. He continued that open-ended objectivity in his major survey, *A History of the Christian Church* (New York: Charles Scribner's Sons, 1918), pp. 44–45.

a description of the external events which he modestly termed a "tentative and fallible" synthesis.[7] He was able to substantiate that the Jerusalem church created a new ministerial office when it set up a committee of seven to care for the poor. But such a declaration pointedly left open the important question: whether the appointment of those men was a temporary expedient designed to meet a special need or whether those men, as deacons, constituted the first members of a new clerical order requiring ordination and involving a lifetime of dedication.[8]

His concluding observation on the growing use of apostolic succession as a standard used to define the orthodox consecration of bishops was equally mild, noting only that "any share in what was originally a charismatic induement indicates a very considerable modification of primitive conditions."[9] At other times Walker did not even bother to compromise with earlier authors or work within their strictures, stating openly that their categories were not relevant to an adequate understanding of the topic and period. Instead of pronouncing on the legitimacy of episcopal authority, explaining its origins or commenting on its theological importance, the objective chronicler contented himself with establishing the simple fact that it had become "generally prevalent," adding: "Of its sources, whether in the guidance of worship, the maintenance of Apostolic teaching, the administration of funds, the presidency of a board of equals, or the natural tendency to concentrate authority in times of danger and of controversy when men of native leadership are rare, it is not needful for our present purpose to enquire."[10]

In his biography of John Calvin, Walker made great use of his

7. Walker, *John Calvin*, p. 90.
8. Williston Walker, *The Validity of Congregational Ordination* (Hartford: Case, Lockwood & Grainard Co., 1898), pp. 22–23. He retains the same tentativeness in *History of the Christian Church*, p. 23. The case under discussion is particularly interesting because Philip Schaff definitely supported the institutional view, while Arthur C. McGiffert, the major figure of chapter 6, saw them as only temporary appointments.
9. Walker, "The Early Development of Church Officers," p. 23. In another place (p. 34) he said that "no period in this changing situation can be pointed out as a model of what Christian institutions should be. There was here no decline from a primal purity. There was a growth, an adaptation to environment and new conditions." The same point of view can be found in *History of the Christian Church*, p. 48.
10. Walker, *Validity of Congregational Ordination*, p. 30.

ability to synthesize material and eliminate the biased half-truths one always finds embedded in reliable documentary evidence. He pushed through thickets of conflicting data on incidental topics ranging from the accurate number of Calvin's brothers to giving a precise date for his conversion, to an assessment of the actual extent of his power at Geneva. In each case Walker paid some deference to each reputable authority he used and then found the truth to lie somewhere toward a stable center of gravity, away from all extreme opinions. The only instance of his making an unequivocal stand on a controverted point appears when he took great pains to scotch the rumor that Calvin fled rather ingloriously from the Italian district of Ferrara.[11] In the perennial controversy that tries to identify the most powerful impetus behind Roman Catholic reforms in the sixteenth century, with its hackneyed phrase "Counter-Reformation," Walker characteristically declared that the full truth lay with no single protagonist:

The lines which that Roman Reformation were to take were . . . clearly marked out, a generation before Luther began his work, in the Spanish Awakening—itself but the most thoroughgoing . . . of several conservative attempts to purify the Church. . . . Yet, had it not been for the ferment of the Protestant revolt there is no reason to suppose that a restoration of the . . . Roman communion . . . would have become a counter-Reformation coextensive with Latin Christendom.[12]

One final example of Walker's tentativeness will have to suffice. He refused to reach a definite conclusion about the Anabaptist background of Robert Browne and the possible influence such a body of doctrine might have had on the early English Separatists, once again disappointing any who wished him to resolve a crucial interpretive issue.[13] In the last analysis, then, it can be said that he not only

11. Walker, *John Calvin*, p. 153. The matter received only passing notice in his *History of the Christian Church*, pp. 394–95. Schaff also rejected the tale as having no basis in fact; see Philip Schaff, *History of the Christian Church*, 6 vols. [vols. 1, 2, 3, 4, 6, 7] (New York: Charles Scribner's Sons, 1882–92), 7:345 (hereafter cited as *HCC*).

12. Williston Walker, *The Reformation* (New York: Charles Scribner's Sons, 1915), pp. 356–57; see also p. 67 for a similar equivocation. In the later volume, *History of the Christian Church*, p. 422, Walker said more emphatically that "Counter-Reformation" was an incorrect way of viewing the matter.

13. Williston Walker, *The Creeds and Platforms of Congregationalism* (1893; reprint ed., Boston: Pilgrim Press, 1960), pp. 15–17. All references are from the later edition. In his *History of the Christian Church*, p. 461, Walker said that "Browne's system so closely resembles the views of the Anabaptists that some connection in thought at least seems well-nigh certain."

shunned the theological issues involved in church historical studies, but he was extremely cautious about the type of historical generalizations the record would support.

Most of Walker's historical interpretations have withstood the test of time, but there is one small area (and that in his special field) which has been revised in recent times. He supported the view that the Puritan church at Salem, Massachusetts, became a Separatist body after being led to emulate the Plymouth congregation by the friendly persuasions and example of physician Fuller.[14] To be fair to Walker, though, he admitted that the Salem church never became openly Separatist. He knew that it never renounced its connection with the Anglican establishment in Great Britain, but he contended that a theoretical loyalty to an institution with no real power or spokesmen had "little practical importance" in the New World.[15] Even though his interpretation of that particular episode has subsequently been disputed,[16] the greater part of Walker's work remains a model of careful historical judgment, and such isolated miscalculations should not be allowed to detract from its essential accuracy. One might even suggest that his works have remained in use because the bare narratives include so few debatable interpretations or personal views in their diffident conclusions.

Perhaps the most revealing statement relevant to a study of Walker's methodological views was made in connection with the sources of his special field. Viewing the records as one wishing to be an unbiased observer and dispassionate reporter, he said there was little concrete value in the historical narratives of Puritan writers like William Bradford and Cotton Mather. He was willing to grant, with all their bias and spiritual orientation, that they could still serve to acquaint the modern historian with the flavor of their times. But he also insisted that their "paucity of definite dates and . . . substitution of indefinite generalities for the concrete facts" gave scientific inquirers little information pertinent to the institutional, cultural, or social

14. Williston Walker, *A History of the Congregational Churches in the United States* (New York: Charles Scribner's Sons, 1894), p. 103.
15. Ibid., p. 109; see also pp. 99, 106.
16. Probably the most significant contribution in this area was made by P. Miller, *Orthodoxy in Massachusetts, 1630–1650* (Boston: Beacon Press, 1959), pp. 127, 131. See also H. S. Smith, R. T. Handy, and L. A. Loetscher, eds., *American Christianity: An Historical Interpretation with Representative Documents* (New York: Charles Scribner's Sons, 1960), 1:86–87, 97–107.

questions they were asking. In a memorable phrase that indicates the ideal Walker held for himself and all modern historians, he said that Mather's biographies were not trustworthy because they were not "always photographically correct likenesses of the men whom he sketched."[17] Thus Walker can be understood as one primarily interested in reproducing a sequence of events, the traits of an individual personality, or the major contours of institutional change with the clarity and precision that photography affords. That ideal of his also serves to illustrate an aspect theological church historians would consider a weakness: photographs are able to depict only the superficial aspects of phenomena. Walker was satisfied with that type of historical analysis which concentrated on external affairs, and he remained convinced that exactitude in empirical investigation was all scientific inquiry could provide. His volumes stand as the greatest embodiment of an attempt to write empirical, objective church history in this country.

Another general guideline of Walker's distinctive approach to source materials was an inclination to stress political circumstances and institutional factors as adequate categories for explaining developments in church history. In keeping with the intellectual fraternity of the AHA he never conceived of a level of historical explanation that necessitated allusions to supernatural agents or providential superintendence. The major emphases of his doctoral dissertation indicate that in 1888, the year when Schaff was trying to give some institutional structure and longevity to his theological views, Walker was writing with the conviction that power politics was actually the determinative factor behind major events. He adjusted that view later to the extent of admitting rare individuals might occasionally draw upon spiritual resources and directly affect the history of a nation or a movement. But even then, for the historical analyst, the "religious and political impulses [were] so intertwined that they [could] scarcely . . . be disassociated."[18] In the majority of cases, he selected and stressed those types of evidence which supported the view that social and political conditions are the most important factors in man's past. In a long chapter ostensibly dealing

17. Williston Walker, "The Services of the Mathers in New England Religious Development," *Papers of the ASCH* 5 (1893) : 81.
18. Walker, *The Reformation*, p. 58; see also his opening statement on p. 1.

with the "spiritual antecedents" of the life of John Calvin, Walker
devoted almost the entire analysis to diplomatic negotiations between
Leo X and Francis I and the subsequent Concordat of 1516 which
virtually excluded papal control from France.[19] In giving a final
evaluation of the various reasons for the success of reformed Christianity in northern Europe, Walker gave some credence to the view
that the pious zeal and theological cogency of solid Christians could
not be stifled, but he allowed equal weight to the defeat of the Spanish Armada at the hands of the English.[20] Thus the former student in
Maurenbrecher's seminar took the dictum that "history is past politics" and applied it to ecclesiastical affairs, producing the view that
corresponding phenomena in churches were the only subjects of
importance.

Even though Walker emphasized the tangible and the institutional
side of church history, he was never doctrinaire enough to exclude
the possibility of God's direct intervention. As a scientific historian,
however, he simply thought it his duty to remain silent on such
matters of faith and confine himself to tangible factors in arriving
at a plausible explanation. Even in recounting the episode of Calvin's
conversion to Protestantism, Walker cast a rather wide net for
secular factors. Whereas authors like Schaff had attributed Calvin's
change of heart to the direct action of the Holy Spirit, Walker
thought the real influence had most likely been the atmosphere of
humanistic scholarship, a climate of opinion that imbued Calvin with
a longing for the religious excellence represented in his studies.[21]
It seemed both natural and reasonable to Walker that the young
lawyer who studied at Paris, Orléans, and Bourges might have
warmed to any number of eminent spokesmen who sought religious
reform by means of purer morals, effective preaching, and greater
fidelity to the literary sources of Christian truth. In attempting to
single out the most influential figures who shaped Calvin's religious

---

19. Walker, *John Calvin*, pp. 3–4.
20. Walker, *The Reformation*, pp. 434–35. There is not much emphasis laid
on the Armada in *History of the Christian Church*, p. 440.
21. Walker, *John Calvin*, pp. 77–78. There is hardly any discussion at all in
History of the Christian Church, pp. 390–91, about conditions that might have fostered a conversion. P. Schaff, *HCC*, 7:312, became so enthusiastic about the spiritual significance of the event that he compared it to the Damascus Road experience
of the Apostle Paul.

convictions, Walker thought it "not impossible" (a favorite ploy to avoid overreaching himself) that Pierre Olivétan and Gérard Roussel might have been chiefly responsible. But then another factor to consider in assessing Calvin's coolness toward the Roman hierarchy was the fact that his father and brother were in open conflict with ecclesiastical authorities at the time.[22] Walker concluded the study with a characteristically complex statement that no single human factor could be deemed outstanding, and yet at the same time no aspect of the general situation could be dismissed as irrelevant. In addition to that, though he saw no means of verifying it, he felt compelled to include Calvin's own statement which placed the conversion within the sphere of God's direct agency. Although Walker's ideas about natural causation might have led him to exclude such references to the spirit, still his respect for source materials would not let him delete Calvin's account from the proceedings. So once again he tried to compromise and include both naturalistic and supernaturalistic interpretations within one overview, saying that, whatever the real sources of his faith and however scientific man might think differently about it, "[spiritualist] conviction might have come to such a man as Calvin in the quiet of his study with no less force than if impressed upon him by [Walker's preference] public discourse or friendly exhortation."[23]

Still in keeping with attempts to construct a narrative that avoided reference to providential causes or theological significance, Walker traced Calvin's steps from Noyon to Angoulême and then to Geneva, concluding in the last case that it was only "the chances of war" that drew him to the Swiss city.[24] The establishment of Calvinism as a way of life in Geneva had nothing to do with its excellence as a coherent system of doctrine or its superiority as a declaration of religious truth; it rose to ascendancy by default:

Undoubtedly a considerable part of the relative ease with which Calvin established his ecclesiastical constitution in Geneva . . . was due to the

22. Walker, *John Calvin*, p. 91.
23. Ibid., p. 97. Schaff's treatment of the conversion episode dealt with it entirely as a religious event and asserted that Calvin was obeying "the voice from heaven" in becoming a Protestant. See P. Schaff, *HCC*, 7:310–11.
24. Walker, *John Calvin*, p. 181. Schaff had said that "Calvin was fore-ordained for Geneva, and Geneva for Calvin." See P. Schaff, *HCC*, 7:348.

loss of several conspicuous leaders of the city-life just before or soon
after his return. . . . The time of Calvin's opening work was one of relative weakness among the older leaders of both parties in Genevan affairs. . . . Under these circumstances, the introduction of the new ecclesiastical discipline was easier than it might otherwise have been.[25]

Even Walker's discussion of the *Institutes* consisted of an analytical
report of the contents of the book without any comment on their
value as a guide for the faith of modern readers.[26] At a later time he
allowed himself to say that, however inadequate the system might
appear to contemporary eyes, it seemed in the sixteenth century to be
the ablest answer to Roman claims and a defensible presentation of
the Gospel.[27]

Walker also stressed the importance of external circumstances
in his field of special concentration, the history of Congregationalism.
In discussing the Savoy Conference of 1658 he was amused to find
that the delegates were surprised at the unanimity which they discovered among themselves. In face of their open declaration that such
unity stemmed from the direct influence of the attendant Spirit of
God, he scrupled to say that it was "easy to discover causes less
clearly supernatural."[28] Among those causes which did not rely on
providential guidance, Walker pointed out that English Congregationalists had been united by a common resentment of both the
Hampton Court decision and the harsh strictures laid against Dissenters after 1604. The proposed alliance between the English crown
and Catholic Spain together with James's refusal to aid German
Protestants served to knit Puritans even more closely together and
give them "a hold on the national affection . . . never enjoyed

25. Walker, *John Calvin*, pp. 258, 281. In Walker, *History of the Christian
Church*, pp. 396–98, there is no concern for reasons why he came to power. Schaff,
on the other hand, said, "His success was achieved by moral and spiritual means,
and stands almost alone in history" (P. Schaff, *HCC*, 7:316–17; see also pp. 349
and 497).
26. Walker, *John Calvin*, pp. 139–45. There are only paraphrases in Walker,
History of the Christian Church, pp. 392–94.
27. Walker, *John Calvin*, p. 377. Schaff's assessment was that the *Institutes* had
been written "under the inspiration of a heroic faith that is ready for the stake, and
with a glowing enthusiasm for the pure Gospel of Christ, which had been obscured
and deprived of its effect by human traditions, but had now risen from this rub-
bish to new life and power" (P. Schaff, *HCC*, 7:330).
28. Walker, *Creeds and Platforms of Congregationalism*, p. 350. The Savoy
meeting is not mentioned in *History of the Christian Church*, p. 473.

under Elizabeth."[29] By the time of Cromwell both the Anglican and Presbyterian factions had suffered a decline, and the various Congregationalist groups were free to convene their own theological conference and discover the unanimity to which events had unwittingly brought them.

Walker followed the same line of interpretation when he turned to the events in New England, saying that he found it "natural" rather than providential that the Cambridge Confession of 1690 resembled the earlier statements composed at Westminster Abbey (1648) and the Savoy Palace (1658). The ideological continuity could be attributed largely to the efforts of a single man, Increase Mather, who had been in England during the Savoy deliberations and who also held a prominent place on the Massachusetts drafting committee.[30] Whether he sought an explanation for New England's theological homogeneity or a factor to explain the emergence of a unique development such as the Saybrook Platform in Connecticut, Walker concentrated on the nonreligious side, noting in the latter case that the determinative event had been the election of a clergyman as governor.[31] This naturalistic tendency of mind in Walker, illustrated here at great length, fused with several of his personal ideals to give a distinctive turn to some of his broad historical judgments. A review of those suggestive judgments will substantiate our interpretation of Walker as a church historian who approximated the ideals exemplified in the AHA.

DISTINCTIVE INTERPRETATIONS IN WALKER'S WRITING

The circumspection with which Walker published proper historical narratives did not allow him much room for introducing personal elements into his matter-of-fact reporting, but there are some interpretations embedded in his studies of Congregationalism that give his work a distinctive flavor. Those viewpoints can best be described as stemming not from theological perspective or confessional ex-

29. Walker, *History of Congregational Churches,* pp. 80, 84.
30. Ibid., pp. 189–90. See also *Creeds and Platforms of Congregationalism,* pp. 181, 420–21.
31. Williston Walker, "Why Did Not Massachusetts Have a Saybrook Platform?," *Yale Review* 1 (May 1892): 81. The title of the essay is a curious one because the point of his writing was to discover why Connecticut did have one. The individual elected to the governor's chair and who brought the ecclesiastical consociation into being was Gurdon Saltonstall.

clusiveness, but rather from a pride in the institutional vitality of American Congregational churches and a personal concern for their future effectiveness in the United States. In keeping with a sociological definition of churches compatible with scientific historiography, Walker's conception of church life in New England emphasized the institutional aspects of religion, and it was given added weight by his private hopes that Congregationalism maintain its independence and continue to increase its numerical strength.

After years of reflection and extensive research Walker came to the conclusion that the main strength of Congregationalism lay in the fairness of its democratic polity rather than in any theological superiority over other confessions of faith. He thought of his denomination as a cohesive system of practical Christian piety nurtured by voluntary gatherings of the faithful in each locality, led by clergymen dependent on popular support, all of which were free to meet new problems with pragmatic innovations because there was an "absence of . . . authority in doctrine or polity save the Word of God."[32] Of course, he did not deny that there was a theological substratum to most denominational activity, but his personal view of church life as well as his historiographical standards led him to emphasize the institutional aspect over any theological frame of reference. To illustrate how few distinctive characteristics he thought his subjects had, Walker said there was little difference to be found between doctrines of American Congregationalism and the Calvinism expressed in the Westminster Confession. In addition to doctrinal agreement he found that Presbyterians and all forms of Congregationalism were essentially the same in their conceptions of proper forms of worship, equal in their opposition to a sacerdotal prelacy and "largely accordant in their views as to the nature of the ministry and its functions."[33] The only new ideas to be found in the Savoy Declaration, a statement of principles written in 1658 without Presbyterian influence, comprised a section of thirty paragraphs dealing with church order, principles important enough to emphasize because Walker designated them as "the main features of Congregationalism": "the headship of Christ, the constitution of the

32. Walker, *History of Congregational Churches*, pp. 1, 162.
33. Walker, *Creeds and Platforms of Congregationalism*, p. 441. The same estimate can be found in *History of the Christian Church*, p. 567.

local church by the union of believers, its complete autonomy, its right to choose and ordain the officers appointed by Christ, the necessity of a call from a church to confer ministerial standing, the consent of the brethren as essential to all admissions and censures, synods and councils for advice but without judicial authority."[34]

Even the religious movement known as the First Great Awakening was assimilated into Walker's overarching scheme that accounted for change largely in terms of institutional developments. The tremendous energy of theological activity that characterized the 1740s and 1750s was seen chiefly as an effort to apply Christianity more effectively to everyday life. While he was willing to grant that Jonathan Edwards produced "the only original contribution of importance given by America to the development of Christian theology," Edwards's contribution was valued for reasons other than its creativity in the history of doctrine.[35] No matter how interested in the realm of pure ideas the initial protagonists of the "New Divinity" might have been, as an institutional historian of New England religion Walker said their lasting impact lay in a successful attempt to intensify popular concern for piety and morals. Thus in an attempt to give Edwardeans a definition they would have preferred and still subsume them under his own view, Walker concluded that "Edwardeanism was not merely, one is almost ready to say not chiefly, a doctrinal system; it was a moral and spiritual force."[36]

Perhaps the basic attitude brought by Walker to historical studies, exemplified above and expressed in numerous places, can be described by means of a general category, "democratic humanitarianism." On occasion he allowed himself the liberty of crossing the invisible barrier which so often screened his own opinions from the narrative. In those moments he disclosed an unmistakable sympathy for gradual progress in matters of religious toleration and a preference for democratic freedom that allowed men of all persuasions to follow the dictates of their own conscience. In such a vein, Walker deplored Calvin's unwarranted "hardness" and "cruelty" in the

---

34. Walker, *Creeds and Platforms of Congregationalism*, p. 351. See also *History of Congregational Churches*, pp. 124, 344–45.
35. Walker, *History of Congregational Churches*, p. 266.
36. Ibid., pp. 304–5. This view was revised in the 1918 *History of the Christian Church*, pp. 572–73, to say that Edwards's influence was primarily theological.

Servetus affair.[37] He praised the Mennonites and other mild groups of the left-wing Reformation for their patient suffering and pacifist views in the face of persecution.[38] Still along lines of this sympathy, though it dealt with democracy more than humanitarian tolerance, he gloried in the history of colonial New England because it vindicated the struggle for local autonomy against the tyrannical claims of Parliamentary interference.[39]

Walker's enthusiasm for democratic procedures and religious toleration did not lead him into a Whiggish interpretation of the history of his denomination. He was realistic enough to see that Puritanism became established in New England as Anglicanism had been in Old England and that it, like its counterpart, used governmental power to curtail the activities of other denominations within its jurisdiction. But whenever denominational loyalty might have posed a conflict with his larger faith in democratic humanitarianism, allegiance to the latter ideal always won. With his understanding of historical precedents he admitted that enforced religious conformity was a logical step in a new land monopolized by zealous rulers who shared common theological views, but such conformity contradicted his private ideals. On the basis of that contradiction he criticized the Puritan identification of political power with New Testament tenets.[40] As a loyal Congregationalist committed to the ideal of democratic humanitarianism, he confessed that an arbitrary power to repress and banish had been wielded in the cases of Anne Hutchinson and Roger Williams. He did not hesitate to label it "persecution as real as it was unjustifiable."[41] The exercise of such power in those

37. Walker, *John Calvin*, pp. 325–26 and 427. Walker blunted the edge of his criticism in *History of the Christian Church*, p. 399, and said only: "However odious the trial and its tragic end may seem in retrospect, for Calvin it was a great victory." Schaff concurred in viewing the incident as an unfortunate stigma on the record of the Magisterial Reformer; see P. Schaff, *HCC*, 7:324, 785.

38. Walker, *The Reformation*, pp. 354–55. He called Menno Simons and Balthasar Hübmaier, "in spite of all their crudities and mistakes . . . prophets of a freedom to come."

39. Walker, *Creeds and Platforms of Congregationalism*, p. 178. He has no theme of republican progressivism in his later *History of the Christian Church* at all.

40. Walker, *History of Congregational Churches*, pp. 125–26; see also *Creeds and Platforms of Congregationalism*, p. 166. There is no such criticism voiced at this juncture in *History of the Christian Church*, p. 567.

41. Walker, *History of Congregational Churches*, p. 145. Neither case is mentioned in *History of the Christian Church*.

early incidents, representative of a large category, produced the short-range effect of a uniform system of faith amd government around Massachusetts Bay. But the liberty-minded Walker disowned a large segment of his denomination's past as an unhappy memory because it did not tally with his hopes for life in a democratic society.

One of the rare instances in which Walker ventured a judgment that can be identified as an indication of theological interest occurred in his account of the Half-Way Covenant. He disapproved of the "illogical and inconsistent position" which lowered qualifications for church membership, claiming on religious grounds that it destroyed all meaning for the church as a distinct group.[42] He obviously relished the collapse of such a fatal compromise in the nineteenth century. It is also interesting in this regard parenthetically to note that Walker considered the Half-Way Covenant to be an exclusively religious controversy. Even though he was generally prone to emphasize social influences and institutional implications as the major factors in historical incidents, and though that particular debate over membership qualifications held great consequences for the political and financial stratification of New England society, Walker insisted that such considerations were incidental to the real issue.[43] Another instance in which Walker disclosed a tendency to criticize historical developments in the light of their effect on denominational strength was his account of the rise of Unitarianism. To his credit, though, it must be added that he treated this latter category with more sophistication than the Half-Way compromise. In evaluating the activities of early Unitarians like Charles Chauncy, he viewed them in the light of their contributions to his ideal of progress. In such a perspective Walker emphasized their social conscience and never pointed up any theological incompatibilities between reformists and the New England Way.[44] But even though he saw noble qualities in some prominent representatives of American Unitarianism, as a Congregationalist churchman he summarized by saying that the movement eventually "lost touch with those needs

42. Walker, *History of Congregational Churches*, pp. 179–80; see also *Creeds and Platforms of Congregationalism*, pp. 249–50.
43. Walker, *History of Congregational Churches*, pp. 172–73; see also *Creeds and Platforms of Congregationalism*, p. 245.
44. Williston Walker, *Ten New England Leaders* (New York: Silver, Burdett and Co., 1901), p. 310.

and feelings that the church universal has always recognized as deepest in mankind."[45]

Walker's account of the rise of American Unitarianism did not mark a departure from his fundamental interest in environmental factors, but it offers a useful comparison with the judgments of Frank Hugh Foster discussed in a later chapter. As far as Walker was concerned, it was not necessary to go any further than a general observation about the gradual shift of values in New England society. He considered the new religious viewpoint to be based on a climate of opinion in which men stopped insisting that a divinely wrought change in human nature be a prerequisite to morality and began hoping that the cultivation of morality might serve as a means to, rather than a consequence of, Christian piety. He concluded simply that Unitarianism owed its origin largely to a major revision in popular notions about the possibilities of human achievement. The Half-Way Covenant and Stoddardeanism had nothing to do with its emergence.[46] Within the limits of that interpretation Walker could not account for the fact that only some New Englanders became Unitarians, while some in that new environment remained orthodox, and still others departed from Calvinism in a number of other ways. Nor did that conception of the movement allow for a satisfactory appreciation of the genuine intellectual differences over trinitarian creedal statements. Those deficiencies did not, however, prevent him from considering his basic analysis a satisfactory one.

Once when he was describing fundamental changes in categories of religious expression, Walker formulated what he called "the law of . . . declining Calvinism," a descriptive device appropriate to many countries but one involving no value judgment at all. It did not matter whether one began his survey with Switzerland, France,

45. Walker, *History of Congregational Churches,* p. 345. It is not surprising to find very little evaluation of Unitarianism in *History of the Christian Church.*

46. Walker, *Creeds and Platforms of Congregationalism,* p. 284. In his later statement about the change (*History of the Christian Church,* p. 577), Walker conceived of the movement as a controversy over ideas, and he mentioned leading spokesmen. For a more thorough treatment along that latter line, see H. M. Morais, *Deism in Eighteenth Century America* (New York: Russell and Russell, 1960), pp. 86–87, 165–66, and especially 177–78. The most thorough book on the subject, one that deals with all the various components of Unitarianism including not only its anti-Trinitarian but its Arminian and various conceptions of the nature and scope of religious values, is by C. Wright, *The Beginnings of Unitarianism in America* (Boston: Starr King Press, 1955).

Holland, England, or America, because in each place Calvinism had begun on a level of intense spiritual zeal and held extreme views on divine sovereignty, human inability, and "special salvatory mercy to the elect." But Walker noted, with no further explanation of possible causes, that in time the original feeling of intensity abated and that men began to concern themselves less with God's irresistible grace and more with what they could do "to put themselves in a position where God is more likely to save them." The third step of declining Calvinism was then an easy accomplishment, introducing the belief that religion is a cultivation of careful habits in church attendance and public morals. That third level, properly termed Arminianism, holds that "if each man labors sincerely to do what he can under the impulse of the grace that God sends to all men, God will accept his sincere though imperfect obedience as satisfactory." The final transition was effected when men came to say that "the essence of the Christian life is . . . the practice of morality, and the need of man is . . . education and culture, not rescue and fundamental transformation."[47] Walker's convenient levels of historical transition provided an interpretive scheme without any apparent evaluation of the state of religion at the various stages. We shall see later in studying Foster that a similar descriptive pattern could allow for an intensely personal evaluation of identical developments.

While Walker did not write church history with the Schaffian objectives of edifying his readers or vindicating theism by exhibiting the gradual development of God's Kingdom on earth, it cannot be said that he thought his narratives were devoid of useful lessons. The major principles which American experience vindicated and which Walker's view of both secular and religious developments confirmed were the broad humanitarian doctrines of democratic freedom and religious toleration. Since that expansive ideology was enough to contain all of his hopes for a peaceful interchange between free churches in a free society, it seemed retrogressive to argue that any particular version of church polity was universally valid.[48] As long as the major goal of freedom remained unchal-

47. Walker, Ten New England Leaders, pp. 229–31.
48. Walker, "The Early Development of Church Officers," pp. 34–35; see also Validity of Congregational Ordination, p. 15.

lenged, he was willing to adopt a relativistic view of doctrinal change, saying that even the deepest Christian verities were subject to "the general rule of modification and supersession which seems essential to all progress."[49] He could admire in a detached way the lucidity or the comprehensiveness of past accomplishments in doctrinal expressions, and he could view with equanimity different systems of church government. But his American sense of experimentation would not allow him to accept any single creed or polity as universally true or binding.[50] In addition to using history as a support for his idealized view of national and ecclesiastical progress, Walker thought church history was worth studying because it afforded the opportunity of meeting some of the more striking personalities in Western civilization. Of course, his biographical sketches did not disclose the hagiographical tendencies found among theological-minded historians, but his treatment of men such as John Calvin, the two senior Mathers or even an obscure missionary like John Eliot implied that their presence gave church history a noble aspect and raised it above the level of a meaningless chronicle. In summarizing his study of New England leaders, he declared that the most admirable quality shared by those men and by prominent individuals throughout Christendom lay "in their thought of the Church as finding its . . . truest expression . . . in self-government and mutually responsible fellowships of Christian men."[51] The highest praise he could award them was to conclude by saying that "not one of them but made New England [in a larger context he could easily have said the United States] stronger, better, freer, by reason of his work."

In another vein altogether and quite at variance with the major portion of his work, there are scattered hints that Walker retained, for all his detachment and empiricism, a small degree of theological sensitivity in evaluating past ecclesiastical activity. Any resemblance to the overtly theological criteria of Schaff and Shea was reduced to a pale shadow, but even the ablest practitioner of a more objective church history could not in the end bring himself to say that the give and take of historical forces was a "mere shuttle-cock play of

49. Walker, John Calvin, p. 425.
50. Walker, Creeds and Platforms of Congregationalism, p. 422.
51. Walker, Ten New England Leaders, p. 455.

chance, beating blindly in one direction or another."[52] Once Walker
stood briefly within a theological frame of reference and confessed
that he was able, with the aid of faith, to discern a providential
superintendence over many developments in the history of Christianity. That statement, which serves as an exception to prove the
general rule of his sympathy for scientific methodology, merits full
quotation:

In spite of all these vagrant turnings, aiming at the same ultimate goal
and steadily moving onward, as if by an irresistible impulse . . . so it
is in the history of the Kingdom of God. Under the guidance of the
divine Spirit the church glides strongly onward toward its completion;
but its course is fretted by bars of human weakness, and turmoiled by
rocks of human passion . . . its current seldom moves long in the same
direction, but bears now to one side and now to the other, so that to the
observer who takes into view only a brief span of the church's progress,
it often appears that its current is reversed, and he almost doubts whether
it can be the same stream.[53]

As for his own denomination Walker expressed the belief that Congregational churches were decidedly in the mainstream of ecclesiastical progress and were directed by the impulse of the Divine Spirit.[54]
But this confession of faith had no real effect on his historical methodology and should be included in a study of Walker's ideas only for
the sake of comprehensive coverage. The great body of his writings
must be taken as evidence to indicate that Walker achieved the
best exemplification of church history written according to standards
set by those who thought they were patterning their work after the
methods of science.

In the remaining chapters of this volume we can turn to individuals who distinguished themselves from the modes of study already

52. Williston Walker, *Three Phases of New England Congregational Development* (Hartford: Hartford Seminary Press, 1893), p. 5.
53. Ibid., p. 4. There is a similar statement at the very end of Walker's majestic
historical survey of the whole Christian church, again out of keeping with the
tenor of the rest of the book (*History of the Christian Church*, pp. 589–90):
". . . no Christian can survey what the church has done without confidence in its
future. Its changes may be many, its struggles great. But the good hand of God
which has led it hitherto will guide it to larger usefullness in the advancement of
the kingdom of its Lord. . . ."
54. Walker, *Three Phases of New England Congregational Development*, p. 22.

mentioned. They valued religious insight and utilized it, but in ways that varied from the theologies and interests of earlier historiographical patterns. They respected the aims of scientific history, and some claimed always to be working within the limits set by its demands. But the unique insights and methodologies that they brought to their task added new departures to the debate over procedure in the historian's craft.

6 &LIBERAL THEOLOGY

The work of Arthur Cushman McGiffert marked the emergence of a fresh perspective in church historiography and indicated that a new vitality had arisen to make theological views and historical methodology once again partners in a common task. McGiffert and the two authors studied in subsequent chapters began their work after the AHA had succeeded in establishing norms for acceptable knowledge within the community of historical scholars. To some degree these younger church historians built on the generally accepted professional attitudes regarding scholarly objectivity and the minute findings yielded by an empirical investigation of human source materials. But they also shared a tacit assumption that theological insights could not properly be excluded from historical studies of religious subjects. Each of the following authors resembled scientific historians in rejecting the overtly theological guidelines so basic to both the investigation and interpretation of events in Schaff's theories. They utilized the dispassionate and detached methods available for securing reliable information about what had actually occurred in the church's past, but they resembled earlier patterns of church history by interpreting those historical events in the light of theological presuppositions. Their new theologies departed significantly from Schaff's ideas about the sacred mission of institutional churches and his concern for an increased emphasis on liturgy, confessions, and ecumenism in the ongoing history of redemption. In the narrow question of ascertaining concrete facts, liberal church historians expressed the wish to abide by standards set by the age of science, giving additional indications that Schaff's interest in blending theological insights with research techniques was falling into disuse. But in regard to interpreting the evidence provided by those rigorous methods, they rested on theological orientations and broached many suggestive ideas. They also kept a recurrent theme alive by maintaining a religious understanding of historical movements.

In the last analysis, then, the ideas of liberal church historians should not be viewed as a compromise within the context of an earlier debate or a synthesis of the most attractive points contained in the above-mentioned scientific and theological points of view. The emergence of a new working hypothesis, which we may call "liberal church historiography," had roots sufficiently diverse to allow it to stand as a major development; yet it can be related to the previous conflict of ideas because it shared problems which have defied solution through several generations of scholars. The work of liberal theologians in the historical discipline tends to substantiate the thesis that theology cannot long be separated from church historians, nor can it be isolated from their interpretation of the collective experience of men and institutions. A basically theological conception of the church inevitably undergirds historical work in that area. In the years between 1876 and 1906 the ultimate impact of ideas attributed to natural science can be said to have greatly affected, but not destroyed, the particularistic quality of church historiography. Without trying to assess the role of science in the origin of liberal theology, it is not inaccurate to say that scientific standards affected liberal church historians in both their methodological approach and in the religious perspective by which they interpreted their findings. Writings of the men in the next three chapters disclosed conceptions that contrasted with earlier ideas about procedure and objectives in church history, contrasts of a more striking nature because they differed on both methodological and theological grounds. At the same time, however, liberal church historians kept alive the perennial issue of combining theological insight with an awareness of one's cultural setting.

ARTHUR McGIFFERT AND THE SHAPING OF A LIBERAL

Arthur Cushman McGiffert was the most lucid thinker and prolific writer of the new wave of church historians who came to prominence in the early 1900s, and he deserves to head the list of liberals as their most articulate spokesman. Graduated from New York's Union Theological Seminary in 1885, he studied in Berlin for a year and then obtained his doctorate under Adolf Harnack at the University of Marburg in 1888. While in Germany McGiffert developed a taste for translating and editing documents of the early church and acquired a knowledge of general church history comprehensive enough to win a post at Lane Theological Seminary in Cincinnati. His first major work was a translation of the *Church History* of Eusebius (to be volume 1 of Schaff's *Select Library of Nicene and Post-Nicene Fathers*), a heavily annotated volume that displayed McGiffert's erudition as well as his skill in translating, but one which gave no indication that the young scholar harbored any liberal theological views. His learned prolegomena and extensive notes accompanying the text established him as a scholar of the first rank, and that reputation led to his appointment as the second Washburn Professor of Church History upon Schaff's death in 1893. Few men could have realized at the time how little Schaff's successor would maintain the historiographical synthesis cherished by the founder of the American Society of Church History.

A genuine affection and professional admiration existed between the two men ever since McGiffert had been a student at Union Seminary. Apparently the work of the young church historian impressed Schaff and convinced him that the cause of scholarship would benefit if more work was encouraged. In 1885, while McGiffert was still a student in Germany, Schaff asked him to edit the Eusebius volume. Schaff tried to have him appointed his assistant in 1887, but failing that, he sent congratulations on his being made church historian at Lane Seminary. There is no record of how McGiffert responded to his patron's advice, but in that letter, Schaff reminded him that his work carried great responsibilities: "I know no higher and nobler calling than that which you have chosen. . . . Church History is the history of Christ and his Gospel in its saving mission, and next to God's word, the richest storehouse of instruction, wisdom, and comfort."[1]

Schaff further indicated his esteem for the younger professor by recommending him for more prestigious academic posts: Princeton Seminary in 1889 for church history, Union Seminary in 1891 for systematic theology, and McCormick Seminary in 1891 for church history.[2] Probably the highest compliment came when he asked McGiffert to write the history of Christianity from 1648 to their day and publish it as the final volume of his own *History of the*

1. Arthur C. McGiffert, Jr., "The Making of an American Scholar: Biography in Letters," *Union Seminary Quarterly Review* 24 (Fall 1968): 37.
2. Ibid., pp. 38, 41, 43.

Christian Church. In that letter, which has only recently come to public notice, Schaff referred to McGiffert as "the finisher of my life work" and offered him full control over any future revisions the series might require.[3] As we shall see, there were significant differences between the two scholars' methods and goals, but that should not be allowed to detract from the sincerity of their personal regard for each other.

A second major publication, the catalytic agent of his subsequent career, was *A History of Christianity in the Apostolic Age* in which McGiffert continued to exhibit his German training, both a fundamental grounding in historical research techniques and liberal interpretations perhaps absorbed from Harnack himself. He utilized all the latest scholarly findings, archaeological discoveries, and linguistic hypotheses relevant to his subject; he discussed textual evidence from the Bible in the light of advanced critical interpretations and presented his conclusions with a clarity and boldness that would become a mark of excellence in his style. There were many students in the United States who recognized his publication as a lucid summary of the most recent interpretations of early Christianity, but much of what he said was denounced by conservatives as too radical for a respectable Presbyterian. From the day of the book's appearance in 1897 until 1900, when McGiffert was forced to withdraw from his denomination, the charge of "heresy" hounded his every move and helped shape the young historian into a confirmed liberal.

G. F. W. Birch, a self-appointed lion of orthodoxy and chief antagonist throughout the affair, was indefatigable in pressing five separate charges. Birch argued that McGiffert's book contained an implicit denial of the immediate inspiration of Scriptures and thus impugned their authority; it suggested that Christ had held mistaken ideas about the immediacy of the approaching eschaton, implying that he might have taught other erroneous views as well; it questioned the traditional conviction that Christ had deliberately instituted the Supper as a memorial of his death;[4] in discussing divergent

3. Ibid., p. 43. The intent of this letter was to soften McGiffert's disappointment at not being chosen to fill the chair in systematic theology at Union. Taking that into account, one might suspect the sentiment expressed is overextended.

4. His position on this question seems to have drawn most of the fire as proceedings began. Moreover, it could not have been in his favor to utilize the works of C. A. Briggs to justify his interpretation. See Arthur C. McGiffert, Jr., "A Mischievous Book: Further Correspondence of A. C. McGiffert," *Union Seminary Quarterly Review* 24 (Summer 1969): 365.

theories of justification it denied that any specific explanation such as
the imputation of righteousness could serve as a universal standard;
finally, the book involved McGiffert in the difficulty of having violated his ordination vows by departing from what was considered
established truths of the Gospel.[5] During its annual meeting in 1898
the Presbyterian General Assembly reluctantly listened to the
charges Birch insisted on publicizing, but no debate ensued because
McGiffert was simply asked either to endorse the explicit doctrinal
standards set for Presbyterian ministers or to renounce his ministerial
status. McGiffert avoided both alternatives by declaring himself innocent of the distorted extrapolations taken from his historical narrative. But as long as theological implications had been brought into
play, he allowed his response to contain an affirmation of beliefs
in Scripture as God's Word, in the deity of Christ, in the efficacy
of the Lord's Supper and in a doctrine of salvation through faith
alone.[6] The General Assembly, unwilling to suffer through another
heresy trial so soon after the Briggs case, passed responsibility for
adjudicating the matter to the local Presbytery of New York. In
June, 1899, Birch saw to it that the charges were reiterated. The
irony of this protracted litigation was that, just as Schaff's experience
fifty-five years earlier had disclosed, neither side really understood
the other. The major defense of McGiffert's position was that scientific inquiry into the early history of Christianity should be free to
discover evidence and interpret material without regard to ecclesiastical censure or approval. Birch contended that any such findings had

5. The best primary source for McGiffert's difficulties with the Presbyterians is
a privately printed series of documents compiled by G. W. F. Birch, entitled *Appeal to the General Assembly to meet in St. Louis, Mo., May 17, 1900: From the
Final Judgment of the Presbytery of New York, Made February 12, 1900* (n.p.,
n.d.). The charges specified in the text can be found on pages 4, 35–36, 43, 44, 47.
Two other useful sources are J. T. Duffield, *The McGiffert Case* (New York, n.d.);
internal evidence indicates that publication must have been after 1898. See also
Dunlop Moore, *Prof. A. C. McGiffert and the Next General Assembly* (n.p., n.d.);
probably printed after March, 1899. For an expert analysis of all the issues involved, see Lefferts A. Loetscher, *The Broadening Church: A Study of Theological
Issues in the Presbyterian Church since 1869* (Philadelphia: University of Pennsylvania Press, 1954), pp. 71–74.
6. McGiffert's statement can be found in Birch, *Appeal*, pp. 73–75, and also in
the unnumbered pages of a pamphlet entitled *Presbytery of New York: In the Matter of the Rev. Arthur McGiffert, D.D.* (New York: Printed by the order of the
Presbytery, 1899).

to agree with established propositions accepted within orthodox Presbyterianism. McGiffert retorted:

I do not . . . claim infallibility for my conclusions—no scholar does— but I do claim that they can be proved incorrect only by historical in- vestigation carried on in the same spirit of loyal devotion to the truth in which the book was written. And I claim still further that the question of first importance touching the results I have reached is not "Do they accord with the Presbytery's standards?" but "Are they true?"[7]

The point at issue was whether one had, within the specific propositions accepted by the majority, freedom to declare what one considered accurate findings produced by the careful investigations of historical science. McGiffert had been willing to affirm generalities similar to orthodox formulations, but Birch insisted on the letter, not the spirit, and would be satisfied with nothing less than a re- traction of the book. In December, 1899, the New York Presbytery pronounced the book's contents to be "erroneous and seriously out of harmony with the facts of Holy Scripture as they have been inter- preted by the Presbyterian Church."[8] But no defender of the orthodox position ever discussed the danger of academic freedom as opposed to the satisfactions of denominational conformity, nor did any con- servative demonstrate exactly what was wrong with denying the theory of verbal inspiration while still accepting Scripture as God's Word. To take another example, no one pointed out what error was involved in holding to a doctrine of salvation through faith alone while declining to explain the process as an imputation of undeserved righteousness. The real issues were never joined, and the case ac- tually devolved to a question of denominational control. Of all the charges and genuine intellectual difficulties which Birch raised, the fifth title on the docket determined the outcome. One of those who defined heresy as a threat to institutional strength said that "how the minister was led to adopt his view, whether by personal critical study or otherwise, is irrelevant to the issue. Higher-critical study, however

7. Cited in a newspaper clipping from an unspecified source, entitled "M'Giffert Leaves Church," one copy of which can be found in the pamphlet collection of the Speer Library at Princeton Theological Seminary.
8. Birch, *Appeal*, p. 76; see also p. 78 where the Presbytery cautioned all schol- ars to "be careful to distinguish between the theories of criticism and the certain- ties of faith."

intelligently and conscientiously pursued, does not absolve one from voluntarily assumed vows."[9] The judicial proceedings had reached an impasse despite the fact that pressure continued to mount. Officials refused to recommend an open trial, but the accusers would not let the matter drop. In the end no trial occurred because McGiffert, dismayed by vacuous critics and their strategy of suppressing diversity by invoking the priority of ministerial allegiance, resigned as Presbyterian minister and became a Congregationalist. The entire affair was another example confirming the thesis that at critical junctures in the intellectual history of the United States proponents of differing systems of thought have failed to grapple with the real issues between them, preferring rather to shift the weight to a question of institutional expediency.[10]

After the controversy subsided, McGiffert retained his position at Union Seminary just as Charles A. Briggs had done earlier, but that clash with calcified orthodoxy accentuated his convictions about a scholar's freedom from religious control. Since his return from studying in German seminars McGiffert had argued that historical investigation should not be subordinated to any system of inherited values or to the ideas of a religious community. His unhappy experience with inquisitors dedicated to a particular brand of Presbyterianism galvanized his determination to rescue historical judgment from the blight of clerical domination. In his own understanding of the relations between scientific criteria and theological values there was to be no confusion of roles. He was convinced that historical method could be kept free of religious interference, while at the same time he thought historical knowledge could aid in the formulation of contemporary theology.

In discussing his conception of the procedure church historians should follow, McGiffert indicated that he was aware of the struggle between the theological and scientific schools of thought, and he considered the latter perspective a better starting point for human knowledge. He thought the volumes produced under the aegis of "theological church history" were faulty because religious objectives

9. Duffield, *The McGiffert Case,* the fifth of nineteen unnumbered pages.
10. S. E. Mead, *The Lively Experiment: The Shaping of Christianity in America* (New York: Harper & Row, 1963), pp. 180, 182–83. For further confirmation see George H. Shriver, ed., *American Religious Heretics: Formal and Informal Trials* (Nashville: Abingdon Press, 1966), pp. 70, 78, 137, 176.

interfered with the historian's investigation, making it "almost impossible for him to investigate objectively and impartially and to reach just and accurate results."[11] The strength of scientific historical procedures lay in their ability to separate scientific criteria from theological concerns and to work strictly within the limits of the former category because, as he put it, "just in proportion as we confound the two methods, are we in danger of misunderstanding those [subjects which] we study."[12] In one of the best statements illustrating the methodological difference between Schaff and this latter synthesis, McGiffert argued that church historians should abandon all theological preconceptions before they could even hope to understand historical subjects: "If we would be historians . . . we must divest ourselves . . . of the theological attitude of mind . . . that thus we may study [religious subjects] without undue bias and may not be tempted to force upon them under the pressure of our own theologies, conceptions which were possibly far from their attitudes."[13] In actual practice McGiffert's works did not bear out this statement, but in theory at least the distinguishing factor between historical and theological investigations was not that they involved the study of different subjects: they applied different sets of questions to the same subject. And in McGiffert's view the historian necessarily performed his task first because, without his contribution, the theologian would have inadequate information upon which to base his set of values. The historian stood within a community of scientists who approached various topics with a shared objectivity, applied the same empirical tools of investigation and drew conclusions by means of universal assumptions about the nature of their evidence. By definition, then, the church historian could not be bound by theology:

The present age is marked by the growing tendency among historians to disregard entirely . . . the question as to the bearing of their results upon their own beliefs, and to examine [the beginnings of Christianity for instance] in the same dispassionate spirit that would be employed in the study of any other period. . . . such a spirit of eagerness to get at the exact historical truth, without regard to its bearing on

11. Arthur C. McGiffert, *History and Theology: An Address Delivered before the Presbyterian Ministers' Association of Philadelphia on April 25th, 1898* (n.p. n.d.), p. 10.
12. Ibid., p. 13.
13. Ibid., pp. 10–11, 19.

present-day thought and life, . . . has wrought a complete revolution in the science, whose results cannot fail to be of lasting significance.[14]

Once he had disentangled history and theology, McGiffert was free to pattern his thinking along the lines set by scientific historians and argue that church history was similar to physics and biology in that it studied empirical phenomena in an objective fashion and based its interpretations on a naturalistic frame of mind. In a classic statement, showing both his acceptance of the theories which Herbert Adams had worked to establish as well as a preference for scientific metaphors, McGiffert presented his case in language that marks a significant development in church historiographical theory:

To study an organism in its antecedents and in its genesis, to trace the course of its growth, to examine it in the varied relations which it has sustained to its environment at successive stages of its career, to search for the forces within and without which have served to make it what it is; to do it all, not with the desire of supporting one's own theory or of undermining the theory of another, but in order to understand the organism more thoroughly, . . . this is the historic method, and this is the way we study the church to-day.[15]

Pursuing that ideal method, the church historian was free to work within the iconoclasm, empiricism, and naturalism so dominant, and apparently so fruitful, in a technological society.

It is a valid distinction to say that the scientific emphasis on objectivity affected church history in two ways. One consequence had to do with an attitude of detachment which all objective students tried to follow, one that repudiated all concern to judge whether past ideas or actions had been right or wrong and concentrated on the simple questions of what had occurred and, as best one could determine, why it happened that way.[16] The other response to the apparent attractions of impersonality took a form which McGiffert seemed self-consciously to emphasize in contrast to Schaff. As one professionally interested in the history of religious thought and at

14. Arthur C. McGiffert, "The Study of Early Church History," *New World: A Quarterly Review of Religion, Ethics and Theology* 8 (March 1899): 9, 10, 12.
15. Arthur C. McGiffert, "The Historical Study of Christianity," *Bibliotheca Sacra* 50 (January 1893): 152.
16. McGiffert, *History and Theology*, p. 7.

the same time committed to a detachment defined on the laboratory model, he stated that he did not intend "to discover and understand the truth of God, but to . . . understand the thought of Christians of the past . . . what they have believed . . . and why."[17] But whether the objectivity of liberal church historians expressed itself in nonjudgmental terms or in an attitude that excluded divine truth from historical conclusions, most practitioners were agreed that naturalistic terminology gave a satisfactory account of events. Ideas begun by Adams and Emerton reached a joint culmination here. Perhaps McGiffert did not realize how far he had really come when he said, "It is a common thing today to deal with religion in a wholly naturalistic way, as one of the forces promoting the development of the race. . . ."[18] In that less exalted but clearer-headed frame of reference, it was no longer plausible for historians to speak of events as "supernatural interferences" or to conceive of their narrative as the account of progress along a predetermined pattern of ordained accomplishments.[19]

Thus far McGiffert's theories have differed very little from Emerton's or Walker's, but his further discussion outdistanced their ideas and broke new historiographical ground. Once scientific methods of investigation provided the student of past events with precise information, he said that the process of reconstructing the total picture depended upon "the insight and constructive genius of the historian" in addition to his accurate use of source materials. McGiffert quickly saw the danger in becoming so "wedded to the documents that one never sees beyond them [thus remaining] contented simply to repeat and reproduce them." His understanding of the historian's role was realistic and candid enough to discern that such a narrow function misconstrued the limited value of historical sources and de-

17. Ibid., pp. 6 and 9.
18. Arthur C. McGiffert, "The Progress of Theological Thought During the Past Fifty Years," *American Journal of Theology* 20 (July 1916): 323. In this vein it is interesting to see how McGiffert turned Schaff's old slogan to his own use. Whereas Schaff had subscribed to the motto: "Christianus sum; Christiani nihil a me alienum puto," McGiffert confined his attention to temporal matters and declared his interests by saying, "Humanus sum, humani nihil a me alienum puto" ("The Historical Study of Christianity," p. 153).
19. A. C. McGiffert, "Divine Immanence and the Christian Purpose," *Hibbert Journal* 5 (1907): 769–70; see also "The Study of Early Church History," pp. 1–2.

pended too heavily on them. He recognized that the raw materials of history have a qualified status. "They are not history itself, they are simply scattered products of that history, and they constitute only illustrations, not exhaustive records, of the process which gave rise to them."[20] McGiffert began moving beyond the theory and accomplishments of Walker's brand of church history when he posited that the best historian was "not simply an annalist" who recorded events, but rather "an intelligent observer" who brought fresh questions and insights to the material.[21] The ideal of objective study was not disturbed by utilizing an author's distinctive ideas. On the contrary, he held that the process of assimilating data was enriched by the historian's ability to "disentangle the elements of which it is composed, to trace them to their origin and study them in their combination, to see how they have been affected by each other and modified by outside influences—all this is necessary if one is to make intelligent and discriminating use of the existing product."[22]

McGiffert's own research included the related tasks of tracing ideas to their sources and then of identifying later modifications which might possibly be caused by outside influences. But he insisted that his interest in comparing later developments with original tenets derived legitimately from the task all scientific observers performed and did not deserve to be classed as subjective interpolation. From time to time a positivist might charge that such historians were unscientific because they included in their account items not mentioned explicitly in the records, but McGiffert dismissed that epistemological narrowness by saying, "the charge frequently means no more than that the historian has thought for himself instead of merely reproducing his sources like a parrot." The crucial factor that decided whether one remained a scientific spokesman or not was how he had arrived at his conclusions, "whether he has actually . . . built his structures upon the basis of his sources, or has simply spun fancies out of his own head." So if the historian could show that his complex reconstruction of the past was based on a solid grounding in the sources, then his insight was not to be rejected as

20. McGiffert, "The Study of Early Church History," p. 13.
21. McGiffert, History and Theology, p. 6; see also "The Study of Early Church History," p. 14.
22. Arthur C. McGiffert, "Theological Education," American Journal of Theology 15 (January 1911): 9.

subjectivism but welcomed as "the greatest of virtues in a historian."[23]

After realizing that even scientific historians contributed new insights to the investigational process, only one more short step was needed to argue that history provided a sound basis for theology. McGiffert always kept church history (now confined to his special interest, the history of religious thought) and dogmatics (a word he reserved to define normative theological statements) as "separate and distinct" headings. He recognized, though, that the difference between studying history and dogmatics was slight, and he warned that constant vigilance was needed to retain a proper relationship between those overlapping interests.[24] Such problems were compounded in studying primitive Christianity because source materials were sketchy, researchers with various specialties presented conflicting views, and despite this confusion, the importance of the subject gave their conclusions added weight. Problems in that area of study placed a great strain on McGiffert's new historiographical synthesis. He saw how subjects related to Christ and his apostles were "peculiarly difficult to deal with . . . in a genuinely historical way, for the results of . . . historical investigations constitute[d] the authoritative material of . . . dogmatics, [further admitting that] we can scarcely avoid a dogmatic bias and interest." But in the last analysis he asserted that he was still working within the strictures adopted by responsible historical scholars.[25]

In studying the history of Christian thought it was important to understand its beginnings, including not only the teachings of Jesus and his apostles but the private experiences and environmental circumstances which influenced their belief.[26] It was particularly important to comprehend the initial stages because those experiences would come to play a large part in the formulation of contemporary theology. After the origins of early Christian experience had been discovered and its content analyzed, then a standard existed by which historians could interpret later developments.[27] Historical

23. McGiffert, "The Study of Early Church History," p. 14.
24. McGiffert, *History and Theology*, pp. 10–11.
25. Ibid., p. 12.
26. Ibid., p. 14; see also pp. 17–18.
27. McGiffert, "The Historical Study of Christianity," pp. 166–67; see also Arthur C. McGiffert, *Primitive and Catholic Christianity* (New York: John C. Rankin Co., 1893), p. 17.

knowledge about early faiths did not determine a set of timeless propositions by which all later ideas could be judged, but it did provide a perspective for measuring the degree of change effected by new spokesmen in various settings.[28] Those changes, however, made the historian aware of how convoluted the development of religious thought actually was. They prompted him to adopt a relativism and a tentativeness that gave priority to no single creed and held no specific idea to be the unchangeable core of dogmatic validity. This attitude helps explain McGiffert's position in the litigation surrounding his book on apostolic Christianity.[29] He had not opposed orthodoxy with another creed of equal rigidity because history had taught him that such machinery was too ponderous to contain the fleet, shifting ideas by which religious men tried to cope with life. He argued that the study of history made man more flexible and provided him with two essentials for contributing effectively to modern civilization. It released one from the dead hand of traditional creeds, allowing serious thinkers to work out new solutions for immediate problems, and in addition to that, history gave one knowledge of earlier human problems as well as the character and fate of their solutions. In discussing the benefits of historical consciousness, McGiffert was careful to legitimize the results by tying them closely to his method. Some might question the source of his resultant iconoclasm, but he argued that it was a direct result of his objective approach: "Tracing in objective fashion the rise and development of the great dogmas to which large sections of the Christian church have pinned their faith . . . we have come to be emancipated from theological tyranny and have learned to think for ourselves in religion instead of simply repeating the thoughts of other generations."[30] From this point, one could argue that one's modernity was proportionate to his knowledge and discriminating use of the past.

Using knowledge of the past in meeting the demands of modern realities was a personal feat accomplished within a single individual.

28. McGiffert, "The Historical Study of Christianity," p. 167.
29. A. C. McGiffert, Jr., "A Mischievous Book: Further Correspondence of A. C. McGiffert," pp. 368–69, substantiates the view that his father was more concerned with judgments on his historical method than on his theological views. In a letter he said, "The attacks—on theological grounds as they have been—have not troubled me in the least. . . ."
30. McGiffert, "The Progress of Theological Thought During the Past Fifty Years," p. 327; see also "The Study of Early Church History," p. 9.

A crucial point in McGiffert's theory concerns exactly how historical and theological roles are related in the same person, and it is unfortunate that his thoughts on the matter are imprecise. But through all the uncertainty, one cardinal fact stands out: he thought the same individual could be both a historian and a theologian without compromising either interest. Whereas Schaff had subordinated all goals to theology and performed the task of writing church history as a form of retrospective prophecy, and whereas Emerton had exalted scientific reporting to a height that made church history too rarified to be effective in theological circles, McGiffert safeguarded the existence of each pursuit and urged that one could, at different times in his life, master both categories. "The theologian lives and works in the realm of ideals as well as in the realm of facts. He is both historian and prophet."[31] It seems further that the theologian's task had the more comprehensive scope because it relied on historical knowledge. A historian might do an adequate job without moving beyond a satisfactory reconstruction of the past, but a theologian could not fulfill his responsibilities without being, indirectly at least, a historian.[32] One decisive statement on that difficult connection affirmed that it was "only after we have honestly and conscientiously . . . studied [earlier religious thought] in the purely historic spirit, that we . . . are prepared to use the results so gained in shaping the theology of our own age."[33] Indeed, McGiffert even went so far as to claim that "the spirit of independent scientific investigation can *govern* theological study as it never could before." He was happy to see the day when men were not "obliged to ask what Bible or church or creed require[d], but what the facts teach. . . ."[34] In keeping with his train of thought thus far, one should be able to conclude that scientific history promised to furnish the reliable data which theologians needed before they could build their inclusive system of values.

31. "Exercises Connected with the Inauguration of the Rev. Arthur Cushman McGiffert, Ph.D., D.D., LL.D. as President of the Faculty," *Union Theological Seminary Bulletin* 1 (July 1918) : 32. In that same context he said: "The study of men's ideals, past and present, is as much a science as the study of their stomachs or their lungs; but when from studying ideals we go on to frame them for ourselves we pass from the realm of science into the realm of creative art."

32. McGiffert, *Primitive and Catholic Christianity*, p. 16. See also *History and Theology*, pp. 9–10; on p. 13 of the latter work he said, "we must first be historians and only afterwards theologians. . . ."

33. McGiffert, *History and Theology*, p. 13.

34. Cited in the inaugural address, p. 31; italics supplied.

But the most important factor linking the two disciplines was the specific topics theologians were to study with the scientific tools available to them. In his discussions of that particular aspect McGiffert seemed to abandon a scientific orientation altogether and move to a theological view of things, showing in yet another instance that the gap cannot be bridged, only crossed by an exertion of will. At various times in his career he emphasized the importance of knowledge about primitive Christianity, but it is impossible to determine which aspects of that early period he thought it was essential to know. McGiffert singled out two topics useful for theological study, neither of which lend themselves to the scientist's verification. In an early essay he defended the theologian's prerogative to "study the past in so far as he believes it to contain authoritative revelations of God which should control or form the bases of his own theology."[35] At another time McGiffert did not presume to discover revealed truths by historical means but proceeded more modestly to analyze the early years in an attempt to isolate a universal religious pattern applicable to all situations. He stated that as a historian he was trying to identify "Christianity's true nature, the eternal principles . . . which must always, through all external changes . . . be preserved pure and unrestrained."[36] Yet even in pursuit of general principles he spoke of "the hand of God in the process" and "the power of the divine germ," terms incompatible with any stretch of a scientist's imagination.[37] But whether he sought specific revelation or a general spirit, McGiffert was convinced history could be a theological tool that provided a core of religious truth useful for interpreting previous religious activity and building new forms for modern man.

In either case, if we would understand Christianity we must know both Jesus Christ and the Christian centuries since his day. . . . We may measure it by its agreement with the spirit and purposes of Jesus or by its adaptation to the needs of the men of today. In either case we can estimate it just only as we know it in its origin and history. We must know it thus if it be only to reject it. We must know it thus if we would reform it and make it conform more nearly to our ideal of it. Much

35. McGiffert, *History and Theology*, p. 8; see also p. 18.
36. McGiffert, "The Historical Study of Christianity," p. 160.
37. Ibid., p. 166.

more must we know it thus if we would wisely and effectively employ it as an instrument for the promotion of God's work in the world.[38]

Despite his careful explanation of how history provided a basis for theology, McGiffert's conceptions disclosed an underlying religious motivation that lay in tense and uneasy relation to his professed admiration for science. The secular spirit of objectivity and naturalism was useful only as it furthered the religious ends which at bottom controlled everything else. The following analysis of McGiffert's religious ideas should not be taken as an exhaustive definition of "liberal theology" as a standard body of doctrines or as a contribution to the debate over whether liberalism was a point of view and not really a system of ideas shared by its spokesmen.[39] The outline merely shows that many of McGiffert's theological opinions were compatible with, if not derived from, a historical methodology he considered scientific.[40] That blend of religious disposition and empirical theory was important, however, because it sustained tremendous scholarly effort.

In conjunction with building his theology on accurate knowledge about Jesus and the history of primitive Christianity there were two major principles guiding the course of McGiffert's religious thought, respect for science and concern for social betterment. An ineluctable tinge of scientific thinking colored all his theological premises and marked a distinct break with Schaff's creedal pietism. It was definitely as a participating member of modern society that McGiffert posited, "the development of modern science has given birth to a need not

38. McGiffert, "Theological Education," p. 10.
39. The best book to date on the matter of discussing both the basic characteristics and different types of theological liberalism is K. Cauthen, *The Impact of American Religious Liberalism* (New York: Harper & Row, 1962); see especially pp. 26–30, 33–37.
40. In a letter to C. A. Briggs, dated 10 February 1891, McGiffert expressed his theological point of view and its relation to historical analysis: "I am and have been ever since I left the Seminary thoroughly in sympathy with liberal principles in theology, and it has been one of my great aims to contribute to the spread of these principles. I have long been convinced that where the essence of Christianity is fully apprehended true liberality must exist, and that the common misconceptions which today discredit Christianity in the eyes of many high minded men, and which constitute the chief barriers to church unity will in the light of that knowledge disappear. It is because I have believed that such knowledge will be promoted by a thorough understanding of Church history especially of the history of the Apostolic Age and of Christian Doctrine, that I have devoted myself to that subject" (A. C. McGiffert, Jr., "The Making of an American Scholar," p. 40).

felt . . . in any other period of Christian history: the need of such an interpretation of the world as shall make religious faith possible to the man who believes in the scientific method and accepts the results of scientific observation and experiment."[41] Acceptance of modern science entailed not only learning by means of a single method but the adoption of generally substantiated observations about the natural world, especially the evolutionary hypothesis. The most recent conception of evolutionary development did not sanction the view that all of modern life had gradually unfolded from innate tendencies contained in the original seed; it held rather that radically new forms of life sometimes emerged from the historical process. Translated into religious terms, such a concept meant that "all is in process of development and change, and [that] . . . each generation must discover for itself the new truths and the new principles by which it shall live." An evolutionary understanding of things in science or religion did not sanction conservatism, "the worship of the old and submission to it." On the contrary it made for "radicalism, the recognition of the new and the welcome of it."[42] Another corollary of accepting science as a standard was "the spread within theological circles of a naturalistic way of looking at things." After having based so much of his thinking on the naturalism implicit in empirical verification, McGiffert did not try to conceal a sense of vindication in his observation that "the older supernaturalism has been outgrown . . . and in the place of it has arisen a naturalism which has transformed our theological thinking."[43] Any new religious posi-

41. Arthur C. McGiffert, "Modernism," in *Christianity as History and Faith by Arthur Cushman McGiffert* ed. Arthur C. McGiffert, Jr. (New York: Charles Scribner's Sons, 1934), p. 78. On that same point but in another essay he said, "Catholic modernists as well as Protestant liberals are children of the modern age, and both feel in their own peculiar way the influence of modern tendencies. The new scientific spirit, the new historical sense and the new methods of historical criticism . . . the new emphasis on evolution, the new estimate of nature and the supernatural . . . all this has made itself felt within Catholic as well as Protestant circles, and the result has been similar in both" (Arthur C. McGiffert, "Modernism and Catholicism," *Harvard Theological Review,* 3 [January 1910]: 26).

42. McGiffert, "The Progress of Theological Thought During the Past Fifty Years," pp. 327–28. Yet here too McGiffert is bewildering in his complexity. While affirming radical departures in religious thought, he also said, "The true historic spirit, as I understand it, is that spirit which makes for *progress,* not by the destruction but by the *fulfilment* of the past, by the conservation of the best that is in it" ("The Historical Study of Christianity," p. 154).

43. McGiffert, "The Progress of Theological Thought During the Past Fifty Years," p. 322.

tion, then, would have to be made consistent with the contemporary vogue of newness and naturalism.

Through his wide-ranging studies in the history of religious thought McGiffert pursued a theological objective in comparing creedal formulations with early beliefs. The procedure was defended as a legitimate part of scientific inquiry, but he utilized it for religious ends. One of the historical observations which he used for contemporary theological benefit was that "Christ's simple gospel of God as His father and the father of His brethren was displaced by a philosophical idea of God as the absolute."[44] Philosophizing about the nature of God had taken different forms like the Alexandrian Logos or Augustine's notions about Supreme Good and Absolute Will, or even found its way into an ecclesiology that tried to perpetuate the Incarnation within itself. But in all such abstractions McGiffert argued that philosophy had shouldered out true religious interests, and the person of Jesus had been forced to take a subsidiary position.[45] In more recent times the idea of divine immanence had replaced transcendence as a basic conception of God's relation to the world, but McGiffert, unlike many liberals of his day, argued that there was no necessary connection between immanentist doctrine and the Christ of the synoptic gospels.[46] Historians knew that earlier theological systems had drawn on environmentally conditioned ideas extraneous to the Christian message, and such knowledge prevented confusing those systems with revelation. Their understanding of the possibilities for innovation allowed by evolutionary development created an even more tentative attitude as to how much the past actually shaped the present. In McGiffert's words, "Now we

44. Arthur C. McGiffert, *The Problem of Christian Creeds as Affected by Modern Thought* (Buffalo: Peter Paul and Co., 1901), p. 5; on p. 12 he said that the Apostles Creed was fairly acceptable by modern standards "because there is comparatively so little theology in it" and thus it had little to challenge a scientific frame of mind.

45. Arthur C. McGiffert, "Theological Reconstruction," *The Christian Point of View: Three Addresses* (New York: Charles Scribner's Sons, 1902), pp. 35–36.

46. McGiffert, "Divine Immanence and the Christian Purpose," p. 777. This should serve as a corrective to any hasty assumption that immanentist ideas were always connected with theological liberalism or that there is any necessary identity between the two categories. For a discussion holding that in most cases after 1870 the conception of an immanent deity was a strong point in liberal theology, see W. R. Hutchison, ed., *American Protestant Thought: The Liberal Era* (New York: Harper & Row, 1968), p. 2.

know there has been no stable past, as there is no stable present, whether in religion or in life."[47] So in the last analysis the process for judging the worth of religious ideas was not to examine their compatibility with some historical creed, but to see if they spoke to problems that really mattered in the modern world.[48]

As if to dispel any possible misunderstanding of his liberal perspective, McGiffert explained very clearly the conclusion to which historical research and involvement in present problems had led him: "The whole structure of the creeds and the underlying purpose of them are alien to our modern way of looking at things. Nothing less than a complete transformation of fundamental principles, affecting not only specific doctrines, but the general drift of the whole, will do. And this means an entire re-writing of the creeds, or, in other words, this means not the revision of old creeds, but the creation of new ones."[49] At the same time, he held that new religious ideas could not be formulated in a completely arbitrary manner. As a student of Harnack it is probably natural that McGiffert had an interest in "the great underlying principles of Christianity" which served to give all theologies validity proportionate to their agreement with that primitive essence.[50] Thus the liberal theologian worked in an optimum situation where there were enough controls to make religious thought meaningful from one generation to another and yet enough freedom to abandon outdated directives.[51]

The content of McGiffert's theology cannot be taken as a micro-

47. Arthur C. McGiffert, "Christianity in the Light of its History," *Hibbert Journal* 11 (1913): 729.

48. Arthur C. McGiffert, "How May Christianity Be Defended To-Day?" *Hibbert Journal* 7 (1908): 152–53.

49. McGiffert, *The Problem of Christian Creeds as Affected by Modern Thought*, p. 17.

50. McGiffert, "Theological Reconstruction," p. 33. Yet here is another place where McGiffert's comprehensive mind defies simple explanations. In "The Progress of Theological Thought During the Past Fifty Years," p. 325, he seemed to be searching for another common denominator: "Agnosticism touching many matters formerly deemed fundamental has come to be a common attitude on the part of religious men, and even of theologians. If we say that in order to be scientific we must take our theological material from religious experience alone, then we must be content to be agnostic about all that lies beyond the range of experience." As we shall see later, Frank Hugh Foster takes that principle much further.

51. Only after the contextual framework has been established by the foregoing discussion can one understand his apparently radical statement that "We are coming to recognize that Christianity has been many and different things in the past, and to expect that it will be . . . in the future, as it becomes the religion of successive generations and civilizations and is reinterpreted by them" ("The Progress of Theological Thought during the Past Fifty Years," p. 328).

cosm of all liberal ideas, but the following sketch fairly represents his own compelling synthesis of three strains of thought: science, the historical Jesus, and social justice. In discussing his mature theological opinions McGiffert took pains to distinguish his ideas about the proper content and utility of theology from what he considered to be the fatal grasp of archaic structures. Whereas too many earlier systems had tried to perfect a body of knowledge about God's nature, economy, and ultimate purposes, liberals began by describing theology not as a speculative exercise in philosophical definition, but as "a strictly practical discipline, dealing with . . . the principles that underlie and govern the Christian life." Actually the most important distinction in that new attempt to construct a relevant body of religious ideals was not its practical bent because even the most abstruse theologian hopes to provide ideas with practical value to his readers. The real difference appeared when liberals insisted that their conception of Christ's personality and activity was the only valid basis for all theological ideas. As if to ensure against any possible misunderstanding about the narrow grounds for conducting meaningful discourse, McGiffert defined theology as "primarily a formulation and exposition of the principles which underlay and governed [Christ's] life." And then he reiterated: "The constructive principle . . . in Christian theology must be the life-purpose of Jesus Christ."[52] History had repeatedly shown how religion could be distorted by various cultural factors, and so historical revisionism aided the procedure of theological reformation by reminding the church of its early days. In the complex mind of a single individual, the various methods and hopes of historian-theologian, revisionist-reformer, radical-classicist, and scholar-preacher converged on a single goal, to assert that Christian theology "should be based, not chiefly merely, but solely, upon Christ. And the Bible, Old Testament and New, so far as it is used theologically at all and not for religious inspiration merely, should be employed, not as an independent source of Christian theology, but simply as an aid to the better understanding of Christ. And the same is true of the religious experience of ourselves and of others in this and other ages."[53] A genuinely Christian

52. McGiffert, "Theological Reconstruction," pp. 41–42.
53. Ibid., p. 39. He was able to emphasize the centrality of Christ that strongly because he considered liberals to be (p. 35) "in a better position than ever before because the life and work of Jesus Christ are better understood to-day than they ever have been." See also *History and Theology*, pp. 20–21.

theology would take the life of Jesus as its source of information and have knowledge about him as its sole content. McGiffert's understanding of what scientific historical methodology made available only strengthened his conviction that the essential "life-purpose" of Christianity's central figure could be found and identified in its untouched, native simplicity.

At this point it is important to notice that, despite his careful description of how theology should be based on scientific inquiry into the New Testament world, McGiffert displayed an unmistakable reliance on Ritschlian pronouncements about which sort of theology was "truly Christian and solely Christian." Some of those standard liberal doctrines included the notion that man's basic problem was a moral one in which "sin is taken as a moral not a religious category."[54] Within that context man was seen as one striving to "win the victory for his ideals and to keep his soul intact and free." Jesus had been such a man whose faith in God and devotion to His will had aided him in achieving victory over the world, not by exploiting it but by serving it. "The ideal of Christ was not spiritual exaltation, the wrapt contemplation of divine things, the conscious oneness with the absolute. . . . [Such contemplative inactivity was a curse to true religion because] both immanence and transcendence are ontological terms, and it is in the ethical, not the ontological, sphere that Christianity moves."[55] Thus all men with similar faith could emulate Christ's active participation in God's will. God for the liberal theologian was one whose moral purpose was to promote the spirit of love among men. Religion was a venture in faith, love, goodness, honesty, and truth.[56] If anyone raised the criticism that a theology based on the life and work of Jesus was too constricted a foundation on which to build a definitive structure of ideas about nature, man, and God, McGiffert was ready to defend the apparent inadequacies of his theological position. His major point, of course, was that much of what his theology omitted had never properly belonged to Christianity; thus his pragmatic view of things not only avoided arguments on unessential matters, it kept modern man in

54. McGiffert, "Modernism," p. 89.
55. McGiffert, "Divine Immanence and the Christian Purpose," pp. 777, 779.
56. McGiffert, "The Progress of Theological Thought During the Past Fifty Years," p. 331; see also "Theological Reconstruction," p. 38.

touch with the few basic issues in which he could work out his salvation. All the rest was considered to be unnecessary verbal baggage. Subsidiary doctrines about primordial events like the creation of the world, the origin of man, the historicity of Adam, his fall from grace, and all post–New Testament speculative exercises on attributes of an Absolute Deity (already mentioned) were given no place in modern conversations about religion: "with all these matters Christianity has absolutely nothing to do any more than with astronomy, or geology or mathematics."[57]

The reason liberal theology claimed the ability to construct a full system of ideas on such a small basis was because the end of much of man's existence seemed fully explicable by reference to issues in social morality. There in that final, mundane, area the most advanced aspects of liberal thought emerged. It is difficult for us to analyze the origins of McGiffert's ideas and decide whether historical studies or existential involvement was more influential in defining Christianity as basically a social program. But for him there was no problem because a happy congruity existed between "interpreting the Christian purpose in accordance with the modern spirit, recognising it as . . . the establishment of the Kingdom of God on this . . . earth [and] the re-discovery of the real Gospel of Jesus, for this was his purpose too."[58] Stated in its most comprehensive fashion, religious activity pursuant to establishing God's kingdom among men was best expressed as service in the temporal world. In modern times chief emphasis had come to be placed on duty not to God or oneself, but duty to one's neighbor.[59] Of course concentrating religion in the temporal sphere involved positive assumptions about human nature and the goodness of progressive achievements within a social framework. McGiffert was willing to affirm them because he thought it marked one of the greatest differences between modern liberalism and the otherworldliness of earlier patterns of thought. He observed approvingly that, once men committed themselves to transforming society into a harmony of love and justice, they grew "relatively indifferent" to outmoded thoughts about personal salvation and immortality that implied escaping from an evil world and

57. McGiffert, "Theological Reconstruction," p. 46.
58. McGiffert, "Divine Immanence and the Christian Purpose," p. 771.
59. McGiffert, "How May Christianity be Defended To-Day?" pp. 153, 160.

everlasting punishment.[60] As one might expect, such a shift of emphasis from individual souls to society at large caused liberals to revise a great many more doctrines that they considered out of keeping with the simple life of Jesus. In one sweeping pronouncement Mc-Giffert indicated how free from traditional shibboleths a socially oriented religious impulse could be: "It has profoundly altered our conceptions of the nature of the gospel, the person and work of Christ, of man and sin and redemption, of the church and the sacraments. And above all it has transformed our interpretation of the character and purpose of God. . . . The reinterpretation of God's character in terms of our own social interest . . . finds its finest expression in Ritschl's description of God as a being whose holy purpose of love is to promote the spirit of love among men."[61]

The only remaining consideration was to define how such a universal humanitarianism could accommodate the more distinctive aspects of Christian self-consciousness. As we have already seen, the conception of responsibility to neighbor in social settings was a compelling one for McGiffert. He gave that injunction a more explicit ideological grounding by expanding one of the few genuinely unique ideas in Christianity (belief that God was incarnated in a single historical person) and interpreting it within a contemporary context. To be sure, his view was that Christ had not been the only manifestation of divine incarnation; the lives of good men and women everywhere exhibited such a force. Thus God could be seen and worshiped not only by prayer, sacraments, and contemplation in churches, but also by service to one's fellow man in hopes of building a society of mutual love, sympathy, and brotherhood.[62] Divinity was diffused throughout humanity, and the means of service were legion. Since that was the case, all well-intentioned men who worked for something other than their own selfish welfare could be called religious, in keeping with the best sense of Christianity's true purpose. The widest application of religion encompassed all humanitarian or cultural activities, whether they went under the

60. McGiffert, "Modernism," pp. 93–94; see also "Divine Immanence and the Christian Purpose," p. 769.
61. McGiffert, "The Progress of Theological Thought During the Past Fifty Years," p. 330.
62. McGiffert, "Modernism," p. 84.

guise of science, art, or philosophy.[63] In the last analysis, then, Christianity could be an acceptable religion if its activities contributed to the overarching and more important goals of moral progress and social betterment. As McGiffert put it in his clear and emphatic way: "Christianity is a true and good religion not if it saves men's souls for heaven and fits them for life there, but if it brings them into communion with God here, makes them more conscious of his presence and more responsive to his will and transforms them into better citizens of this world."[64] So the usefulness of Christian history was judged finally by modern standards: a scientific naturalism, an emphasis on the simple gospel of Jesus, and a concern for the good of society. A brief look at some of McGiffert's interpretations of church history will illustrate the interaction of theology and historical judgment in his work. It will also bring into sharper focus the imprecision as to which way the two were actually connected.

A LIBERAL'S VIEW OF MAJOR EVENTS IN CHURCH HISTORY

A friend once observed that McGiffert considered Christianity to be composed of three unequal time periods—early beginnings when the Spirit of God acted freely without regard to institutional confinements, then an arid middle age marked by conformity to a closed canon and apostolic authoritarianism, finally modern times which returned to the original spirit of religion because human conscience could cooperate freely with divine inspiration again. His friend thought it unfortunate that the second Washburn Professor of Church History produced his most important scholarly work in studying the second epoch rather than concentrating his efforts in the latest phase where most of his sympathies were placed.[65] But regardless of the topics one wishes McGiffert might have chosen, his studies of the past provided knowledge that was part of a calculated effort to bolster the gains made by modern religious thought. All of his research and comparative studies were based on the assumption that

63. Arthur C. McGiffert, *The Rise of Modern Religious Ideas* (New York: Macmillan Co., 1915), p. 79.
64. McGiffert, "Modernism," p. 86.
65. Ambrose W. Vernon, "Arthur Cushman McGiffert," *Hibbert Journal* 32 (January 1934): 286.

"knowledge progresses by error."[66] At the beginning of this brief review it should be stressed that one of the primary functions of his
history was to inform the present generation about earlier eccen-
tricities, misunderstood ideas, or faulty themes in order to guard
against repetition. In what was probably his best statement of a hope
for contemporary intellectual liberty that resulted from applying the
lessons of history, McGiffert said: "The true test of the present is
the future. The question is not whether we agree with our fathers,
but whether we so live that the world we hand on . . . is better for
our living. All questions of orthodoxy are out of place in a living
and growing organism. Not to be true to its own past, . . . but to
be true to its opportunities—this is Christianity's business."[67] He began his work with a basic conviction that the history of Christianity
consisted of nothing more than a wandering narrative in which
succeeding ages discovered new objectives and defined new truths.
With the help of such a perspective he hoped to convince men of
the remoteness and practical irrelevance of historical events. In that
way he could prepare them to live in the present and plan for the
future.

The main contribution of McGiffert's scholarship was the production of a manageable compendium of Christian thought, itself a
gesture characteristic of many liberals because it implied that religious ideas were more important than shifting patterns of institutional change. Another preliminary consideration which should be
mentioned is that McGiffert displayed a curious ambivalence in his
assessment of the results of historical study. At an early stage in his
career he sought to determine what was vital and permanent in
Christianity and decided that it was not the history of hierarchical
institutions that mattered but rather the history of what he called
"the Christian idea" or "the Christian spirit."[68] After many projects
conducted along the lines of that conceptual framework, in the light
of ideas discussed earlier, McGiffert reached a more relativistic position, saying that Christianity had not been univocal in its fundamental principles. In the end he concluded that it had shown many,

66. Arthur C. McGiffert, "A Teaching Church," *Hibbert Journal* 19 (1920):
131.
67. McGiffert, "Christianity in the Light of Its History," p. 729.
68. McGiffert, "Theological Education," pp. 9–10.

often contradictory, sides and that there was "no such thing as Christianity in general."[69] The only thread linking centuries of believers together was the fact that they all recognized Jesus Christ to be "in some sense their master," but that minimal common denominator afforded no basis for a historian to write a sustained narrative on perennial themes.[70] Since there was no such thing as timeless faith, "no unchangeable essence, no static form by which one could test its every varying aspect," modern man was free to formulate religious principles which might be more effective in a contemporary situation.[71] McGiffert's judgments in each period of church history reflected the insight of a liberal theologian who intended his observations to be remedial as well as instructive, to produce freedom from, instead of allegiance to, earlier conceptions of religious truth.

Despite this equivocation, it seems valid to distinguish between Christianity as an expression of spontaneous communion of individuals with the unmediated Spirit of God and Christianity defined by specific beliefs and prescribed activities. McGiffert probably assumed that difference. Although much of his work described fundamental changes in the content of various Christianities, in the last analysis he still thought that, at rare moments in the history of western religion, some individuals had succeeded in regaining the basic essence of which Jesus was the best exemplar.

Beginning with primitive Christianity, an area in which he had already caused a stir among religious spokesmen who required certain interpretations to bolster their theologies, McGiffert produced a sustained and consistent view of the evidence. The most important figure of that embryonic stage was of course Jesus of Nazareth who embodied, in a phrase that has come to be a classic characterization

69. A. C. McGiffert, "What is the Christian Religion? An Historical Approach to the Question," in *Christianity as History and Faith*, pp. 12–13.

70. McGiffert, "Christianity in the Light of its History," p. 729; "The Progress of Theological Thought During the Past Fifty Years," p. 328; also *The Problem of Christian Creeds as Affected by Modern Thought*, pp. 13–14.

71. McGiffert, "Christianity in the Light of Its History," p. 730. He even went so far as to say (pp. 727–28) that "these are not simply different phases of the same faith; these were often altogether different faiths. They were not the mere development of an original principle, the life and work and teachings of Jesus of Nazareth; they were many of them fresh creations. . . . Often forces entirely alien to Christianity had their part in producing them, and few of them would have been recognized by Jesus himself as an interpretation of his own faith or of his own ideas."

of liberalism, a "vivid realization of God as his father and the father of his brethren."[72] The lasting influence of his earthly career had been built on the simple principles of devotion and service, of "making righteousness a faithful and joyful doing of the Father's will," a life expended "in terms of love and service of one's fellows."[73] But that simple and unstructured life of love and service which Jesus embodied did not transfer itself easily to the lives of his followers. There was a loose connection between Jesus' original purity and what followed in the sense that his piety was taken to be a primary factor behind the activities of the apostle Paul. But after sober reflection McGiffert found Paul's teachings to have been "totally at variance with Christ's."[74]

Some of the new ideas antithetical to Jesus' simple approach which Paul introduced were that God was remote and wrathful, that humanity in its depraved state was utterly helpless to improve itself, that salvation was an undeserved gift, and that the only good life was one devoted to otherworldly concerns. Since later generations followed Paul's pessimistic view of human nature more than they relied on the activistic assumptions of Jesus, McGiffert judged Paul to be the "real founder of historic Christianity." That form of "historic Christianity" was a corporate phenomenon distinguishable from both original and modern forms, but it had attracted popular support during most of the intervening centuries.[75] Two other developments departed even further from the original. Jesus had never made any claims to messiahship, but Paul and succeeding adherents made much of his divine nature and declared that belief in such a cardinal doctrine was essential to being considered a true Christian. Finally, Jesus had no thought of establishing a church to serve as a vehicle for his ideas about God

72. One source from which McGiffert possibly drew his ideas about the nature of Jesus' teachings was his major professor, Adolf von Harnack. See his *What Is Christianity?* (1911; reprint ed. New York: Harper & Row, 1961), pp. 6–7, 10–14. All references are from the later edition. See also his *History of Dogma* (London: Williams and Norgate, 1905), 1:59, 67–68.

73. Arthur C. McGiffert, "Was Jesus or Paul the Founder of Christianity?" *American Journal of Theology* 13 (January 1909): 18, 20.

74. Ibid. There seems to be a degree of consistency on this point through McGiffert's career, from *A History of Christianity in the Apostolic Age* (New York: Charles Scribner's Sons, 1897), chapters 3 and 4, all the way through to the latest distillation of his interpretation in a more mellow tone. *A History of Christian Thought* (New York: Charles Scribner's Sons, 1932), vol. I, chaps. 1 and 2, especially pp. 19–20.

75. McGiffert, "Was Jesus or Paul the Founder of Christianity?," pp. 15–16.

and human brotherhood. An institution arose, however, and declared that God's word could be equated with canonical writings, grace with sacraments, and salvation with membership.[76] Such developments departed significantly from the original gospel, and McGiffert despaired of finding much of Jesus in the changes of thought and action urged by his followers. He was forced to admit there was little evidence through the centuries to support any interpretation that men in "historic Christianity" worshiped the same God, followed the same ethical motives, held the same concept of salvation or even shared the same ideals as its founder.[77] The only connection was a verbal deference to idealized notions about a historic figure. But church historians with liberal sympathies took heart in the fact that the personal example of Jesus' life would occasionally pierce through the accretions of ecclesiastical and messianic pretensions to touch the lives of sensitive individuals. That possibility was, in McGiffert's view, the only element that continued to make institutionalized Christianity interesting.

The earliest phase of Christianity maintained its original thrust wherever men were left free to pursue the life of "religious individualism . . . lived with God and under his direct control." McGiffert thought that the men who best followed Jesus' examples were ones who expressed their love toward God by a charity toward neighbors, one which did not include a program of influencing the Roman world at large.[78] But the outside world had such an impact on original Christian attitudes that it, along with Pauline theology, changed the spirit of Jesus into "the spirit of Catholicism," an unheroic attitude that submitted to external authority in matters of faith and ethics and looked to an official hierarchy for spiritual guidance. One of the more important factors in that transformation from Jesus to "historic Christianity" had been the threat of Gnosticism. That ideological alternative caused Christians for the first time to claim that their organization and ideas were of divine origin and thus superior to Gnostic categories of less exalted derivation. McGiffert termed a second factor, "Romanism." That latter baneful influence covered a

76. Ibid., pp. 4–5.
77. McGiffert, "What is the Christian Religion? An Historical Approach to the Question," pp. 6–11.
78. McGiffert, *Primitive and Catholic Christianity*, p. 19. See also Arthur C. McGiffert, "The Influence of Christianity upon the Roman Empire," *Harvard Theological Review* 2 (January 1909): 28–29, 35, 39.

wide range of attitudes including a genius for government, a command of legal procedures and a tendency to think in absolutist
categories.[79] So the true influence of Jesus' life came to be stifled by
external circumstances and by apparently loyal followers who erected
a concrete, external organization under the pretext of defending
genuine Christianity. McGiffert's view of the origins of Catholicism
were obviously facile and stylized, but the ultimate objective he
sought was to free men from the idea that such a church ever monopolized grace and revelation to the degree that it alone could dispense
them through sacraments and preaching. He wanted to show modern
men they no longer needed to accept notions of the church as the ark
of salvation, of man as corrupt, of earthly life as evil, of Christ as
divine or of any previous religious orthodoxy as binding because it
had enjoyed long and popular support. Throughout his many studies
of medieval thought, McGiffert sustained that basic interpretive
framework, allowing for variations on common themes but insisting
that the dominant categories were secondary to Jesus' example in both
time and importance.

The Protestant Reformation had been, in McGiffert's estimation,
a revival of the spirit of primitive Christianity in the sense that it
tried to restore to the individual believer a spiritual freedom of which
the Catholic church had deprived him, and to make the Holy Spirit
once again the only source of religious truth. The Magisterial Reformers had succeeded in bridging a spiritual gap between Jesus and
their own time by stressing a "recognition of the central place of
Jesus Christ in all Christian living and thinking." In that manner, they
broke the shackles of theological antiquarianism and once again gave
men freedom to serve their neighbors in this life.[80] Martin Luther had
been one of those individuals who achieved that rare goal of embodying the true spirit of Jesus. He was successful in "really substitut[ing]
for all external authorities the enlightened conscience of the individual Christian," and in his achievement "lay the promise of a new

79. McGiffert, "Christianity in the Light of Its History," p. 721; "Modernism
and Catholicism," p. 40; "Catholicism," in *Christianity as History and Faith*, pp.
34–43; finally, see Arthur C. McGiffert, *Protestant Thought before Kant* (1911;
new ed. New York: Harper & Row, 1961), pp. 1–7. All references from the later
edition.
80. McGiffert, "Theological Reconstruction," pp. 36–37.

age."[81] A statement which illustrates McGiffert's conception of Luther's main contribution to Christian history is one that also outlines those salients he hoped later generations would accept as determinative. The historian observed: "This is the heart of the gospel as Luther understood it—liberty in order to service. Set free from all bondage, . . . from all those things which keep a man cautious about himself and careful lest he . . . imperil his future salvation, he gives himself in disinterested love to the good of others. This is essential Protestantism."[82]

But the Reformation as a historical movement, in contrast with individual lives of reformers, did not succeed in eliminating the two principles which had distorted essential Christianity, viz., emphasis on the divinity of Christ and undue ecclesiasticism in the religious life. Even though Protestantism rejected the authority of the pope, substituted two sacraments for seven, abandoned transubstantiation and purgatory, and reduced the veneration of Mary and other saints, McGiffert judged sixteenth-century organizations to be basically the same as their predecessor. "Luther's principle of liberty failed to work out its legitimate results. The old which he retained was too strong and the new was overlaid and hidden."[83] But the fact that some men had succeeded in reaching God despite the strictures of organized religion was seen by liberal theologians as a source of hope and challenge for men living in the age of science.

McGiffert judged the modern age to have begun when the spirit of rationalism succeeded in establishing a new standard for human truth, breaking through the shell of dogmatic scholasticism and substituting the alternative of knowledge based on direct human experience. Clear-eyed thinkers like Hume and Kant had demonstrated that religious values could never rise above the world of

81. Arthur C. McGiffert, Martin Luther: The Man and His Work (New York: Century Co., 1911), p. 144.

82. Arthur C. McGiffert, "Protestantism," The Unity of Religions, ed. J. H. Randall and J. G. Smith (New York: Thomas Y. Crowell, 1910), p. 271. See also "The Progress of Theological Thought during the Past Fifty Years," pp. 323–24; Protestant Thought before Kant, pp. 21, 24, 86, 88, 97. In the same volume he said similar things about the Anabaptists (p. 105) and about John Wesley (p. 163).

83. McGiffert, "Protestantism," in Christianity as History and Faith, pp. 72–73; see also Protestant Thought before Kant, p. 9.

sensory data by the mere power of speculation.[84] Human values, not the venerable eminence of accumulated dogma, became the gauge of truth, and man's attitude toward the natural world changed from one of ascetic detachment to an appreciation of its intrinsic values. McGiffert approved of all those changes because that basic shift succeeded in "banishing theology altogether from science and substituted mechanical for final causation in the explanation of . . . phenomena."[85] Another major factor that had struck at traditional systems of theology was German Pietism which fostered a deep interest in personal relationships with God, an emphasis on the inner man which tolerated nonconformity and opposed rigidity in either its intellectual or institutional forms. Pietism combined with rationalism to bring down the last vestiges of medieval conceptions about man, God, the natural world, and the church. By 1800 the healthy result was that traditional Christianity had been dismembered beyond recognition by the forces of the modern mind.

McGiffert thought that an epoch of such destructive proportions had been necessary to allow religious forces the opportunity to develop new areas of interest outside the confines of moribund dogmatism. In his estimation, religious thought in the nineteenth century gave occasion for a great deal of optimism because men were turning from fruitless speculations about the attributes of God to concrete knowledge derived from their own experience.[86] Darwinian hypotheses about the evolution of mammalian species further bolstered theistic philosophy and provided additional weight to encourage ideas about a providential design in the natural order.[87] By the turn of the twentieth century modern men had utilized their intellectual freedom and simple piety to such an extent that they succeeded in grounding religious ethics on a concern for humanity rather than on fear of everlasting punishment.[88] "The modern reading of Christianity is at

84. McGiffert, *Protestant Thought before Kant*, pp. xiii, 186. It will be remembered that Schaff, far from being pleased by the influence of rationalism on Christianity, thought the modern age was one in which the faith had been seriously threatened by such intellectual self-sufficiency.
85. McGiffert, *The Rise of Modern Religious Ideas*, p. 31; see also pp. 14–15.
86. Ibid., p. 165.
87. Ibid., pp. 176–78.
88. McGiffert, "Modernism," pp. 87–89.

three important points a return to the original Protestant platform—
in its recognition of a present salvation, in its gospel of liberty, and
in its emphasis on social service."[89] McGiffert concluded his detailed
study of the history of Christian thought with the observation that
religion in the Western world was better for having undergone such
changes. Three centuries of modern life had produced a Christianity
that deliberately avoided useless arguments over doctrinal formulae
and preferred to stand on the ground originally exemplified by Jesus:
a moral activism dedicated "primarily for the promotion of the
Kingdom on this earth,—that is, the reign of sympathy and service
among men."[90]

After having made a brief survey of the distinctive interpretations
in McGiffert's historical narrative, it is possible finally to assess his
claim that conclusions always derived from inductive research procedures. By now it is clear that there were significant differences
between the work just reviewed and interpretations held by Emerton
or Walker, and even further differences separating all those writings
from those of Herbert Adams. So we find four historians, all claiming
to follow scientific standards of investigation, who arrived at different
conclusions regarding the nature of Christianity in general, the function and meaning of its institutional structures, the role of new ideas
within that framework, and even the practical value of its history. If
those historians had actually studied phenomena along the lines of a
single method, the structure and direction of their work would have
shown more similarity than can be found. It is reasonable to conclude
that there were other components in one or perhaps all of their different approaches to account for the differences in the way each man
studied the same historical topics. The differences separating scholarly
narratives in the decades after 1876 stemmed from those fundamental
preconceptions and emphases by which various men supplemented
their common allegiance to scientific objectivity. In the case of
McGiffert it seems that a liberal theological perspective which had
specific doctrinal content (not just a Cartesian attitude of intel-

89. McGiffert, "Protestantism," in *The Unity of Religions*, p. 273.
90. McGiffert, "How May Christianity Be Defended To-Day?," p. 152.

lectual freedom) was added to and actually controlled the scientific aspects of his complex procedure in historical reconstruction.[91]

Since theological values were present in the criteria by which the relevance of data was judged and the meaning of events determined, they helped distinguish this new type of church historiography from earlier ones. It was not fully scientific because it incorporated too many obviously theological considerations in its interpretation of historical materials. But it differed from the old theological approaches, too, and thereby sacrificed some of its consistency, by holding exclusively to a theoretical objectivity and ignoring the presence of theological ideas in actual practice. That theology, even if it had been incorporated into a methodological theory, was itself enough to separate liberal church historiography from the systems of Schaff and Shea. The impact of science on modern life had so thoroughly altered the basis of learning and making judgments for the generation of students after Schaff that a blend of empiricism and creedal confessionalism seemed no longer possible. All attempts at writing about earlier religious activity tried to build accurate historical knowledge and religious values on the scientific standards which dominated the day. McGiffert's unconvincing combination proves the indeterminate status of faith assumptions and indicates the necessity of recognizing their independence if one wishes to reach a realistic understanding of how church historiography can be studied.

McGiffert's approach was less consistent than Schaff's because he did not claim theology as a working partner in historical study. In point of fact, it was a partner and proved workable because of its congruence with scientific assumptions. Despite his own conception about the origin, content, and working relationships of historical method and theological perspective, McGiffert's ideas depended on a broadly liberal religious orientation. Historical study did not produce theological tenets, but it seemed to because both aspects of his thought were based on an affirmation of science. The compatibility is clear;

91. The Catholic Modernist, George Tyrrell, is reported to have made a remark about the predictable historical revisions of Harnack: that he looked at the Jesus of history down a deep well and saw his own face reflected at the bottom. The same could be said about McGiffert who best represented the Ritschl-Harnack synthesis of historical study and liberal theology in the United States. The reference can be found in Alec R. Vidler, *The Church in an Age of Revolution* (Baltimore: Penguin Books, 1965), pp. 213–14.

the derivation is not. Despite their differences in theory as to the place of theology in historical scholarship, McGiffert did continue one tradition Schaff embodied by applying religious goals in the study of the church's past. His complex mind was able to comprehend an emphasis on moral obligations to social service which he termed "the Kingdom of God." At the same time he argued for intellectual freedom to investigate current needs and to construct new doctrines for contemporary situations. The following studies will indicate how two historians each took an aspect of McGiffert's general outline and produced more concentrated historical work within the framework he established.

7 &CHURCH HISTORY
AND THE SOCIAL GOSPEL

Walter Rauschenbusch has long been considered a leading spokesman in the Social Gospel movement because most of his writing embodied an eloquent appeal for social reform based on Christian principles. Even though Rauschenbusch has been known primarily as a social activist and theologian, he held the position of professor of church history at Rochester Theological Seminary from 1902 until his death in 1918. From that post he influenced a generation of seminary students and was recognized by the scholarly world on two continents as one of America's most important church historians.[1] There is no evidence that any of Rauschenbusch's ideas about research or interpretation were influenced by McGiffert, but their writings exhibited a similar tendency to employ religious insight as a standard for assessing the contemporary usefulness of historical phenomena. Both of them belong to that emerging group of church historians who embodied new attempts at creating fresh theological emphases. At the same time Rauschenbusch, just as unwittingly as McGiffert, continued the old attempt to blend his theological perspective with the latest scientific methodology as defined by secular historiographical theorists. The scope of historical productivity was more limited in the case of Rauschenbusch because he did not follow the standard method of insisting on first-hand knowledge of original materials, nor did he publish any work considered to be essentially a product of historical research. But even though much of his information about events was derived from secondary sources, the interpretation he placed on those events was his own. In the last analysis he should be considered a historian of fresh and creative judgment, one who furnished new perspectives on the history of religious activity in the

1. His biographer, Dores R. Sharpe, pointed out that Rauschenbusch was one of the few invited to sign an appeal to observe the sixtieth birthday of Adolf von Harnack. As one might guess, A. C. McGiffert was the other American church historian similarly honored. See Sharpe, *Walter Rauschenbusch* (New York: Macmillan Co., 1942), pp. 189–90.

United States. In addition to that, his historical productivity can be seen as an expression of the theological renascence that was gathering force in this country at the turn of the century.

RAUSCHENBUSCH'S CONCEPTION OF THE CHURCH AND ITS HISTORY

The academic training which Rauschenbusch received prepared him more for the ministry than for historical scholarship. He was born in this country, but a family preference for German educational opportunities led him to study at the Gymnasium in Gütersloh from 1879 to 1883. After attending some classes briefly in Berlin, he returned to the United States and completed his senior year at the University of Rochester in 1884. While a student at Rochester Theological Seminary, he indicated that the preaching ministry seemed to hold greater attractions for him than other possible openings. After earning a B.D. in 1886, he must have felt his future confirmed by accepting a call to serve a German Baptist church in the city of New York. After five years in the pastorate, he went on leave to study in England and Germany. From 1891 and thereafter his theological and social ideas seemed to have become more self-consciously liberal.[2] He assimilated the views of Schleiermacher, Ritschl, and Harnack. That new orientation provided a basis on which he could reconsider previous interpretations of church history, and a teaching career at his old seminary afforded the opportunity to carry out those revisions.

In studying historiographical patterns in this area, one should begin by knowing that there were at least two levels on which Rauschenbusch conceived vital centers of religious activity to exist. On one plane there were organized churches trying to cope with their various social circumstances; at the same time, on a level distinguishable from institutional considerations, there was a transcendental community of faith shared by individuals of all ages who were dedicated to the timeless ideals of original Christianity. Beginning with the fundamental axiom that "the essential purpose of Christianity was to transform human society into the kingdom of God by regenerating all human relations," Rauschenbusch had a standard

2. The best short biographical sketch can be found in Robert T. Handy, ed., *The Social Gospel in America, 1870–1920* (New York: Oxford University Press, 1966), pp. 253–55.

by which he could judge the success of any institution claiming to follow Christian precepts.[3] The relationship between institutional
churches and the perennial standard of the Kingdom of God could
be gauged by the degree of determination churches manifested in trying to fulfill their mission. Both the earthly church and its divine
purpose had to be kept in view for an adequate understanding of all
the ramifications of church history.[4] In his own view of that history
Rauschenbusch did not envision a continued advance or dialectical
progress toward achieving God's will on earth. At times ecclesiastical
organizations embodied and advanced the ideals of the Kingdom,
while at other times they had abandoned their Christian origin and
pursued goals irrelevant to the chief end of their existence. But in
the question of a basic definition of the true church, there was no
doubt in Rauschenbusch's mind that "the saving power of the Church
[did] not rest on its institutional character, on its continuity, its
ordination, its ministry, or its doctrine." He made it clear that a mundane group could be considered a part of the true church only if "the
presence of the Kingdom of God within it" could be ascertained.[5]
Even though the connection between earthly agents and theological
prototype was often difficult for historians to determine, the divine
mission which churches tried to follow made the relationship sufficiently tenacious to ensure continued interest in their activities and
possibly afford useful religious knowledge.[6]

    In discussing empirical churches as objects for study Rauschenbusch
had almost no theological standard for identifying institutions that
claimed to be Christian. He was willing to accept as a church any

    3. Walter Rauschenbusch, *Christianity and the Social Crisis* (New York: Mac-
millan Co., 1907), p. xiii.
    4. Another student who noticed this double vision in Rauschenbusch is Rein-
hart Müller, *Walter Rauschenbusch: Ein Beitrag zur Begegnung des deutschen und
des amerikanischen Protestantismus* (Leiden/Köln: E. J. Brill, 1957), p. 65.
    5. Walter Rauschenbusch, *A Theology for the Social Gospel* (1917; reprint ed.
New York: Abingdon Press, 1945), p. 129. All references are from the later
edition.
    6. A certain amount of ambiguity will probably always remain over that aspect
of Rauschenbusch's ideas where he tried to define the nature and importance of
churches. A good example of the confusion can be found in *Christianity and the
Social Crisis*, p. 207, where he said: "The churches are profoundly needed as
generators of the religious spirit; but they are no longer the sole sphere of action.
. . . They exist to create the force which builds the Kingdom of God on earth,
the better humanity. By becoming less churchly Christianity has, in fact, become
fitter to regenerate the common life."

group of individuals who claimed to have experienced a personal confrontation with Christ and who afterward joined together in order to follow his teachings.[7] Such a permissive definition on the phenomenological level avoided many interdenominational disputes about orthodoxy and conflicting allegiances to confessions of faith. Its simplicity further allowed the historian scope to include a comprehensive selection of viewpoints in American experience. The lack of predetermined identity also allowed him to think of churches as social organizations, groups of like-minded citizens rather than sacerdotal bureaucracies, whose chief end was to establish justice and brotherhood in society at large. In addition to the methodological usefulness of such a simple, flexible working definition, Rauschenbusch defended his viewpoint by saying there was good theological precedent for assessing church activity in terms of their application of Jesus' teaching to local surroundings.[8] As in the case of McGiffert we begin here with a theology compatible with scientific method because theology has been formulated in a manner that could accommodate it. Churches could be studied in a way that was congruent with science, and the knowledge derived from such study was prized for the possible implications it held for the practical faith of religious activists. Once having arrived at a definition that blended earthly wisdom and heavenly meaning, historical knowledge and theological value, we find that this conception of churches was reiterated in several publications:

The chief purpose of the Christian Church in the past has been the salvation of individuals. But the most pressing task of the present is . . . to lay a social foundation on which modern men can live and work in a fashion that will not outrage the better elements in them. Our inherited Christian faith dealt with individuals; our present task deals with society.[9]

7. Walter Rauschenbusch, "Why I Am a Baptist," *Rochester Baptist Monthly* 20 (January 1906): 107.
8. Rauschenbusch, *A Theology for the Social Gospel*, pp. 124–25. The precedent to which Rauschenbusch was alluding can be found in F. D. E. Schleiermacher, *The Christian Faith* (Edinburgh: T. & T. Clark, 1948), pp. 587–89. For precedents in American religious history, see Helmut R. Niebuhr, The Kingdom of God in America (1937; reprint ed. New York: Harper & Row, 1959), p. 194. All references are from the later edition.
9. Walter Rauschenbusch, *Christianizing the Social Order* (New York: Macmillan Co., 1912), pp. 41–42.

The Church is the social factor in salvation. It brings social forces to bear on evil.[10]

All professions will have to go into the business of salvation and experience a call to the Christian ministry. Town officials and chiefs of police must become secular bishops and pastors. The church then would not be the only agency of salvation, but it will always occupy a unique place. . . . It is by far the greatest voluntary institution in our country. . . . If it is against any social movement, it can retard it terribly. If it gets behind any move, it is a decisive force.[11]

Rauschenbusch never attempted a systematic analysis and defense of his own research technique, but his language indicates a sympathy for scientific expressions and patterns of thought that were encouraged by the AHA. In a rare moment of introspection he seemed indirectly to reflect the common attitudes of scientific historiography when he said that "historical study trains the critical faculty. . . . The capacity to be accurate in stating the truth is a late and rare development of the human mind. Modern scientific and historical methods have greatly increased this capacity." The iconoclastic and empiricistic aspects of modern historical methods come through clearly in his statement that "what we call criticism is trying to separate truth from falsehood, and those who denounce criticism ask us to accept the assertions of a past generation without testing them."[12] The question of naturalism in his approach to evidence is not definite because he was willing to build on the facts uncovered by the research of others. But long after becoming a professional historian he went on record in favor of the position that "the scientific study of history is also the best method for training the scientific temper and the critical faculty of theologians," stating moreover that such a critical

10. Rauschenbusch, *A Theology for the Social Gospel*, p. 119.

11. Walter Rauschenbusch, "Enoch Pond Lectures on Applied Christianity" (1915), Walter Rauschenbusch Papers, American Baptist Historical Society, Rochester, New York. See also Vernon P. Bodein, *The Social Gospel of Walter Rauschenbusch and Its Relation to Religious Education* (New Haven: Yale University Press, 1944), p. 24.

12. Walter Rauschenbusch, "The Value and Use of History," *The Record* (November 1914): 38. In another, less forceful, definition he said, "The history of Christianity is the orderly and scientific narration of this great historical movement. . . . It will be scientific in the measure in which it brings events into causal connection and shows how the future has always grown out of the past" (Notes of Prof. Walter Rauschenbusch . . . Re-copied for Church History Class, for Prof. A. J. Bretschneider, Rauschenbusch Papers, chap. 1, no. 2).

faculty was "absolutely necessary" for modern men attuned to the times.[13] Further, his use of naturalistic metaphors helps reinforce the view that he stood fundamentally within the definition of history shaped by scientific modes of thought. Perhaps the best expression of that usage was made at the peak of his influence as a national figure:

History is the biological laboratory of humanity. We can cross rabbits or sweet peas and in a few years we have many generations on which we can base our deductions. In human life we cannot follow the final effects . . . until several generations . . . and that takes more than a century. The biological study of social institutions and ideas takes far longer still. For instance, no one could judge adequately of the historical effects of Protestantism when it was merely a hundred years old. Many of its effects are still maturing to-day in the rise and decline of nations. Therefore all sciences dealing with human life have adopted historical methods. . . . This is the special mark of the modern intellect.[14]

Even though one cannot discern a conscious and carefully reasoned acceptance of scientific procedures, as in the cases of Emerton, Walker, or even McGiffert, Rauschenbusch's understanding of history should be viewed as grounded in the same ideological structure that influenced his fellow historians. The unique contribution which he brought to the area was an interpretation of the data which those generally accepted principles furnished.

The historical study of Christianity for Rauschenbusch consisted of basing a narrative on empirical knowledge and at the same time interpreting that factual narrative line from the perspective of transcendental ideals. Since churches were conceived as existing on two levels, and historical research could provide information about only one of those planes of existence, he thought the church historian could legitimately draw on theology to supplement his categories of interpretation and judgment. In discussing what he called "the ultimate qualification for the study of church history," Rauschenbusch posited that "the spirit of Jesus is the ultimate canon by which every historical personality, institution, or movement must be judged, and our personal absorption of his mind and spirit is the ultimate

13. Walter Rauschenbusch, "The Influence of Historical Studies on Theology," *American Journal of Theology* 11 (January 1907): 119.

14. Rauschenbusch, "The Value and Use of History," p. 38.

qualification for a really useful study of the history of the Church."[15]
Just as in the perspective from which McGiffert wrote, Rauschenbusch stressed the fact that the life of Jesus heralded the introduction
of a new, creative force in history. That new force could be seen at
work transforming individuals into a community which relied on his
ethical teachings to build a new kind of society. "The Church," he
said, "by teaching Christian ideas and uniting men in Christian worship and work . . . sought to be the organized social expression of
the Christian life."[16] Ideally speaking, it sought to conserve and trans-
mit Christ's exalted goal for humanity, but its history indicated how
often it had failed that calling. Even a brief survey of ecclesiastical
annals would reveal how often men had become engrossed in petty
objectives due to "the deflecting influence of alien forces" that stifled
the moral power of churches and negated their primary reason for
being.[17]

Paralleling a fairly common liberal interpretation of church history, Rauschenbusch attributed the corruption of primitive Christianity
to a number of standard factors: a hostile environment, an otherworldly millennial hope, monastic asceticism, sacramentalism, the loss
of democratic polity after becoming a state religion and an unfortunate lack of scientific understanding of social dynamics.[18] His general treatment of the bulk of church history contained nothing new
in its basic definitions, selection of materials or insights applied to
them. He also repeated the liberal's optimism about prospects for a
contemporary recovery of the original Christian impetus, noting that
"all the causes which have hitherto neutralized the social efficiency of
Christianity have strangely disappeared . . . in modern life." Though
he did not bother to identify the causes behind the modern revival, he
shared the contagious and sanguine conviction that Christianity had
been able to overcome its problems "as an insect sheds its old casing
in passing through its metamorphosis." He was confident that "with

15. Rauschenbusch, Notes . . . Re-copied for Prof. A. J. Bretschneider, Rauschenbusch Papers, article VIII.
16. Ibid., chap. 1, no. 1.
17. Rauschenbusch, *Christianity and the Social Crisis,* p. 198. See also W. Rauschenbusch, "The New Evangelism," *The Independent,* 12 May 1904, p. 1055.
18. Rauschenbusch, *Christianity and the Social Crisis,* pp. 198–99. He also repeated McGiffert's view about the freshness of Luther's insights and the subsequent
loss of that vision to Protestant orthodox scholasticism. See ibid., p. 201.

the disappearance of . . . these causes, Christianity [had] become fitter to take up its regenerative work."[19]

Rauschenbusch taught a range of topics considered normal in his day covering early, medieval, and modern church history. He eventually added special courses on English and American developments but apparently never considered his work in those areas interesting enough to warrant publication.[20] The American Baptist Historical Society recently acquired a set of classroom notes taken during the years 1911–13 by George C. Fetter, one of Rauschenbusch's students. These valuable manuscripts include notes on a series of lectures on American church history delivered in 1912. The Fetter notes are sketchy and disconnected at times, but in most cases they are coherent, retaining salient points of the interpretive scheme and quoting verbatim many of the professor's remarks. The following reconstruction is based almost exclusively on these handwritten notes. They are the single known source for understanding a unique and distinctive historiographical phenomenon, Rauschenbusch's ideas regarding the past and future of American churches.

Throughout the lectures on American religion there are references to problems of social justice rather than any sequential treatment of isolated topics. Rauschenbusch confined most of his narrative to conventional episodes of denominational growth, evangelistic awakenings, and theological debates, but those historical topics also provided the opportunity to comment on contemporary issues such as land speculation, Christian socialism, alcoholism, and the single tax. One of his continual interests was the question of clerical attitudes toward different forms of slavery. Another was a concern that ministers avoid the stultifying effects of grasping after wealth and position. A third social motif recurring in the survey was a keen interest in the increased democratization of polity in the American branches of many different ecclesiastical organizations. Those three concerns about the

19. Ibid., p. 201.
20. Rauschenbusch wrote the sections on North and South America in *Handbuch der Kirchengeschichte,* ed. Gustav Krüger (Tübingen, 1909), 4:25–27, 100–104, 125–26, 165–66, 169–71, 270–84. Those entries do not, however, afford any insight into his distinctive interpretations of church history. They consist of statistical reports on appointed topics with a summary of denominational numerical strength in 1909, involving no opportunity for bringing his distinctive point of view into play.

social aspects of religion converged to undergird a second major interpretational category, one similar to Schaff's historiographical objectives in that it hoped to foster unity among denominations in the United States. But there seems to have been a more pragmatic "Americanness" about Rauschenbusch's point of view in that he looked for a unity that could utilize the advantages of democratic action to attack problems of social welfare.

It is important to notice that Rauschenbusch did not interpret church history in this country as a series of episodes in the gradual establishment of the Kingdom of God as a physical reality. A theological conception of God's ultimate directives gave him particular insights and allowed him to select certain subject materials over others, but there are only two explicit references made to the Kingdom in the entire set of notes on American church history.[21] One can readily see how the Kingdom shaped Rauschenbusch's historical perspective, but it is difficult to determine its precise role in his narration of past events.[22] The course concentrated on concrete historical information, but it was used to quicken the social conscience of students. Rauschenbusch tried to utilize historical precedents as a means of moving ministerial students to greater activism and to encourage them by showing how some diseases had already been isolated and effective cures administered. Despite the fact that other problems showed a more stubborn tenacity, he said their recurrence demanded constant vigilance lest the churches' sympathy for the welfare of common man be lulled into accepting such malefactions as a natural part of earthly life. His lectures had the general effect of alerting students to social injustice and of urging them to act in the

21. Taken from a set of classroom notes by G. C. Fetter, entitled "American Church History," Rauschenbusch Papers, pp. 15 and 62. Throughout the remainder of the chapter all references to "Fetter Notes" will concern the 1912 lectures on American church history.

22. *Rochester Theological Seminary Bulletin.* The annual catalogs for 1913–14 and 1914–15, pp. 48–49 (identical pagination) list a course on "Social Interpretation of Church History," saying that it would be offered in the fall term of 1915. Fetter had graduated by that time and thus did not attend those lectures, as he probably would have since he took all of Rauschenbusch's courses. The annual catalog for 1915–16, p. 49, indicates that Rauschenbusch offered a course entitled "The History of Social Redemption" which may have been more explicitly oriented to the idea of the Kingdom. Apparently this course was also offered for the first time in 1915, but unfortunately there seem to be no surviving notes pertaining to that set of lectures either.

name of religion and humanity.[23] Those studies never allowed an audience to lapse into a comfortable assumption that the Kingdom of God would succeed inevitably. The tone of prophetic urgency about working for the future was one of Rauschenbusch's lasting contributions to the study and writing of American church history.

AMERICAN CHURCHES, SOCIAL PROBLEMS, AND UNITY

Slavery was an important issue with Rauschenbusch because the theme of human exploitation was tangled in the roots of American history and continued to be a major factor in social change. He found that topic important also because he thought forms of slavery still existed in his day. On the question of origins, Spaniards were identified as being first to cultivate the peculiar institution in this hemisphere because they needed cheap labor. The Spanish government tried to check the practice of enslaving Indians, but the "greed and selfishness" of the settlers prevailed over the humane attitudes that tried to shape policies in the home office.[24] During the sixteenth century, when the supply of Indian manpower dwindled under brutal living conditions, Negroes were imported from Africa to serve European interests. In the North American colonies Virginia proved to be the most profitable area for exploiting slave labor because its broad fields of cotton and tobacco could easily be tended by slaves under an absentee supervision. The owners of slaves and plantations thus were freed from the drudgery of subsistence farming, and, in contrast to their northern countrymen, Virginians established an aristocratic way of life, dominated by a few men who controlled large tracts of land in virtually a feudal hegemony. Like their Spanish counterparts those feudal lords blocked any reforms the English Parliament tried to initiate, and they continued to bleed the land and their fellow man for personal profit.[25]

Throughout the history of such oppression Christian churches never stood idly by, permitting slavery to go unchallenged. Rauschenbusch wanted to stress that point in order to meet the charge (made in his own day by labor leaders) that churches always had leagued with

23. For another example of this aspect of his utilizing history, see "The Influence of Historical Studies on Theology," pp. 125 and 127.
24. Fetter Notes, Rauschenbusch Papers, p. 2.
25. Ibid., pp. 9–10.

affluent classes to exploit the poor. It was an unhappy fact of modern life that "labor says that the men who oppress them are those who pay their dividends to churches and build theological seminaries."[26] Attempting to answer such a misconceived charge, Rauschenbusch marshaled historical evidence to show that Christianity from its very inception had championed the cause of social justice.[27] In that area, he said, churches had many "honorable scars."[28]

One of the earliest champions of human rights for the Indian had been Bartholomé de las Casas. He opposed the cruel methods of human exploitation in the colonies and defended the Indians' cause at the Spanish court, but his isolated heroics had little effect against the heavy odds of vested interest lobbying there. The brightest spot in South America during the colonial period had been Paraguay where in 1608 the Jesuit order gained control of the country and defended the Indians against white settlers and slave traders. They were able successfully to organize approximately 100,000 Indians along the monastic ideals of simple communism and social equality. Paraguay flourished under that Christian plan, and the Indians achieved a standard of living unequaled in the New World. Rauschenbusch proudly singled out the success of Jesuit social planning as proof that "wherever the Christian spirit gets a strong foothold, there is an immediate leap forward towards a larger amount of fraternity in property relations."[29] In 1750 Spain ceded Paraguay to Portugal, and the Jesuits lost their influence; the work of one hundred and forty years was undone. Apparently this historical view implied that it remained for Protestants to deal adequately with the slavery question.

By mid-nineteenth century all the great Protestant church groups in the United States had become "deeply stirred" over the slavery issue. The fact that the largest denominations—Methodists, Baptists, and Presbyterians—split over slavery was evidence enough to support

26. Ibid., p. 3.
27. It would be helpful here to remember what he said in *Christianity and the Social Crisis,* pp. 139–40: "The spirit of Christianity did not spread only sweet peace and tender charity, but the leaven of social unrest. . . . Christianity must have had a strong social impetus to evoke such stirrings of social unrest and discontent. It was not purely religious, but also a democratic and social movement. Or, to state it far more truly: it was so strongly and truly religious that it was of necessity democratic and social also."
28. Fetter Notes, Rauschenbusch Papers, p. 11.
29. Ibid., p. 6.

Rauschenbusch's contention that churches had long been sensitive to major social problems.[30] He held that American Protestantism played an essential role in molding the nation's social conscience and in bringing about the abolition of slavery. There was some truth in the boast that Christianity had freed the slaves, but the professor of history was quick to warn that the problem had not really ceased to exist; it had only changed shape. Modern examples of slavery and the exploitation of human labor were less blatant, but just as real: "Contract labor in our prisons is one of the greatest moral evils. The prisoner is driven, works for nothing and is exploited by the contractor. In so far as it is a question of 'get to work' and having no other option, it is slavery."[31] Thus by historical and contemporary examples Rauschenbusch stressed both the success which Christianity had achieved in abolishing overt forms of slavery and the need to be constantly alert for other types of the same oppression.[32]

The attitude of the churches toward human bondage was only one of the interests comprising the course in American church history; another assessed the worth of ecclesiastical leaders themselves as they functioned in social contexts. Anglican colonial policy was chosen to acquaint students with a prime example of clerical negligence and social apathy. Virginia, a colony which offered few opportunities for implementing any liberalizing ideals, compelled its citizens to attend Sunday services and pay taxes to support the established church. Each clergyman received a generous grant of glebe land, tobacco, and corn to provide the services he monopolized. Such a policy seemed to work against itself because it produced an indolent, self-centered clerical class which grew insensitive to the needs of the people.[33] The

30. Ibid., p. 43.
31. Ibid., pp. 5–6.
32. Perhaps one of his best statements on this point was in *A Theology for the Social Gospel,* p. 128: "The world is full of stale religion. It is historically self-evident that church bodies do lose the saving power. In fact, they may become social agencies to keep their people stupid, stationary, superstitious. . . . Wherever an aged and proud Church sets up high claims as an indispensable institution of salvation, let it be tested by the cleanliness, education and moral elasticity of the agricultural laborers whom it has long controlled, or of the slum dwellers who have long ago slipped out of its control."
33. One calls to mind the acid remarks in *Christianity and the Social Crisis,* p. 7: "A very large part of the fervor of willing devotion which religion always generates in human hearts has spent itself on . . . religious acts. The force that would have been competent to 'seek justice and relieve the oppressed' has been consumed in weaving the tinsel fringe for the garment of religion."

Church of England compounded its error by ordaining priests only in England and by never sending a bishop to the colonies.[34] America had no college for training effective priests during most of the early decades, and few devoted men of high caliber came to the new continent. Rauschenbusch described the Anglican regulars as "a motley company of discouraged representatives . . . a set of profligate men."[35]

Since no bishop resided in the colonies, discipline was lax and parishes deteriorated under poor leadership. Rauschenbusch exposed the social indifference of the established church against a background of religious neglect and misdirected values. He noted that, despite the need for a self-sacrificing clergy, English priests seemed to be interested primarily in their social standing and financial privileges: "The clergy fought for nothing but their salary. They did not develop spiritual, moral or intellectual life. All they wanted was salary. . . . Finally the laity managed to get some control over the clergy by lay-courts. *Then* the clergy clamored for a bishop."[36] Whenever crop yields were poor, the market value of the small quantities of goods which could be produced spiraled upward. Clergymen were able to extort great profits in poor years by insisting that their salaries be met in full. Rauschenbusch was saddened by the fact that churchmen, of all people, would "try to get an unearned income" by taking advantage of misfortune. He contrasted Jesus' teachings about personal property with those of the Anglicans and

---

34. As we shall see later, Rauschenbusch admired the efficiency of episcopal polity, if it was balanced with lay participation in church affairs. Thus he considered the weak structure of colonial Anglicanism a tactical miscalculation and did not see that the failure to send bishops was also the result of other factors. Dissenting bodies in England and in the colonies opposed the introduction of a bishop because of the restrictions it might place on their own religious freedom. The Anglican laity also resisted the move because it would have lessened their control over ministers. See Winthrop S. Hudson, *Religion in America: An Historical Account of the Development of American Religious Life* (New York: Charles Scribner's Sons, 1965), p. 34. See also G. M. Brydon, *Virginia's Mother Church and the Political Conditions under Which It Grew* (Richmond: Virginia Historical Association, 1947), 1:125.

35. Fetter Notes, Rauschenbusch Papers, p. 48. One ought to supplement this interpretation by looking at a more accurate view of the facts involved; see H. S. Smith, R. T. Handy, and L. A. Loetscher, eds., *American Christianity: An Historical Interpretation with Representative Documents* (New York: Charles Scribner's Sons, 1960), 1:14–17, 52–55, 68–70.

36. Fetter Notes, Rauschenbusch Papers, p. 48; italics supplied.

reminded his students that in every case "when the church applie[d] business methods, the people stood *aghast*."[37] Such methods failed to serve the people and eventually made them enemies of almost every form of religion.

After the Protestant Episcopal church lost most of its privileges as a result of the American Revolution, it slowly began to realize that it had been neglecting its most important duties. It eventually abandoned all claims to social preferment and, by the early years of the twentieth century, had assumed a more respectable prominence as a church deeply concerned with social equality. But Rauschenbusch reminded his students that vestiges of the old, callous attitude still remained. One example of the ethical lag was Trinity Church in New York City which used shrewd business tactics regarding its land holdings. Instead of using its property in the Wall Street district for parks and low-income housing, the church collected immense profits by means of high rents and unearned increments.[38] Such capitalistic collaboration, he observed, disregarded the needs of workingmen and endorsed unchristian business methods.

Rauschenbusch believed that churches became more attuned to the spiritual and social welfare of the people as they adopted the principles of religious liberty and democratic government. At an earlier point in his career he almost equated the democratizing forces of history with those of the Kingdom of God.[39] So it is natural to see that in his history lectures he also stressed the importance of those forces which produced religious liberty and worked for vital, effective churches in the United States.

In the light of such liberal ideas, all types of intolerance and pressures to induce religious conformity understandably stood condemned. Rauschenbusch recognized the Puritans of Massachusetts Bay Colony as intellectually vigorous men, but he remarked in a vein quite unlike that of Walker that intolerance "darkened their reputation." He admired their physical hardihood and their democratic town meetings, but he also gravely reviewed "cases of men being dragged to church in chains" and of "men hanged or whipped for

37. Ibid., p. 47; italics and verb tense in the original.
38. Ibid., p. 55.
39. The best statement of that view is in "Die Geschichte der Idee des Reiches Gottes" (Paper delivered at Rochester Theological Seminary, Rochester, N.Y., 1902), see especially p. 19.

religious dissension."[40] In the judgment of the Baptist historian, Congregationalist ministers had stifled the spirit of American freedom for many decades by establishing themselves as "the aristocracy of the New England town." Ministers had originally been supported by voluntary gifts, but they abandoned that wholesome practice and began drawing their pay from the public treasury. They gradually became men of substance and were less inclined to sympathize with the common people.[41] Such a static aristocracy could not easily find a place for ardent souls like Anne Hutchinson and Roger Williams.

In the judgment of a historian dedicated to the ideals of democracy and toleration, Roger Williams was interpreted as the greatest exponent of religious liberty in colonial America. Contrary to the estimate of Shea, Rauschenbusch viewed Maryland as essentially an aristocratic colony and said that any semblance of toleration practiced there was intended primarily to facilitate trade. Lord Baltimore's policies stood for utility and profit rather than high religious principles. The liberal ideals of the early proprietors of Maryland and even the 1649 "Act Concerning Religion" were, in Rauschenbusch's interpretation, expedient maneuvers combining "self-protection on the part of a repressed religion and a business enterprise."[42] Roger Williams, by way of contrast, rose above such petty motives because he was a man of "utter idealism." He had argued that religion could not be forced on men and that uniformity dimmed "the inner eye which perceives the truth."[43] Williams's defense of the principles of "freedom, spontaneity and independence" eventually led him to establish the free colony of Rhode Island "not merely for religious liberty, but also for political and social democracy."

Rauschenbusch greatly admired the erstwhile Baptist because he "shared property with others and gave all an equal chance."[44] But after praising the egalitarian policies that would win the admiration of any liberal-minded historian, Rauschenbusch was forced to admit that Rhode Island's colonists actually contained "an undue supply of cranks" who created governmental and social crises. The observation was offered in defense that a free Rhode Island might have seen hard

40. Fetter Notes, Rauschenbusch Papers, p. 14.
41. Ibid., pp. 16–17.
42. Ibid., p. 11.
43. Ibid., p. 19.
44. Ibid., p. 20.

times, but its social structure had never been as deplorable as that of the crown colonies: "Democracy always brings with it its dangers. Yet the dangers of democracy are open and on the surface, while the dangers of aristocracy are hidden and deeper rooted."[45] Because of his love for democracy and religious liberty Williams did not try to force his fellow citizens into supporting a dominant theology or church system. His broad concept of Christian piety gave Rauschenbusch another occasion to condemn parochialism and to speak of the democratizing forces at work in religious activism: "When ministers stand for the church, they oppose democracy. When they stand for the Kingdom of God, then they push the causes of righteousness in the advance guard of Christianity."[46] Thus in Rauschenbusch's estimation of American religious history, Roger Williams had been an outstanding Christian soldier who achieved prominence by struggling to establish the Kingdom of God on these shores.

A very large section of the lectures on American church history was reserved for only two denominations, the Episcopalians and Methodists. Almost every lecture had some denominational focus, dealing variously with Baptists, Quakers, or New England Congregationalists, but Rauschenbusch chose two denominations because he considered them leading examples of the best type of democratic church action. He was willing to grant that Congregationalists usually embodied the principles of democratic church government and a "resolute love of social justice," but he justified their exclusion by saying that "their loose organization [made] united action more difficult for them."[47] Methodism, on the other hand, and its parent church maintained a more realistic balance between efficient organization and lay participation, thus making them more flexible in actualizing their social zeal.

Rauschenbusch thought the Episcopal denomination deserved special scrutiny because by his day it had become active in the two most important areas of modern development, social reform and church union. In their early history Episcopalians had been too lenient on the problems of slavery and alcoholism, but they had begun to realize the extent of the social crisis during the latter part of the nineteenth cen-

45. Ibid.
46. Ibid., p. 15.
47. Rauschenbusch, *Christianizing the Social Order*, p. 23.

tury. Evidence of their awakening was the formation of the Church Association for the Advancement of the Interests of Labor in 1887, one of the first groups of its kind in the United States. In 1886 they had also become "one of the bravest and earliest expounders of church unity."[48] Even though there were some conservative elements which still tried to prevent needed liturgical renovations, a broader historical view disclosed an encouraging growth of liberal tendencies within an episcopalian power structure.[49] Those tendencies, "in harmony with the American spirit," had taken root in local churches, diocesan conventions, and general synods. Low church theology and American democracy had combined to reduce the power of bishops from supreme rulers to executive officers of popular will. Rauschenbusch stressed the significance of such developments, concluding that "the reason the Anglican church has grown so much in America is because the laity has been given so much power."[50]

Of course, Rauschenbusch was realistic enough to see that certain elements in the Anglican communion were incompatible with his hopes for democratic American churches. The High church party, emphasizing its Catholic heritage, apostolic succession, and exclusive claims to correct doctrine, opposed cooperation with other American denominations. It could be admitted that there were "many fine men" in the High church faction, but on the whole their claims to superiority seemed "a reversion to heathenism" which leaned toward Rome and "despised the work of Protestantism."[51] About such exclusivism Rauschenbusch produced a memorable quip: "An ecclesiastical point of view is the cork that bottles many minds. It can swing around in an ocean of water and never get a drop inside."[52] Since isolationists would hardly cooperate with other churches, the future was seen to lie more in the hands of Broad church men who "represented the distinctly modern elements of the Episcopal church."[53] The Broad church party adopted an evangelical emphasis on vital personal faith, and at the same time it retained a more catholic view of grace and the sacraments. Broad church men appreciated the value of episcopal

48. Fetter Notes, Rauschenbusch Papers, p. 61.
49. Ibid., pp. 51–52.
50. Ibid., p. 52.
51. Ibid., p. 57.
52. Ibid., p. 60.
53. Ibid., p. 59.

organization, but they were thoroughly democratic in their sympathies and encouraged lay participation in church affairs. They cooperated with other denominations on social problems and thus placed their church in the most important currents of American history.

Rauschenbusch thought that "the Methodists [were also] likely to play a very important part in the social awakening of the American churches." He was convinced that they combined the best of "the democratic spirit of the Congregationalist group with a much stiffer and more centralized organization." More importantly, "their field [had] always been among the plain people."[54] Throughout its history, Methodism had flourished because of its concern for the common man. The heartfelt preaching, study classes led by laymen and its emphasis on family devotions sustained a spiritual life second to none. He praised their noble itinerant ministers who "gave themselves to America and allowed themselves to be plowed in."[55] Their pioneering spirit led them over the Alleghenies and established them as the most representative denomination in the United States.[56] Methodism had also developed an efficient, democratic organization of exhorters, elders, deacons, itinerant ministers, district superintendents, and bishops. Rauschenbusch termed their hierarchy an "episcopacy of utility" which made no claims to divine sanction.[57] Historically speaking, a number of Methodist offices had originally carried over from Anglican usage, surviving as vestiges which were referred to in the lectures as "the egg shell which clings to the Methodist chick to show what it came from."[58] The metaphor is misleading because it could

54. Rauschenbusch, *Christianizing the Social Order*, p. 23; see also Fetter Notes, Rauschenbusch Papers, pp. 30, 35; and Krüger, *Handbuch der Kirchengeschichte*, p. 100.

55. Fetter Notes, Rauschenbusch Papers, p. 32.

56. Perhaps this reconstruction of classroom notes too easily allows the reader to form the impression that Rauschenbusch's interpretation of American church history was extreme and therefore unsound. It should be noted that many of his judgments have been substantiated by more exhaustive and comprehensive research. For example, his interpretation of Methodist itinerancy, stated as a contemporaneous rebuttal to the Turnerian "frontier thesis," has been corroborated by W. C. Barclay, *Early American Methodism, 1769–1884* (New York: Board of Missions and Church Extension of the Methodist Church, 1949), 1:78–92, 100–109, 121–57, 258–67; 2:9–14, 287–99, 367–72, 428–30. See also R. M. Cameron, *Methodism and Society in Historical Perspective* (Nashville: Abingdon Press, 1961), pp. 112–14, 120, 123–35.

57. Fetter Notes, Rauschenbusch Papers, p. 39.

58. Ibid., pp. 39–40.

give the impression that, as a chick eventually rids itself of the shell, Methodists might be expected to abandon the use of bishops. But nothing was farther from the estimation Rauschenbusch made of their utility. Bishops were a necessary element in the Methodists' efficient structure, and the historian had to admire their effectiveness. He especially approved the practice of appointing men to one locale for a few years and then transferring them to another part of the country. In that way Methodist bishops gained the advantages of wide acquaintance with the needs of different people and a more comprehensive view of the challenges confronting the church.

History had also shown that Methodist theology held the best promise for church unity in a democratic society. Its "Arminian" emphasis successfully opposed the aristocratic doctrines of election and limited atonement by preaching the more egalitarian doctrines that Christ had died for all and that grace was available to anyone who accepted it in trusting faith. Methodist theology also preserved a special function for the church by viewing the sacraments as visible signs of God's pledge rather than an efficacious participation in symbolic rituals. Baptism and the Lord's Supper were defined as acts "by which He doth work invisibly in us . . . and by which He increases our faith in Him."[59] At the same time Methodism stressed the importance of Christian nurture. The denomination thrived on revivals and emotional religious experiences, but it laid constant emphasis on religious education and the quiet application of Christian virtues to all facets of society. Originally, the Methodists had been "solitary" in their demands for total abstinence, fervent religion, lay participation in church government, and involvement in problems of social reform, but the piety and theology which they had long embodied eventually came to characterize all progressive American churches.[60] Rauschenbusch was convinced that Methodism had harnessed the forces of social consciousness and democracy so effectively that it held the keys to successful church union in America.

The entire course on American church history culminated in a lengthy consideration of the problem of church unity. Rauschenbusch was convinced that the most powerful historical forces behind the development of modern Christianity, namely concern for social justice

59. Ibid., p. 41.
60. Ibid., p. 44.

and increased democratic cooperation, had converged in his day to unite churches in the United States. There had been, however, little success in outlining an adequate plan of union or even a declaration of doctrine persuasive enough to convince all denominations of the benefits of unity. His lectures on religious history culminated in an effort to supply that ecumenical rationale.

The most important doctrinal advance toward ecumenism had occurred in 1886 when the General Convention of the Protestant Episcopal church adopted four articles suggesting there was some common ground all Christian groups could share. Rauschenbusch analyzed and commented on most of these tenets which came to be called the Lambeth Quadrilateral, but apparently he accepted the first proposition—which declared the Old and New Testaments to be God's revealed Word—without equivocation because his lectures contained no objections. The second article of the Quadrilateral declared the Nicene Creed to be a sufficient statement of Christian beliefs. Rauschenbusch demurred in accepting that standard because he thought such creedal rigidity unjustly excluded believers like Unitarians and Universalists.[61] He also objected to the third point, holding the sacraments of Baptism and the Lord's Supper as instituted elements of faith, because it failed to include contemporary spiritualistic antinomians such as the Quakers.[62] The fourth article of the Quadrilateral declared itself to favor "the historic episcopate" which could prove useful to all churches if it were "locally adapted in the methods of its administration to the varying needs of the nations."[63] As a Baptist churchman and as a historian Rauschenbusch could give

61. It is doubtful Schaff would have included Unitarians and Universalists in his ecumenical plans, even though he did not consider the Nicene Creed a barrier to union.

62. On this point too there is a parallel with McGiffert in the shared optimism about the tendency of contemporary religion's becoming more relevant and centered on the right issues. Even the matter of liturgical changes could be fitted into Rauschenbusch's hopes for social activism. See *Christianity and the Social Crisis,* p. 205: "The present tendency to a more ornate and liturgical worship in the radical Protestant denominations of America is aesthetic and not sacramental in motive. It is proof that sacramentalism is so dead that Protestant churches no longer need to fear the forms that might revive it. The priest is dying. The prophet can prepare to enter his heritage, provided the prophet himself is still alive with his ancient message of an ethical and social service of God."

63. One accessible record of the original articles is in C. C. Tiffany, *A History of the Protestant Episcopal Church* (New York: Christian Literature Co., 1895), p. 559.

only qualified assent to that last proposal. If cooperating with "the historic episcopate" involved acceptance of the view that bishops had been an office indigenous to the primitive church, then it was based on an untenable historical thesis and favored the view supported by only a few communions: Greek Orthodox, Roman Catholic, and Swedish Lutheran. Rauschenbusch declared that no historian could have a very high view of episcopal dogma because "at the year 40 the historic episcopate [had been] a shadow."[64] He denied any doctrine which supported episcopacy as the single legitimate claimant to ecclesiastical authority, remarking that "when you see a dogma put together, then you cannot fall down and reverence it."[65] But he did not deny that the office of bishop, correctly understood, might play a significant role in the future vitality of church life in the United States. So his analysis of the Lambeth Quadrilateral concluded with tacit approval of its fourth point, with the stipulation that episcopacy be interpreted only in terms of Methodist utilitarianism.[66] After stating his objections to the Episcopalian prospectus, Rauschenbusch did not discuss any other plans, apparently deciding that specific ecumenical platforms were still too vague or exclusive to merit comment. He did not offer any plan himself, but his students were invited to come to grips with ecumenism as one of the most pressing questions of contemporary ecclesiastical interest.

The lectures did include an original contribution to thinking in that area, labeled "motives for seeking union," which make clear one thing about Rauschenbusch and the ecumenical movement: he never thought in terms of church *union* at all. He was interested rather in unity of purpose, collaboration, cooperative action among separate denominations, not the creation of a single American church. Rauschenbusch suggested three reasons for promoting cooperation. The first was simply an attack on the excuses used to rationalize sectarian contention. He regarded the doctrines and practices which kept denominations apart as "antiquated and trivial," and in a strikingly reductionist disparagement of denominational differences he declared that "questions of doctrine and organization have been outgrown.

64. Fetter Notes, Rauschenbusch Papers, p. 62.
65. Ibid., p. 60; see also "The Influence of Historical Studies on Theology," pp. 116–17.
66. Fetter Notes, Rauschenbusch Papers, p. 62.

No particulars are left any more. Churches have gone through a remarkable process of assimilation of doctrine, feeling, spirit, etc. Why then maintain the divisions? Anyone open to the real problems loses interest in the trivial squabbling."[67] It was to be admitted, of course, that Lutherans and some Episcopalians did not fit into such a facile interpretive scheme, but history seemed to indicate a diminishing self-consciousness and increased cooperation among the more important groups. The second and more weighty argument in favor of ecumenical activity was the fact that denominational rivalry was wasteful. In the historian's view, it was simply a "waste of horseflesh" to erect six churches in one small town. Such thoughtless competition prompted Rauschenbusch to lament: "We peddle the milk of the gospel over the same road."[68] He urged denominations to realize the insignificance of their distinguishing features, cease their dissipating dissensions, and pool their resources to face the common enemy. That common enemy afforded an opportunity for discussing the third and most important motive for seeking union, namely "the tremendous need of united social action." In the face of widespread social oppression and deteriorating social effectiveness, the churches could not afford, he argued, to waste their energies on fruitless dissension and interdenominational rivalries.[69] If each denomination went its separate way, Rauschenbusch saw that such a diffuse Christianity would make little impact on society, fail to implement Jesus' teachings about responsible brotherhood and stand doubly condemned, for its contentiousness as well as its irrelevance.

Most of the "motives for seeking union" were arguments drawn from expediency and designed to promote "united social action." The emphasis Rauschenbusch laid on interdenominational cooperation provided little basis for liturgical renewal or theological synthesis. He

67. Ibid., p. 68. See also Walter Rauschenbusch, "The True American Church, Great Christian Groups which Belong Together," *The Congregationalist*, 23 October 1913, pp. 6–7.
68. Fetter Notes, Rauschenbusch Papers, p. 67.
69. Curiously, the lecture notes include no mention of the Federal Council of Churches. The organization, founded in 1908, consisted of thirty-three denominations and based its existence largely on the same ideas Rauschenbusch expressed (Smith, Handy, and Loetscher, eds. *American Christianity*, 2:394). Rauschenbusch considered the council proof of "the spread and strength of the social awakening in the churches" (*Christianizing the Social Order*, p. 16). Apparently he was preoccupied with its opportunities for social reform and unable to appreciate its possibilities as an ecumenical agent.

recognized the limitations of his ecumenical ideas, but it is clear his sense of values placed that limited goal above institutional considerations. He evaluated different ideas about church unity and chose those platforms which were congruent with his primary goal of social relevance. A lingering note of self-conscious justification is embedded in his remark that "there is a great difference between the man who sees a mere ecclesiastical . . . form of unity and those who have a social point of view."[70]

There is an important similarity between the ideas held by Rauschenbusch and the ecumenical vision of Philip Schaff. Both men refused to be distracted by arguments over the future autonomy of present denominations or the mechanics of institutional mergers. In Schaff's case the primary goal before all churches was to have all forms of Christianity confess the lordship of Christ. Institutional forms were of secondary importance because "even where two or three are gathered in his name, he is in the midst of them. *Ubi Christus, ibi Ecclesia.*"[71] The two historians agreed in their view that denominationalism and confessionalism were simple consequences of natural differences in human attitude and preference. Both also thought that different orientations could coexist under the aegis of a true catholicity and a large-hearted charity. If the spirit of divine love could overcome petty discord, then men of differing viewpoints could "be Christian after the pattern of Christ, and best promote the work for which he came into the world, and for which he established the Church."[72]

The main obstacle to a more workable relationship between churches, in the estimation of each of these thinkers, was the divisive spirit of sectarianism. Neither Schaff nor Rauschenbusch wished to see Christendom united under a single organizational framework. A return to some pristine pattern did not seem useful, and a merger into one overarching corporation was not possible. But the question was largely irrelevant because both Rauschenbusch and Schaff stressed an ecumenical attitude rather than a specific structure.[73] Schaff thought there could be "variety in unity and unity in variety" if the primary

70. Fetter Notes, Rauschenbusch Papers, p. 68.
71. Philip Schaff, *The Reunion of Christendom* (New York: Evangelical Alliance Office, 1893), p. 21.
72. In James H. Smylie, "Philip Schaff: Ecumenist. The Reunion of Protestantism and Roman Catholicism," *Encounter* 28 (1967): 13.
73. Ibid., p. 14.

factor holding groups together were "unified in the creed of Christ."[74] There seems to be fundamental agreement, then, on the ecumenical priorities and patterns of Rauschenbusch and Schaff. While they emphasized different aspects within that viewpoint, the following statement by Schaff could stand as a characteristic expression of the hopes of both: "We must . . . expect the greatest variety in the Church of the future. . . . The world will never become wholly Greek, nor wholly Roman, nor wholly Christian, and will include every type and every aspect, every virtue and every grace of Christianity—an endless variety in harmonious unity, Christ being all in all."[75]

Rauschenbusch's ecumenical view was cross-hatched with another notable element that distinguished it from the early goal of the ASCH. It was a conception of church unity based on volitional rather than ontological terms. He was concerned that churches act decisively in society instead of embodying any essence peculiar to itself and trying to benefit society somehow by simply existing in it. He thought nothing could be accomplished by assertions that the Christian church was a holy institution, one that existed to draw men's minds away from the problems of everyday life. With such presuppositions and utilitarian goals, the ideas Rauschenbusch had about church unity were understandably limited and short-lived, but they indicate the area in which many ecumenical thinkers were working at that stage of development within the movement.

The emphasis throughout the latter part of the course, dealing with church history and future unity, was one that drew observations from a study of concrete realities, past and present, rather than theological theory. Rauschenbusch knew that venerable denominations would be slow to relinquish the autonomy they had gained and that a true union of American churches might never be realized.[76] His optimism about the future stemmed from the conviction that denominational collaboration was at least within the realm of possibility, whereas the creation of a single church might never be accomplished. Thus in his view it was better to achieve cooperative action and begin dealing with the social evils at hand rather than

74. P. Schaff, *The Reunion of Christendom*, p. 29.
75. Ibid., pp. 11–12.
76. Fetter Notes, Rauschenbusch Papers, p. 69.

prolong suffering while seeking the elusive chimera of complete synthesis.

The classroom notes giving us some knowledge about the course in American church history were taken in 1912, and they embody a sense of optimism about the tendency of circumstances that augured well for the utilitarian position. Rauschenbusch seemed to be hopeful that a unity of purpose was possible among denominations in the United States because of the historical fact that they had come to respect each other. Their experience in the American pluralistic society tended to eliminate exclusive attitudes in all but the most impractical of parties. Their work to alleviate suffering from common social ills worked to produce instead a tolerance which could possibly form a foundation for ecclesiastical unity. That tolerance could not be stressed too often, and the historian concluded that no major faction or doctrine remained to prevent effective interdenominational cooperation any longer: "We have what we might call an American Protestant church—Congregational, Presbyterian, Methodist, Baptist [groups] . . . have gradually converged . . . have learned Christian equality. . . . Christian toleration has been schooled in us by denominationalism."[77] In the light of all the social problems which he considered to have priority, Rauschenbusch's ecumenical ideas were limited to achieving the goal of having different denominations accept each other as partners.[78] The working unity he found attractive did not go beyond a cooperative pooling of resources to cope with social injustice. He never moved to the con-

77. Ibid., p. 70.
78. For some reason, perhaps one attributable to his Baptist heritage of congregational autonomy and denominational distinctiveness, Rauschenbusch always thought in terms of similarity rather than of any merger that would have destroyed any of the existing separate groups. And he thought that was enough to mount an offensive for the last great task, realizing the Kingdom in society. He summarized: "In their [Methodist, Baptist, Disciples of Christ, Congregationalists, German Reformed and Dutch Reformed] form of worship they have also converged. . . . These denominations have all outgrown sacramentalism, and since the interest in the old questions is fading out, the next 20 years are almost certain to bring them still closer together. . . . The religious thought and teaching heard in these churches belongs to the same type. Their ministers draw their ideas and inspiration from a kind of common reservoir of religious thought. . . . These churches have all developed the same form of evangelist appeal, the same type of religious experience, the same methods of teaching the young, the same organizations inside of the local church, the same social meetings for the culture of the spiritual life" ("The True American Church, Great Christian Groups which Belong Together," p. 6).

ception of creating a single American church sometime in the future, preferring rather to work for short-range programs of cooperation to alleviate the suffering of humanity.

The theological viewpoint held by the great leader and spokesman for Christian social reform and his practical goal of church unity placed him a great distance from the earlier theological versions of church historiography. But he and other liberal historians on the continuum should be considered closer to Schaff and Shea, approximating their basic pattern more than the ideas of Emerton and Walker. Rauschenbusch had a basically religious motivation for trying to renew interest in church history as a field of study. His work served as additional evidence that the turn of the century was marked by a resurgence within the craft of attempts to utilize theological substrata as a means of gaining insight into mazes of documentary material. For Rauschenbusch, perhaps even more than for McGiffert, the process was not a conscious one, nor were all its implications carefully explored. Perhaps the fact that Rauschenbusch's historical activity was so innocent of methodological complications was its greatest significance; it marked the rise of scholars who were so certain of their theological orientation and at the same time so comfortable within the main strictures laid down by scientific history that they felt no uneasiness about blending two viewpoints which had originally been considered mutually antagonistic. The approaches of theological liberalism, of the Social Gospel, and as we shall see in the next chapter, of modernism all indicated that science had not eliminated the fruitful interaction between objective-minded research and theological interpretation in the fascinating craft known as church history.

8 &CHURCH HISTORY
AND THEOLOGICAL
POLEMICS

The contribution of Frank Hugh Foster to American church historiography has not been noticed primarily because he produced few book-length publications. His work failed to have lasting influence because there has also been uncertainty about his theological positions and the consequent lack of a precise pattern in his interpretation of historical events. Nevertheless, in the history of ideas, the research he conducted stands as a logical development along the line initiated by McGiffert because it moves consistently to a use of history as a basis for making theological pronouncements. Foster was one of the first scholars who gave serious attention to a distinctively American strain of religious thought. He broke new ground as a historian of ideas in this country and opened a field (which many others soon began to cultivate) by writing a sustained analysis of New England theology. In the estimation of one student of the field, Foster's work constituted the "most exhaustive scholarly research concerning the New England theology" published before 1940.[1] Foster distinguished himself in works on Calvinistic thought as well as studies of liberal religious ideas arising in the decades between 1860 and 1920. In those areas his work was always based on a close scrutiny of primary source materials. During most of the time in which he was laying the groundwork for his historical publications, Foster stood within the theological tradition he chose as a subject. His effort to comprehend changes of religious thought from that interior perspective was faced by formidable obstacles, and the resulting material warrants our including his ideas in this survey.

In addition to the fact that Foster's activity was a significant historiographical endeavor, his open use of theological polemics made it distinctive. Few church historians of his generation tried to unite

1. G. Hammar, *Christian Realism in Contemporary American Theology: A Study of Reinhold Niebuhr, W. M. Horton, and H. P. Van Dusen, Preceded by a General and Historical Survey* (Uppsala: Appelbergs Boktryckeriaktiebolag, 1940), p. 8.

the fields of history and theology as closely as he, or to use them for the ends he wished to serve. In terms of the continuum we have been employing, Foster should be placed in the general area between Philip Schaff and Walter Rauschenbusch. For over three decades Foster was a loyal defender of conservative Calvinistic doctrines. Later, during the period in which his two major historical works were published, his viewpoint was altered, and he became an advocate of what he termed "thoroughgoing radicalism." A study of the content and the reasons behind that fundamental shift has a rightful place in the development of religious doctrines at the turn of the twentieth century.[2] But a comprehensive study in that area should include an analysis of the various interpretations which Foster placed on historical data and the reciprocal impact which historical evidence might have had on his emerging theological system. The historiographical activities of Frank Hugh Foster provide a symmetrical conclusion to our studies because he exhibited the influence of science on both historical and theological patterns of thought. At the same time his work also supports the paradoxical observation that theologians who began with scientific method rather than biblical confessionalism continued to produce workable combinations of historical research and religious insight.

FOSTER'S SCIENTIFIC AND THEOLOGICAL ORIENTATION

In 1888, the same year in which Schaff organized the American Society of Church History to help keep church history a separate discipline and use it for ecumenical purposes, Foster published one of his most important statements about methodological procedure. In it he espoused the general rubrics of scientific investigation and urged the general conclusion that nothing separated church history from other historical studies. He was convinced that empiricism and inductive reasoning were universally applicable methods of research and that they legitimately belonged to any careful study of ecclesiastical phenomena or religious activity. In summary, he said: "In all these disciplines the method of original study is the same that is practised

2. A solid piece of work has been accomplished in this area; see Henry C. Brockmann, "Frank Hugh Foster: A Chapter in the American Protestant Quest for Authority in Theology" (Ph.D. diss., Union Theological Seminary, New York, 1967).

in historical seminaries. It differs as to details, but it is the same in its principles. . . . the application of the laws of inductive logic . . . are the same everywhere. . . . when the facts are obtained, they are treated in the same way, whatever the science."[3] One corollary to affirming the universality of inductive reasoning and detached observation involves the question of whether religion actually lends itself to such methods of study. Foster made his naturalistic sympathies explicit by stating that churches were simply parts of their various social environments and thus well within the scope of critical, scientific inquiry.[4] On all three counts, then, Foster can be seen as one who approached both the institutional and intellectual aspects of his special field with the cast of mind admired by scientific historians. In pioneering the history of American religious thought he followed the rule that "the students of church history and of the history of philosophy have . . . exactly the same problems before them."[5] Other studies in the general field of religion such as systematic or practical theology might seek ultimate values or pose normative questions, but Foster argued that historians of theological activity were limited by preference and by their methodology to ascertain facts in a more restricted but publicly verifiable area. For historians the question was not "What is the truth?" but rather "What have men believed?"[6]

3. Frank H. Foster, *The Seminary Method of Original Research in the Historical Sciences: Illustrated from Church History* (New York: Charles Scribner's Sons, 1888), p. 2; see also pp. 4, 7.

4. Ibid. Compare the procedures he discusses on pp. 52–66 with those appropriate to other subject matter on pp. 66–79.

5. Ibid., p. 12. On p. 7 we find a basic but meager discussion, including the statement that "history is the explanation of events. Annals, which merely record events, can only form the basis upon which history rests. History is a science, which, like every other science, takes the facts peculiar to its sphere, reduces them to order, and gives them their due explanation. The understanding of history is the understanding of this explanation. . . . What is meant by 'explanation' here is just what is meant by the term in any other inductive science, viz., the exhibition of the significance of the event as seen in its causes and its effects."

6. Ibid., p. 1. A striking example of Foster's ability to separate the two approaches, in theory at least, can be seen in his treatment of Christological theories. In 1892 he published an essay written largely according to the canons of scientific historical methodology, "Studies in Christology: With Criticisms upon the Theories of Professor Adolf Harnack," *Bibliotheca Sacra* 44 (April 1892): 240–75. In that same year he became professor of systematic theology at Pacific Theological Seminary and published a sequel to the essay, written this time according to a different norm; see "Studies in Christology," *Bibliotheca Sacra* 52 (July 1895): 531.

Foster's book was intended to generate enthusiasm among students of religion for the kind of historical studies proposed by the American Historical Association, and so he spent a great deal of time defining and discussing the rudiments of basic research for a rather specialized circle of readers. In that discussion he disclosed not only empiricist and naturalistic habits of thought, but also a healthy iconoclasm and an inclination to employ scientific metaphors, all of which marked him as a thinker who developed his standards of truth and accuracy in keeping with the rubrics laid down in the age of science. His promotion of new research techniques followed a confident tone similar to Herbert Adams and other university spokesmen. Foster singled out Adams's seminar at Johns Hopkins as a perfect model of "a laboratory for history . . . a workshop where the student is taught to make history . . . a place where the beginner may acquire methods, and where the advanced student may do work which shall contribute to the sum of human knowledge."[7] Foster urged that students of church history could use such laboratories to test old opinions and discover new truths in their field by a critical scrutiny of primary source materials. His conception of what constituted acceptable sources underlined his naturalistic approach to historical phenomena: "By original sources of history we mean the testimony of the original witnesses to the facts. For political history they are statutes, treaties, . . . etc. In church history they are the writings of the Fathers . . . the acts and decrees of councils, . . . the original depositories of church doctrine. . . . Decrees, reports, minutes, letters, monuments, . . . art, churches, etc."[8] He made no mention of spiritual forces at work in the historical matrix because he discounted the possibility of discussing such intangibles on the basis of empirical investigation. The ideal seminar in church history was intended to yield, just as it was in other historical investigations, undistorted truth derived from original sources by means of inductive reasoning. Foster may have relied on the process of induction too uncritically, but he never wavered in the conviction that it afforded students precise knowledge about the history of religious thought just as it yielded accurate information concerning earlier thinking on social, political, economic, ethical, and aesthetic questions.

7. Foster, *Seminary Method*, p. 18.
8. Ibid., p. 16.

Unscientific histories, based on the predigested conclusions of religion, politics, or any other exterior interest, were of little use to
Foster. He permitted new students to consult earlier works based
on such misleading interests, mentioning Philip Schaff's as an example of those in which there was confessional interpolation, in order
to gain some bearings in the field. But he forbade reliance on such
works because they did not provide what he called the "control or
appreciation" which an objective historian expected to derive from
a scientific treatment of the sources.[9] Foster thought that historical
studies in religion were especially prone to distortion and said that
one of the major problems in the discipline was a tendency for
theological loyalties to take priority over scientific accuracy. He insisted therefore that church historians readjust their values and pursue
independent research with an open mind toward the evidence, following the principle: "Never use another man's results till you know for
yourself."[10] He persisted in such dicta because futile disputes over
points of emphasis and interpretation had taught him "nothing was
more likely to disturb . . . historical judgment than theological
prejudice."[11]

Throughout his career as a historian Foster tried to avoid the
methodological pitfall of trying to blend theology with the selection,
study, or interpretation of topics in religious history. Of course, he
never succeeded in realizing this ideal separation because his major
interests seem always to have been in debating theological points.
After studying in Germany, he came to respect historical scholarship
as a discipline to be valued in its own right, but recent studies have
confirmed the view that Foster did not pattern his research after any
historiographical school.[12] His theories, though, were drawn from
some of the most respectable precedents and practices of his day. The
iconoclastic aspect of his scientific objectivity was best expressed in

9. Ibid., p. 15.
10. Ibid., p. 35. On p. 49 Foster said that one should read introductory works
only after one has finished his own research. Another good example of his attitude toward theologically determined history can be found in his "Studies in
Christology: With Criticisms upon the Theories of Professor Adolf Harnack," pp.
242–43.
11. Foster, *Seminary Method*, p. 41. An especially trenchant criticism of a position that allowed dogmatics to distort historical evidence, in the case of Harnack,
can be found in Foster, "Two Histories of Christian Doctrine," *Bibliotheca Sacra*
45 (January 1888): 174–75.
12. Brockmann, "Frank Hugh Foster," pp. 46–47.

the advice he gave about how to deal with the narratives of pre-scientific historians:

Gain close enough view of his methods, test his general ability . . . and examine his alleged proofs critically enough, to have a reasonable ground for an opinion about him. If you see that he has written history to gain support for some preconceived opinion of his own, reject him at once. If he has first laid down certain fundamental laws according to which history must develop, give him the go-by. Nothing can more discolor the simple facts of history than philosophic or dogmatic goggles.[13]

In addition to distinguishing himself from conventional church history, particularly regarding attitude and general investigative approach, Foster also embodied a non-Schaffian perspective on the subject matter by distinguishing between two levels of history, rather loosely designated as "external" and "internal." Of course, Schaff had also drawn a distinction between an ideal church and actual ecclesiastical bodies, but he always insisted that the perfect spirit of religion manifested itself in physical forms and could not be understood without them. Whereas Schaff thought a study of ecclesiastical structures and their cumulative experience through the history of western Europe was indispensable for achieving religious truth, Foster considered the external appurtenances of religion a distraction which was not germane to understanding relevant ideas on questions of vital significance. External historical events, such as the church's territorial expansion, changes in polity, periodic reform movements or fluctuating church-state relations were valid enough topics for some understanding of religious activity, but in Foster's view they failed to come to grips with the real significance of religion in history. On a more important level, the one which he chose as his own field of research, church historians were expected to deal with the "chief intellectual and moral movement of man." As a modern thinker interested in the science of history, Foster thought the discipline gravi-

13. Foster, *Seminary Method*, p. 40. Perhaps it would be useful to point out that Foster's criticism does not apply to a great part of Schaff's writings. The most conspicuous examples of good work are those which minimize his interpretive prose and reproduce documents at length. See his *Bibliotheca Symbolica Ecclesiae Universalis: The Creeds of Christendom with a History and Critical Notes*, 3 vols. (New York: Harper & Brothers, 1877) or the first eight volumes of *A Select Library of Nicene and Post-Nicene Fathers of the Christian Church* which Schaff supervised in collaboration with Henry Wace of King's College, London.

tated toward a study of ideas and asserted that "the careful student is called away from . . . whatever attracts his attention most at first, to the course of human thought. . . . So history, in its development as a science, has come to deal more and more with the internal facts of the life of man."[14] That more vital area of investigation did not lend itself to a survey of some grand organic development of an institutional structure which progressed along preconceived or foreordained lines; it was rather the story of individual achievements and failures in a vast and complex "unfolding of the thought of man as to God and duty."[15] The most important facet of that subject which Foster called the inner history of the church was, to judge by his preference, a chronicle of developments in systematic theology. Foster spoke warmly of that aspect of history, justifying his choice of subject by saying that "we can perhaps in no better way gain a living apprehension of the theology . . . handed down to us, and make our theology alive, than by watching it in its original genesis."[16]

Foster thought of churches as human institutions, important centers of thought which contributed to the world's theological and moral deliberations. Since scientific methodology apparently could be applied to all such phenomena in human history, he considered it an adequate tool for the study of church history. But, still on the methodological level, he said that church historians needed additional powers of insight, a capacity which placed his ideas close to Schaff's notion of "sympathetic union." Foster theorized that historians of theology should "put [themselves] so completely into the situation of the writer that [they could] think his thoughts after him and find his language natural."[17] Thus the actual process of doing intellectual history required a blend of scientific objectivity and a subjective empathy which was never made explicit or fully elaborated. The similarity between Foster and Schaff is a superficial one, however, and the former never concluded, as the latter had done, that church historians needed the credentials of Christian allegiance before they could interpret the past or present meaning of Christian

14. Foster, *Seminary Method*, p. 11.
15. Ibid.
16. Frank H. Foster, "The Eschatology of the New England Divines," *Bibliotheca Sacra* 43 (January 1886): 4.
17. Foster, *Seminary Method*, p. 36.

thought. Foster's use of empathetic rapport marked a step beyond the ideals of a fully detached object-observer model fostered by historians such as Herbert Adams, but it did not cross over the line of secular historical theory into an avowedly theological one. This point about insight is the crux of two of his important assertions: that historians can reconstruct previous ideological systems accurately and that anyone interested in contemporary theology could rely on such information for his deliberations.

The connection between historical study and creative theological activity was stated in terms similar to those laid down by A. C. McGiffert. In the case of Foster, however, theologizing seems to have followed much more closely the same contours as historical inquiry. At times Foster waxed eloquent about history as the basis for sound theology, saying that it served as "an oracular divinity" or that the assiduous student could actually learn from "the prophetic office of history."[18] In a more sober delineation he acknowledged that religious spokesmen were unable to avoid their antecedents or even define themselves outside of those circumstances, and since all men were thus "entangled . . . in the meshes of the net of history," virtue could be derived from necessity if theologians would "draw profit" from a study of the past.[19] But whereas McGiffert used historical knowledge to show contemporary religious man that he really did not need history, Foster wanted to utilize selections of the past by gleaning from them certain elements of truth which he found to have existed at various times in the history of Christendom. The resulting study ended not in a relativism or special definitions supported by private interpretations of Scripture; it stood rather on a more settled theory about the usefulness of Christian antiquity. Foster held that religious truth could be grasped by those who were discerning enough to find it among raw historical data. The basic assumption separating Foster and McGiffert was on the problem of whether human history contained information pertinent to the ongoing task of defining religious values. The key to this significant difference seems to lie in their conceptions of the evolutionary process. McGiffert favored the

18. Ibid., pp. 17 and 9 respectively. See also *A Defense of the Catholic Faith Concerning the Satisfaction of Christ against Faustus Socinus of Sienna, Written by Hugo Grotius,* trans. Frank H. Foster (Andover: W. F. Draper, 1889), pp. lx and lvii. [Originally published in *Bibliotheca Sacra* 36 (1879).]
19. Foster, "The Eschatology of the New England Divines," pp. 1-2.

Darwinian notion that nature exhibited many varieties produced for
no good reason at all, and thus he concluded that spontaneous generation destroyed all serious reliance on continuity or the idea of
providential control. Foster, on the other hand, seems to have supported a view that antedated Darwin and viewed all events as occur-
ring in a more direct line of progress which preserved the best
aspects of each succeeding generation. The implication for theology
is perhaps best set forth by a cogent and indicative piece of Foster's
argument:

The theory of evolution, in the broadest sense of that word, has created
for us a new interpreter of the experience of the church, the science of
the history of Christian doctrine. The various opinions held in the
Christian church have been so many and apparently so conflicting, that
the impression has been left upon the careless observer that all is chaos,
everything in dispute and nothing known. But evolution has brought
order out of confusion, marked out the historic course of development,
distinguished between the essential and the non-essential, the nascent
and the mature, the voice of the individual and the voice of the church,
and has thus enabled us to employ the history of doctrine as one of our
most efficient allies in the defence, and one of our most instructive
teachers in the unfolding, of Christian truth.[20]

The scientific study of any segment of past events produced a body of
knowledge with intrinsic merit, but as a church historian Foster
maintained that "history render[ed] its chief service to constructive
theology in . . . interpreting Christian experience."[21] He never made
clear the distinction between "individual thinker" and "the church,"
nor did he explain the exact nature of "Christian experience;" but
those were pivotal points on which he relied in his own radical shift
in theological opinion.

In 1888 Foster's primary aim was to acquaint his readers with the
latest scientific procedure in historical investigation and to provide
the basis for a reliable American church history, "one wrought with
American problems in mind, and filled with lessons prepared for
American use."[22] His own histories of theology in the United States

20. Frank H. Foster, "Evolution and the Evangelical System of Doctrine,"
Bibliotheca Sacra 50 (July 1893): 419–20.
21. Ibid., p. 421.
22. Foster, *Seminary Method,* p. 90; see also p. 100.

were offered in the hope that men might eventually produce a body of thought that profited from the accumulated wisdom of church thinkers. But at the same time Foster's unique theological viewpoint, derived from considerable study and years of effort, gave a distinctive shape to his historical narrative. Before surveying his interpretation of American theological history, it will be useful to understand the religious orientation which controlled his interpretation of historical and scientific data.

If there was a single thread of continuity in Foster's theological development, whatever the varying content and changing emphases, it is to be seen in his concern to build a logically consistent and comprehensive metaphysics. The stress on comprehensiveness was particularly important because Foster attempted nothing less than a survey of the full range of knowledge in both the scientific and religious aspects of modern experience. In the course of his lifetime he underwent fundamental changes in his theological orientation, moving all the way from a conservative expositor of some sort of consistent Calvinism to a forthright radical. Though his earlier orientation laid the foundation for parts of his first historical study, a major historiographical undertaking in its own right, Foster's later position as an extreme rationalist colored the greatest part of the interpretations which he made as a historical scholar.

Graduated from Andover Theological Seminary in 1877 and the University of Leipzig in 1882, Foster had long considered himself, because of manifest intellectual capabilities and devotion to time-honored tenets, the logical successor to the Abbot Chair of Systematic Theology at Andover. In his biography of Edwards A. Park, Foster's favorite professor and at that time incumbent in the chair, he described in impersonal language the relationship between a student and the old theologian. The major events paralleled his own experience at almost every turn:

The Bibliotheca Sacra was his [Park's] ready instrument in the double work of giving young men opportunities and of trying them out. He first gave them work as proofreaders. . . . he would suggest an article . . . probably some translation, perhaps from the Latin.[23] Then a review

23. Foster's translation, as mentioned above, was "A Defense of the Catholic Faith Concerning the Satisfaction of Christ against Faustus Socinus of Sienna written by Hugo Grotius."

article on some important book.[24] Meanwhile the young man graduated and was looking for a parish. Park advised a small one.[25] Then if the fire caught, the young man might form the plan of going to Germany.[26] . . . Then more articles[27] . . . and finally when some college president or trustee came to him for advice regarding a vacancy . . . Park had his nomination ready . . . the appointment was as good as made.[28]

But his own career was doomed not to follow this classic pattern. When Professor Park retired in 1881, Foster was not offered the position at Andover, although he certainly considered himself the leading candidate.[29] The prevailing theological attitude at the seminary had undergone great change, becoming increasingly opposed to Park's Edwardean categories and thus to all who supported that point of view. So in 1884 Foster, along with the *Bibliotheca Sacra* which continued to favor articles on conservative theology, moved to Oberlin College in Ohio. As an editor of the journal, Foster tried to use its influence and respectability in supporting opposition to encroaching liberalism.[30] While at Oberlin Foster continued to pursue some minor investigations into earlier religious debates about Christology and into differing views on future punishment, viewing them as contributions to contemporary theological inquiry. He also taught church history there and began work on what was to become his

24. Not fitting the pattern with exact chronology, Foster's review article, "Is Eternal Punishment Endless?," appeared in *Bibliotheca Sacra* 35 (April 1878): 353–80, discussing a book by J. M. Whiton.

25. Foster became pastor at North Reading, Massachusetts, and remained there until 1878.

26. From 1878 to 1882 he studied in Germany.

27. Just to keep in touch, Foster sent Park some translations from Germany: "Calvin's Ethics, an Abstract from the German of Lic. Theol. P. Lobstein, Univ. of Strasbourg," *Bibliotheca Sacra* 37 (January 1880): 1–47; and "Old Catholicism," *Bibliotheca Sacra* 38 (July 1881): 401–33.

28. F. H. Foster, *The Life of Edward Amasa Park, S.T.D., LL.D.: Abbot Professor, Andover Theological Seminary* (New York: Fleming H. Revell Co., 1936), p. 199.

29. One historian of the changes at Andover in this period does not mention Foster as a probable candidate to succeed Park. The trustees nominated Newman Smyth, but the Visitors refused to approve the appointment; eventually George Harris was found to be mutually acceptable. See D. D. Williams, *The Andover Liberals: A Study in American Theology* (New York: King's Crown Press, 1941), p. 28; see also Brockmann, "Frank Hugh Foster," pp. 48–49.

30. Frank H. Foster, *The Modern Movement in American Theology: Sketches in the History of American Protestant Thought from the Civil War to the World War* (New York: Fleming H. Revell Co., 1939), p. 172. See also his *Life of Edwards Amasa Park*, p. 244.

monumental study of the fate of New England Calvinism. Those
early articles tended to confirm Foster in a rather pedantic style of
writing, offering little new in the way of ideas or personal views and
consisting primarily of lengthy book reviews with comments limited
to a merciless criticism of logic. Once that pattern was set, all of his
publications followed a meticulous plan that suffered from a tedious
and unimaginative presentation.[31]

Foster changed his theological position slowly because at first he
still tried to retain traditional Congregational emphases on divine
sovereignty and human depravity in a rational system that was open
enough to be challenged by the latest developments in psychology,
natural science, and biblical criticism. Eventually he concluded that
it was impossible for Calvinism to survive within such a synthesis,
and he abandoned many aspects of his earlier commitment. As early
as 1893 he began making explicit the principle that open-ended con-
temporaneity served as an important criterion in the emergence of a
responsible theology: "History tests doctrines by their power of survival. A doctrine is evolved in the heat of a great controversy. Has it
anything more in it than the adaptation . . . to a passing phase
of thought? . . . when the doctrine appears again under dissimilar
circumstances, . . . as the one persistent answer to the same kind of
question in various ages, then the historian begins to see in it the
divine teaching. Equally instructive is history as to that which does
not survive."[32] It is not altogether clear how one may take an idea
that has survived various historical epochs and identify it as nothing
less than "the divine teaching." But the important thing to notice in
Foster's guideline is the negative aspect: if ideas fail to maintain
adherents, it must be for good reason. Foster's personal experience
should be viewed in the light of this principle. His sense of being

31. In order to keep footnotes at a minimum I shall cite a short list of examples
to point up Foster's pedantic comments on the logic of different authors. See
Frank H. Foster, *A Genetic History of the New England Theology* (1907; reprint
ed. New York: Russell and Russell, 1963), pp. 75, 133–34, 148, 174, 238, 240,
310. All references are from the later edition. See also Foster, *Modern Movement*,
pp. 62, 77, 86, 121, 149, 151–52 and 169–70.

32. Foster, "Evolution and the Evangelical System of Doctrine," pp. 420–21.
For another good example of Foster's ability to change, see his essay, "The Experiential Theology," *American Journal of Theology* 12 (October 1908): 626. It
is worth noting that Foster's theological shift is signified by his changing from
a frequent contributor to the *Bibliotheca Sacra* to one whose essays appeared in
American Journal of Theology.

excluded from Andover and the results of his historical inquiry slowly forced him to admit that much of his original theological position was being destroyed in the age of modern science. A great deal of his mature historical narrative was structured with that conclusion in mind. Consider for example his explicit recognition of the principle of survival at work and his forthright acceptance of its conclusions, a passage that also serves to introduce Foster's ponderous mode of expressing himself:

Descendant of Puritan and Pilgrim as I am . . . it would be strange if I had not begun this history with a feeling of the warmest appreciation of our New England Fathers. . . . These sentiments are reflected upon the earlier pages of the book. . . . With the progress of the work my point of view and my feeling have changed together. The final historical review of the whole period has made me a critic of the school and its work, and led me to the perception of a fact that was long hidden from me—that it was not without reason that a strong reaction set in against this theology about the year 1880. I find myself no longer reckonable to its adherents.[33]

After 1906 Foster began slowly to assimilate scientific information about man and the structure of the natural world which led him to endorse what he considered a more realistic and logically respectable theological position. He was willing to use modern scientific findings as a basis for revising fundamental doctrines because he thought they provided "a new body of truth, possessed of a new and altogether unanticipated degree of certainty" for the serious inquirer.[34] In the light of such unerring methods and results, Foster scorned the efforts of those who tried to defend those tenets accepted back in the days of Professor Park. He criticized another theologian for being behind the times, but he might have had his former position in mind when he charged that, even though a new age had dawned marked by "exact observation of facts" and which demanded "that all reasoning was to take on new forms," the implications "had entirely escaped him." The situation was tragic for any such person because "as an apologist for the new age he was

33. Foster, *Genetic History*, p. vi.
34. Frank H. Foster, "Theological Obscurantism," *American Journal of Theology* 15 (January 1911): 98.

incapacitated by the fact that he did not live in it."[35] But history was kind to Foster in one way at least. It let him see the error of his ways while there was still time to abandon outmoded procedures and advance with the empirical sciences to solid theological respectability. Far from continuing Schaff's reverence for ancient creeds and earlier doctrinal formulations, Foster embodied the Cartesian icono-clasm in much the same way Moses Tyler had done, by trying to "di-vest himself of all his beliefs . . . and begin at the beginning of all thinking." There is no uncertainty that he wished to effect a throughgoing revolution in metaphysics and then to "lay anew the very footing stones of the edifice of thought." If one cannot ac-knowledge Foster's success, one must at least respect his determina-tion to construct a new edifice, this time "committing no leaps and admitting no fallacies, till all [would be] equally sound and the whole [furnished with] . . . answers to the perplexities of the times."[36]

There is sufficient pattern in Foster's theological publications to al-low students a view of how he developed from "New England ortho-doxy" to a position that helps define and exemplify "modernism." Completing his survey on the fate of high Calvinism had a liberat-ing effect on Foster, and by 1906, or shortly thereafter, he undertook the task of giving "the whole system of theology a new and thorough examination in the light of the persistent objections of modern scholarship." So he tried to begin theologizing on a completely fresh page and proceeded to reconstruct his ideas from a "purely non-supernatural or rationalistic standpoint."[37] At the start of this analysis of the thought of a modernist, it is important to notice that Foster always conceived of theology as a body of accurate and publicly verifiable knowledge, not a set of beliefs. Rejecting the traditional distinction invoked by Christians since the days of Tertullian be-tween truths held on faith and truths derived from observation, he argued that "religious truth is discovered in the same way as all other

35. Foster, *Genetic History*, p. 448. This particular statement is rich with irony because most of the particular theological categories which interested Foster were hopelessly out of date by the time he rose to defend them. He is victim to his own judgment. For a corroborative assessment of how antiquated some of Foster's polemics was, see Brockmann, "Frank Hugh Foster," pp. 27–28.
36. Foster, *Modern Movement*, p. 94.
37. Ibid., pp. 204–5.

truth, by the experience and study of man."[38] When he changed the content of his theological categories, he did not alter his conception of proper method or the rational character of its legitimate results. Whereas Foster had originally based his proofs on a rather literal biblical exegesis, he eventually supported conclusions (which he considered as demonstrable and conclusive as the others had been) based on psychology and the observable phenomenon known as the Christian experience.

It would be a mistake to conclude that his move from biblical theology to one derived primarily from human experience involved a lessening of the value of theology per se. Foster did not mean to imply that a scientific orientation excluded considerations of divine guidance or denied the possibility of finding "illumination of God" in the natural sphere. One could still value modernistic theology as something more than human speculation because all that Foster did was to shift the focus of his attention from a transcendental to an earthly sphere. He still sought truth about divine-human relationships, but as a modernist he held that the only legitimate and compelling information was to be derived from the earthly realm of everyday realities in which man found himself to be enmeshed. Further, that world of concrete phenomena had been investigated most profitably by natural scientists. So all future religious thought necessarily depended on the gains science had already made, gains in the form of exact data and more importantly in the epistemological strictures established to evaluate truth-claims:

It may be said that our traditional theology, like all the early thinking of men, is seriously marred by its entire lack of conception of what facts are, and how a knowledge of them is to be obtained. . . . methods of the laboratory to determine what the facts actually are . . . to the present day have remained . . . unappreciated, if not unknown, and generally unimitated by the expounders and defenders of theological systems. . . . when it comes to a fact or a principle upon which scientific reasoning is to be built up, it is the habit of the modern times to demand cogent proof. Often it is said that a man ought not to believe a position if he can doubt it.[39]

Most of Foster's dominant ideas follow the pattern characteristic of modernists—religious spokesmen who depended on contemporary

38. Ibid., p. 89.
39. Foster, "Theological Obscurantism," p. 97.

ideas about the proper approach and possible content of truth. He confirmed this identification when he openly rejected "all systems which depend upon authority" and adopted the more defensible method of empiricism and inductive reasoning. Instead of accepting church dogma or even having a positive opinion about the creeds of Christendom, he asserted that science had reduced past theological systems to guesswork and had confronted religious men with the task of bringing about a "readjustment of Christian thinking to the demands of modern thought—by rational processes alone."[40] Since the actual growth of scientific knowledge seemed limitless and the universal validity of its methods were thereby affirmed, Foster considered his approach to theological presentments free from the intellectual flaws which had debilitated the efforts of earlier theologians. His acceptance of modern scientific standards for every type of investigation cut all ties with a particular confession or denomination and made him appear to be fully a citizen of the world. Perhaps the best example of how emphatically he insisted on uncontrolled inquiry into all aspects of religious thought was when he laid down the positivistic dictum that "the authority of any principle . . . resides in its perceived truth. It can be true to me only as I see it to be true; and only that which I perceive to be true can control my actions."[41] On the basis of such forthright principles he rejected many traditional doctrines as being unintelligible or unbelievable by the lights of scientific criteria. Then in what could be nothing more than a pious afterthought, he added that an attitude of stringent naturalism "carried farther the Protestant correction of Romanism, [by removing] all mediators between the soul and God and [giving the independent thinker] immediate access to God."[42]

One consequence of modernistic revision in the area of religious propositions unfortunately involved rejecting major concepts esteemed by Western Christianity. It is a small irony that they included several which Foster had defended earlier. A full list of changes would be difficult to compile because Foster did not reach a clear understanding of what his new religious outlook ought legitimately to include. But the direction of this type of modernism should be clear when one

40. Frank H. Foster, "The Theology of the New Rationalism," *American Journal of Theology* 13 (July 1909): 405–6.
41. Foster, *Modern Movement*, p. 63.
42. Foster, "The Theology of the New Rationalism," p. 412.

sees that he rejected credence in categories like the Trinity, Incarnation, and Christ's Work of Atonement because he thought science had made them "totally unintelligible."[43] In the light of modern advances in biology and chemistry he was led to reject the New Testament account of miracles, showing with an astonishing amount of energy that water cannot turn into wine. Then on another tack and with even less restraint, he rejected miracles as inapplicable to the general problem of relating the Scriptures to religious truth.[44] Still on the negative side, Foster saw "no shred of a reason" for believing in the divinity of Jesus of Nazareth. The critical historian and scientific-minded rationalist could trace such notions about deifying him to his sincere but misguided disciples who had "not a particle of proof to show that they were right."[45] Of course, the modernist could still admire Jesus as an expert teacher of religion and morals. Foster insisted that "the rationalist who starts out by denying any absolute authority except that of perceived truth, ends by acknowledging the authority of Jesus *as an expert*," a skill that did "not involve . . . any infallibility" on his part.[46] But his demand for "cogent proof," evidence of the sort that was repeatable, publicly verifiable, and free from honest doubts, was rarely satisfied in his assessment of pre-scientific formulations of religious knowledge.

There is less precision in discussing the positive side of modernist thought because, in Foster's case at any rate, few specific ideas seem to have emerged from the working principles he laid down. In a frank admission that religious thought was in a "confused state of things" at the turn of the century, he described the situation as one in which modernists could agree only on which general direction to follow. The negative aspect involved abandoning such topics as Trinitarian Christology, predestination, original sin, prevenient grace, and future punishment because present modes of thinking rendered

43. Ibid., p. 411.
44. Frank H. Foster, "The New Testament Miracles: An Investigation of Their Function," *American Journal of Theology* 12 (July 1908): 370–71, 391.
45. Foster, "Theological Obscurantism," p. 106. In another important essay he said that "the critical study of the New Testament history [would bring one to] the conception that the whole supernatural apparatus of historical Christianity is the product of the times in which it originated, and that literally taken, as the creeds and confessions take it, it is without proof." See Frank H. Foster, "The Christology of a Modern Rationalist," *American Journal of Theology* 15 (October 1911): 586.
46. Foster, "The Christology of a Modern Rationalist," p. 595; see also p. 598.

them uninteresting or unnecessary. Positively, the search for a scientific understanding of religious truth was seen as relying on three basic components: acceptance of the biological evolution of mankind, application of evolutionary principles to the study of historical development, and reliance on "some of the results" of biblical criticism.[47] Probably the most forceful statement embodying the new outlook was made when Foster announced that "biology has been permanently set in its place among the essential elements of a theological education."[48] But after those general principles were given, it is difficult to see what specific religious ideas Foster wished to derive from them. It is clear that rational religion intended to sift the ideas of earlier periods and select those compatible with the age of science, making revisions in doctrine that were "demanded by the call for *proof,* which is the call for *truth* in theology and for *reality* in life."[49]

One might object that Foster equated religious and scientific experiences too rigorously. He is open to the criticism that religion includes emotions and activities where science cannot apply. In addition to that demurrer, it seems the task of building a body of knowledge for a community of faithful could never be accomplished in such a manner because natural science is itself in a state of flux and revision. Any theology that waits for other disciplines to furnish materials with which it can work must suspend all activity until it acquires the requisite data and guidelines. It is indicative of Foster's logical consistency and loyalty to principle that he did not inject, as McGiffert did, a religious system based on different and unrecognized criteria.

The only constant at work in this approach to religious knowledge, providing validity to future theologizing and rescuing it from nihilism, was a concentration on what Foster called "Christianity," those ideas dealing with sin, salvation, and the new life. In that way he singled out an area that might be termed "awareness of recon-

47. Foster, *The Modern Movement,* p. 144.
48. Ibid., p. 170.
49. Foster, "The Theology of the New Rationalism," p. 413. See also the indicative statement made in "The Christology of a Modern Rationalist," p. 598: "The rational Christology becomes a Christology of values, and will prove more effective than the old, we may hope, in helping humanity on to a more intimate fellowship with God, a loftier morality, and a more abundant service to man."

ciliation" as the realm for greatest emphasis and fruitful understanding of humanity—ancient and medieval as well as modern.[50]

The experience of man is his real religion, and, since theology is the
attempt to explain and justify that religion, its subject matter is Christian
experience. . . . Thoroughgoing radicalism will, therefore, clear the way
for a better understanding of what Christianity is, and for a greater display of its spiritual power than has ever been known, since by its prevalence, theology must become *the explanation of Christian experience.*[51]

Emphasizing experience gave the modernist a perspective for achieving a unified metaphysical overview that would be both transhistori-
cal and interdisciplinary. The different scientific, religious, aesthetic,
and political experiences of men in a cultural setting could become
common elements of human life, to be experienced by all others who
wished to enrich their vision of themselves and their world. The use
of experience as a common denominator was also valued by modernists because it resisted any attempt to divide human life into various compartments, allowing some to be oriented toward coping with
mundane affairs and others to seek understanding of supernatural
powers without any necessary connection between the two. Foster's
theologizing did not follow the line of reasoning (which had begun as early as Schleiermacher) that utilized human experience as
grounds for defining religion as an area sui generis. His view of religion as part of human experience was shaped by the scientific assumption that all of life was part of a naturally homogenous totality.
The advantage to his theology was that it provided a single standard,
valuing all knowledge which took man as its topic and the benefit of
man as its goal. In addition to relating separate fields of inquiry, the
modernist's concentration on human experience made it possible to
overlook distinguishing circumstances and to appropriate valuable
ideas from wherever they could be found in different cultures or
earlier historical periods. But an effort to justify his position on
this point caused Foster to reveal a pragmatic existentialism that
proved to be more unhistorical than any scholar we have discussed:

Truth cannot be something which depends upon the existence of the
person who first spoke it to the world, because it is true only as it shines

to the mind by its own light. . . . Though Jesus should be proved never to have existed, the truth which has come down to us, and which we have received because of its own self-evidencing value, and which we have found to work out such great results in the liberation of our spirits . . . it would still be true, and its effects would remain unaltered. In this sense a historical Christ is unnecessary.[52]

This then is the result of the decades Foster spent in search of a theology that could incorporate all phases of human experience and selectively assimilate earlier wisdom with the canons of modern science. The objective and its standards for inclusion are clear, but specific tenets of the new theology, either systematic or practical, never emerged to form a synthesis. Perhaps the stance of "radical rationalism" will come into sharper focus as we see how it actually functioned by providing a pattern for interpreting the data of church history. Of course, Foster claimed that both the research methods and the canons for interpreting historical data were governed by scientific standards. It is the duty of students of historiography to distinguish between investigation and evaluation in order to show how his theological convictions supplemented laboratory accuracy in the historical writing he produced.

FOSTER'S INTERPRETATION OF AMERICAN RELIGIOUS THOUGHT

In 1907 Foster published his most important and lasting historical work, *A Genetic History of the New England Theology.* He began its preparation at Oberlin around 1885 in sympathy with the conservative position of his former champion, Edwards A. Park, but recognizing that his opinions had altered by the time of the book's appearance, he declared himself to be "no longer reckonable to its adherents." Since earlier chapters were allowed to stand as they were written, the *Genetic History* did not benefit from a final revision that might have given it a unified interpretation written from a consistent point of view. The end result unfortunately included varying interpretations. For example, early in the writing Foster expressed his belief that the doctrines of Jonathan Edwards had received divine sanction;[53] but by the time the book reached final form he an-

---

52. Foster, "The Christology of a Modern Rationalist," p. 587–88.
53. Foster, *Genetic History,* pp. 3, 47, 49.

nounced himself an indefatigable critic of such traditional views.[54] Despite his eventual disapproval of the ideas and solutions studied, however, Foster never departed from Professor Park's formulation of the issues involved. He relied on Park for a definition of what New England Theology actually was and adopted the latter's conception that problems of atonement, freedom of the will, and possibilities for human virtue were crucial to its history.[55] The *Genetic History*, then, embodies Foster's remarkable process of theological metamorphosis, but it never completely abandoned its dependence on Professor Park for several controlling ideas.[56]

The lasting impression made by this history of New England Calvinism is similar to that of a classical tragedy. Once begun on their fateful way, the events followed an inexorable cycle toward destruction because of "forces" at work in history and because truly admirable individuals possessed flaws of judgment that doomed them to ineffectiveness.[57] And though he usually viewed events with the unforgiving eyes of a modernist, Foster wrote at times with the wistfulness of one who hoped the result might have been other than its tragic denouement. One fundamental lesson which Foster drew from studying the entire episode was that subsequent theologians should avoid the mistakes made by their predecessors. Perhaps it was a distinctly American characteristic to wish to move beyond pity and terror as the more classical consequences of tragedy, to utilize that

54. Ibid., p. 470.
55. On p. vi of the *Genetic History* Foster acknowledged that Park had supplied "the dogmatic point of view of the whole period." In a more open statement (p. 269) he said that his history, "but for the light which Professor Park's work [threw] upon it, could not have been written. It is his completing work which shows the meaning of the course of the whole school." Foster's chapter on Park (pp. 477 ff.) was a careful report on a full set of classroom notes, and the chief value of the chapter is that it preserves Park's ideas from obscurity. The historian of ideas may resort to one of Park's essays and see how accurately Foster related the old master; see E. A. Park, "New England Theology," *Bibliotheca Sacra* 9 (January 1852): 170–220.
56. In his significant contribution to this area, Brockmann, "Frank Hugh Foster," pp. 5–7, 11, indicates that Foster's admiration for Park involved primarily an approbation of his method rather than acceptance of Park's theological system. While such an observation is an accurate assessment of Foster's priorities and of the relationship in general, it should be supplemented at least to the extent of noting that Foster accepted Park's definitions as guidelines within which he was content to work.
57. Foster, *Genetic History*, p. 47.

catharsis by adding a resolution for more discerning action in the future.

The conception of a "genetic" study of history was not striking as a new or significant idea at the time of Foster's publication, but it does indicate his special conception of science. The meaning of the term intended by him was simply that there was development and change in the history of ideas. While introducing the study he observed that "an adequate history cannot . . . be mere annals, a 'chronicle,' an unconnected heap of opinions. A history of doctrine is not the same thing as a register of discordant and meaningless theories. Ideas grow. . . . A true history must therefore be genetic. Ideas in their genesis, their growth, and their fruit are its theme."[58] In the last analysis, "genetic history" involved nothing more than standard assumptions about the organic relation between past and present life.

Drawing on biological metaphors, Foster outlined four broad stages of organic historical development: construction, systematization, corruption, and restoration. He thought those stages could be applied to early New England thought as well as to continental Lutheranism or Calvinism in other settings.[59] Though he was never explicit about how the four stages applied in a precise way to thinkers in his study, Foster seemed to think that Jonathan Edwards represented the constructive stage, while Samuel Hopkins, Nathaniel W. Taylor, and Edwards A. Park worked to perfect its systematization. Then suddenly and almost without warning, corruption set in. Restoration never occurred.[60] There is some confusion here because at another point Foster seems to say that all his thinkers, from the elder Edwards to Park, represented the fourth stage.[61] At any rate Foster was not content to describe the fall of Edwardean theology by appealing to such loose generalizations. More specifically, he saw its demise resulting from inconsistencies in the system itself as well as from a series of strong assaults from the outside. The inner weak-

58. Ibid., pp. 9–10.
59. Ibid., pp. 6–8.
60. Ibid., p. 543. Perhaps the fourth stage was posited while Foster was still an adherent of some Calvinistic persuasion. As a liberated rationalist he might have dispensed with restoration as an unwanted category.
61. Ibid., pp. 10–11.

nesses made it impossible to defend the system from deft theological attack, and so the body of ideas crumbled under the simultaneous pressures of decay and frontal opposition. At times Foster spoke as if he thought the doctrinal system could have been saved, if theologians had made as logical and coherent a synthesis of the various parts as he would have constructed. But the chief protagonists in the drama were never able to resolve inherent difficulties, and the vigorous theology died like a lion in a net.[62]

Foster conceived of historical analysis primarily as a search for ideas that could survive through the ages. His researches along that line disclosed that the chief difficulty in New England Theology was a tension between two of its parts, apparent since the days of President Edwards. Edwards had emphasized "the absolute and universal dependence of the redeemed upon God as the cause, and only proper cause, of all their good."[63] But while stressing God's grace, power, and direct agency so heavily, Foster was convinced that Edwards had left humanity utterly unable to affect their condition; his doctrine of election thus destroyed that modicum of self-respect that is an essential element in virtuous conduct.[64] Edwards had been so eager to retain divine sovereignty in his system, he considered human inability a consequence worth accepting and worth defending against Arminians and optimistic humanists. But Foster deemed Edwards's arguments against free will a "logical failure," even while noting that such a stern position had helped "bring the theology of New England back to Calvinism" during the days of the Second Great Awakening.[65] As Edwards's theological system stood, Foster judged it to be sadly out of order and unproductive, but he saw the possibility of a distinction between natural and moral ability in human ac-

62. Ibid., pp. 225, 240, 248.
63. Ibid., p. 51.
64. One should notice at this juncture that Foster misunderstood Edwards's use of the categories of "will" and "virtue." Brockmann ("Frank Hugh Foster," pp. 19–23) has demonstrated this at length. In addition to that valuable analysis, Brockmann has brought to light a statement (used on pp. 41–42 and 295–96) which Foster made when he was sixty years of age. He admitted then that his personal convictions had occasionally prevented him from understanding the precise meaning of ideas at variance with his own.
65. Foster, Genetic History, pp. 75, 77. In a less guarded statement, Foster called Edwards's emphasis on divine sovereignty at the expense of human freedom "a travesty of the Gospel." See his essay, "Zwingli's Theology, Philosophy and Ethics," in Huldreich Zwingli: The Reformer of German Switzerland, 1484–1531, ed. S. M. Jackson (New York: G. P. Putnam's Sons, 1900), pp. 392–93.

tivities which actually occurred later and provided fruitful ground for Edwardean systematizers.

Samuel Hopkins expanded Edwards's theory of volition by distinguishing between regeneration and conversion. This distinction made it possible to hold the strict principle that a sovereign God regenerated men without their help, while at the same time it allowed one to say they took some of the initiative in conversion. Foster was in basic agreement because he thought Hopkins's distinction placed human ability in its "proper place," and rightly taught free men that "conversion was their own work, and that they could . . . repent, believe, and be saved."[66] New England theologians were thus provided with a rationale for revival preaching and energetic activism corresponding to opportunities in the new world. The intellectual dexterity of Calvinists during the Awakening period also ensured the eminence of their ideas for yet another generation. But Foster criticized them for failing to make a more thorough break with outmoded doctrines, lamenting the fact that flaws in their judgment caused them to retain an uneasy allegiance to ideas about God's absolute sovereignty and election. He also chided them for insisting on a particular view of the atonement, one that held redemption had been brought about by Christ's suffering. He thought such a theory was largely accountable for recurring threats about everlasting punishment for human sin.[67]

Nathaniel W. Taylor departed even further from Edwards's theory of the will by arguing that man's moral depravity was not created in him as an innate tendency or disposition to sin. For Taylor, a man's sinfulness was a product of his "own act, consisting in a free choice of some object other than God, as his chief good."[68] That explanation seemed more satisfactory to Foster because it avoided saying God decreed sinful acts in the lives of his creatures, while at the same time it made man a free agent who could choose for himself and possibly attain Christian virtue. To be sure, Taylorism admitted that God's creating men as moral agents necessarily involved the possibility that sin might occur; one could still say God

66. Foster, *Genetic History*, p. 184.
67. Ibid., pp. 258–59.
68. From Taylor's 1828 sermon, "Concio ad Clerum," in Foster, *Genetic History*, p. 370.

was the "cause" of everything, including evil. But the indirect divine activity did not make sin inevitable. By the means of such distinctions and subtle argumentation Taylor attempted to preserve God's perfections and still hold that men could act on their own initiative. Foster thought Taylor made his greatest contribution to revitalizing theology when he "vindicated the freedom of the will, and made this to reside in a true power of original causation."[69] During his long and influential career at Yale, Taylor contributed to other areas of New England thought as well, but in Foster's view of the history of the system, he was important because he led directly to Edwards A. Park.

As "the greatest representative of the unmodified New England strain," Professor Park finally succeeded in arranging Edwardean theology, as it had come to him, into a system of almost perfect symmetry and cogency. But, since he already knew the end would not be long in coming, Foster was forced to observe that one tragic, fatal flaw remained. Park brought the full force of his insight and systematizing ability to bear on the theology he inherited, but he had been unable to fashion a true union of its components. The most insurmountable obstacle facing him was, as it always had been in Foster's estimation, a "failure to compose the strife between the idea of liberty . . . that of the nature of virtue, and its [the system's] theory of the will."[70] Despite the respect he always held for his former professor and champion, Foster was compelled to admit that Park was an anomaly in his later years.[71] But even then he did not condemn Park, as he had others, for ignoring recent developments in psychology and natural science which might have aided his theology. At times he deplored Park's lack of attention to scientific advances and regretted his reliance on outmoded Edwardean conceptions, but he ended by praising his system as cogent (his highest accolade) and forceful.[72] In the last analysis, though, the modernist in Foster forced him to conclude by observing that Park's attempt was destined to fail because no effort of will or intellect could "free Calvinism, while it still retained its characteristic features, from the paralyzing load of inability."[73] Such statements as this indicate a

69. Ibid., pp. 399–400.
70. Ibid., p. 539.
71. Ibid., p. 511.
72. Ibid., p. 524.
73. Ibid., p. 540.

major weakness in Foster's own treatment of the history of ideas. He deserves attention and credit for pioneering in that new field, but he failed to reach a mature understanding of causal relationships. His poor explanations of important developments—especially his inability to account for the total collapse of orthodox Calvinism as it apparently reached its highest expression in Park's system—never afforded a thorough or realistic comprehension of the facts involved. Foster's books may be valued as compendia of earlier theological treatises, but not as analyses of the historical forces which produced them.

There was another element, added to its manifest logical weakness, that eventually brought New England Theology to earth. A series of controversies arising in the 1820s revealed most orthodox theologians to be rather dull and unable to defend themselves in open discussion. Foster thought their resulting panic and rigidity lost them respect and adherents. From a historian's perspective in 1907 it was plain to see that the Unitarian controversy had been "by far the most important event in the history of Congregational theology."[74] Faced with the challenge of explaining a unified Godhead that incorporated three distinctive natures, New England theologians never achieved a lucidity acceptable to contemporary or later critics. Foster, ever vigilant to mark the latest victim in wars of attrition, concluded that excessive debate had reduced Trinitarian doctrines to abstractions. Eventually such abstractions lost their place in the Edwardean system, and thinkers became embarrassed by their presence. As vestiges of a once-vigorous past, they came to be regarded as "a burden upon the system of Christianity."[75] Most orthodox defenses of Trinitarian views fought their way back to the last trench, a literal interpretation of Scripture, and did not provide effective answers for the many questions following a serious consideration of the nature of Christ. Arguments reiterating proof-texts did not give adequate thought to questions about God's benevolence, human freedom, or the exact nature of the atonement, that is, all the questions Foster deemed urgent in the modern setting. His view was that the orthodox were really beaten in the Unitarian controversy because they lacked the logical rigor to think out their position: "Not

74. Ibid., p. 281.
75. Ibid., p. 300.

all points were clear; not all antitheses as sharp as later. . . . Hence their reply, when they were first attacked, was bungling, confused, and largely ineffective. . . . the favorable moment . . . of pointing out what was extreme in the positions of the Unitarians, and thus of winning them back to the evangelical theory, was lost."[76] Foster's summary opinion was that New England Theology continually lost prestige in the eyes of nineteenth-century religious men because as a system it was hopelessly confused, outdated, and unable to understand or defend its own ideas.

Foster concentrated on the decay of Calvinism in the *Genetic History*, but in his later book, *The Modern Movement in American Theology*, he discussed its decline in a broader context—one similar to, but no more satisfying than, Walker's earlier attempt. Following the direction in which his own interests had led him, he condemned orthodox theologians for not appreciating the significance of scientific discoveries. Foster even charged them with failure to accept Copernican astronomy. That remark must have struck descendants of members of the Royal Society as a curious charge for a historian to make. Nevertheless, rapid advances in sociology, psychology, and historical research had created a new climate of opinion, and New England Calvinists were judged culpable of a failure to assimilate the new knowledge.[77] After using history to show that such a backward-looking theology was no longer entitled to his allegiance, Foster gave a parting glance at the position he once held, now reduced to a state of stagnation. The final judgment, substantiated by events, read like an epitaph: "Perhaps they were merely too incurably conservative. . . . the pitiless logic of facts quietly swept the propounders of such a new theology as Andover had to offer [Park's improved system] aside, and the great current of investigation and discovery went on, neither helped by them nor hindered."[78]

Foster began writing the *Genetic History* with the intention that his readers might familiarize themselves with a great theological tradition and "appropriate its good and . . . avoid its evil."[79] But he became less hopeful in the years after 1906 as his increasing

76. Ibid., pp. 282–83.
77. Foster, *Modern Movement*, pp. 11–13.
78. Ibid., pp. 3–31.
79. Foster, *Genetic History*, pp. vi–vii.

rationalism depended less and less on a study of the past. By the time he wrote sections of *The Modern Movement*, published post-humously in an age which no longer provided a context for his thought, he had reached such an extreme position that he criticized most liberals for not rejecting old conceptions as quickly as he had done. Indeed much of the book points up ways in which modern thinkers had failed to approximate the "true liberalism" that Foster had acquired. Thus a study of history allowed at least one serious intellectual to come full circle, back to the task of constructing a unified metaphysics that would be both cognizant of the past and re-sponsible to the present. The history of religious thought had its place in providing the basis for acquiring a comprehensive perspective, one that comprised "nothing more than the persistent search for the truth. . . . We have found some failures in the efforts of the think-ers we have been studying. Their great failure is but one, lack of thoroughness, and this we ascribe to their conservatism. They have generally failed to face all the facts."[80] Foster's historical writings as well as his polemic publications reveal a lifelong attempt to face the facts as he saw them. And it was his view of the facts, together with attempts to construct a natural theology on the basis of scien-tific data, that effectively distinguished his work from earlier his-torical studies of religious thought.

The end result of such a plan of historical study brought one to the same general conclusions that religious thinkers reached when they used human experience as a common denominator for relevant information. In both historical and psychological studies, Foster wished the reflective thinker to go "back to the facts, . . . to the grim facts of the actual world" because only then could liberals "go forward to a new consideration of these facts and to a new formula-tion of truth in relation to them."[81] Thus the facts and one's experi-ence of them coincided to facilitate an inductive process of coping with the natural world in which men existed. Foster's theological and historiographical procedures were obviously congruent with the atti-tudes produced in the age of science, including those of iconoclasm, empiricism, and naturalism. He hoped his critical and thoroughgoing radicalism would "clear the way for a better understanding of what

80. Foster, *Modern Movement*, p. 213.
81. Ibid., p. 214.

Christianity is, and [prepare] for a greater display of its spiritual power,"[82] but he left the question open as to what that new under-standing would be. At times he hoped the ageless truths of reconcilia-tion, forgiveness, and brotherhood could be preserved.[83] But at other times he seemed to doubt that ideals fashioned in the age of science could be made to resemble traditional Christianity.[84] He never doubted that modern religion would rest ultimately on the rational treatment of empirical fact and that it would be the better for it.

82. Ibid., p. 105.
83. Ibid., p. 147.
84. Ibid., p. 95.

9 ♂OVERVIEW

The decades between 1870 and 1920 were ones in which significant historiographical ideas developed in this country. Largely through the initiative of a small group of German-trained scholars, a new conception of the proper method and legitimate goals of historical inquiry came into prominence. The new approach to historical materials followed the practical example of critical European scholarship, but it drew its inspiration from the marvelous advances made by modern science. The name "scientific history" does not indicate the origins of new research techniques as much as it connotes an admiration for the values and attitudes fostered in scientific inquiry. While there was no single standard for defining scientific history, and no nationally acclaimed theoretician to give it systematic expression, the central ideas of that general scheme are clear. Scientific history, as it was understood by Herbert Baxter Adams and other founders of the American Historical Association, comprised three basic points. They were an iconoclastic attitude toward earlier historical narratives, especially toward the romanticized literary efforts of the previous generation; a professed objectivity that tried to exclude all presuppositions from the historian's mind as he began research and to prevent his reading into the record anything disallowed by the evidence; a naturalistic understanding of the evidence that held all possible explanations to a single, homogenous world of measurable phenomena and denied appeals to unnatural or miraculous intervention. This cluster of ideas and attitudes came to be accepted by a great many historians during the last decades of the nineteenth century. These historians wanted to pattern their work after the leading ideas and activities of their age. Their numerical strength gave weight to the popular notion that there was only one proper approach to historical research and writing. General guidelines for critical historical scholarship became accepted slowly, and the new rubrics for respectable work were exemplified by the research accomplished in university seminars and in the papers read at annual sessions of the AHA.

Studies in the field of church history during the 1870s and 1880s were conducted by men whose priorities were shaped largely by theological considerations. Materials related to the historical experience of Christian churches were considered by most of them to require theological evaluation for proper assimilation. Volumes written in that area were intended primarily to enrich the patterns of a religious world view and to heighten the level of one's devotional life. More to the point, the unique fact that the church was a divine institution made it necessary for historians to conduct their historical inquiries in a manner different from those confined exclusively to earthly subject matter. Since God was confessed to be directly involved with the activities of his appointed representative, any history of that institution seemed inadequate without references to him as one of the chief factors at work in its life. The leading spokesman of that viewpoint was Philip Schaff, and his tremendous erudition and scholarly publications lent a great deal of prestige to such a historiographical plan. When he died in 1893, there were no sympathizers of sufficient ideological scope, intellectual power, or productive capacity to succeed him. Traditional arguments as to the uniqueness of church history and the special ends that it could serve seem to have entered a serious decline by 1895.

Philip Schaff was the most important figure active in founding the American Society of Church History, and his ideas about the profession were congruent with his hopes for the work of the organization. The ASCH was not, however, the instrument of one man or the vehicle of a single point of view. One of the broad conclusions of this study is that none of the various historiographical ideas held by influential thinkers of the period assumed an institutional form. There were many differences of opinion both between and among secular and religious historians, but there was no organizational entrenchment and no attempt to perpetuate a point of view by collective means. Nevertheless, Schaff's death in 1893 and the dissolution of the ASCH in 1896 marked the end of an era. Debates on the general subject continued, but no one after Schaff supported a dichotomy between church history and other kinds of history *on methodological grounds* as eloquently as he.

It would be claiming too much to conclude that scientific history and its supporters outperformed or argued down those committed to the goal of writing a different kind of history on religious subjects. There were no open controversies over questions of method, admissible evidence, the legitimate uses of historical knowledge, or the exact nature of different historical topics. And since there were no contests, one cannot expect to find conclusive results. But in the main, the prevalence of church historians like Emerton, Walker, McGiffert, and Foster indicates that a trend away from Schaffian conceptions was taking place. To be sure, these later historians differed among themselves as to proper methods and goals within their discipline, but the collective weight of their influence leads to the conclusion that a watershed in intellectual history had been passed. Science provided the context in which men adopted a new orientation toward their craft. Dominant historiographical ideas in the latter part of the nineteenth century were formed in a scientific milieu, and they greatly affected historians of the church as well as students of other phenomena. The end result was a greater compatibility of methodological procedures and more cooperative interaction between what had originally been conceived as separate disciplines.

This limited study has been conducted in a manner that concentrated primarily on methodological considerations. The ideas expressed in this area deal not simply with questions of method; they also afford considerable insight into respective views regarding the nature of history and of historical cognition. One of the lasting values of such an analysis is to understand how a selected number of historians dealing with a specific conceptual problem brought out the basic issues confronting every practicing historian. Their answers did not resolve the issues, and we may not remain content with their solutions, but it is instructive to see how men faced perennial problems and, in their various ways, came to terms. Such a methodological analysis could be constructed to view the effect of Marxian convictions on historiographical procedure. It could be made sensitive to the political sympathies of particular historians or to some overarching conceptual pattern like the significance of frontier conditions, the importance of sea power, the effects of capitalism, the importance of demographic distribution as worthy of more attention than individual efforts. All such theses have emerged in American historiography, and each could be analyzed by the basic questions brought to light in this volume. It would be a relatively simple task to replace "providence" with an appeal to "dialectical materialism" (or any of a number of theses) and see how that world view influenced the work of historians. The problem of church history vis-à-vis other kinds of history has been chosen because, in addition to its providing instructive comparisons of the sort already mentioned, it provides another element as well. The historian's religious orientation inevitably plays a part in his research procedure and finished publications. An analysis of his works sheds light not only on his interpretation of men in historical contexts, it also demonstrates how each was able to reconcile his religious concerns with those canons of professional conduct he felt obliged to follow.

The major questions applied in this study have pivoted on the possible uniqueness of church history among other types of history shaped in the age of science. The general tendency among most thinkers after 1876 was to deny that such a specialized category had a legitimate basis on which to employ special methods not acknowledged by the historian's guild. The publications of many post-Shaffian church historians did not actually reflect the new resolution, but in theory at least, scientific procedure dictated that faith assumptions and rational inquiry be separated, confined to mutually independent spheres of activity. Another means of analyzing this material could concentrate on the various ways in which historians used language in their narratives, attempting thereby to define the general effect they wished to achieve. A great deal could be illuminated by discovering whether a historian was employing language as a mode of poetic expression or as a matter-of-fact means of scientific reporting, whether he wished to create empathy for his subject or rather coldly to relate information pertinent to its essential features. The student of historical writing might try to ascertain the results an author wanted to produce, whether he hoped to move his readers to action along a predetermined line or simply to provide them with accurate data. If it were the former goal, it would shed some light on the historian's conclusions if one could determine whether he intended to encourage unstinted service to an ecclesiastical organization or to arouse citizens and urge contributions that might improve the social setting of all residents. The uses of language are many, and the possible modes of inquiry in this field invite further research.

Another point of departure for exploring historiographical patterns during this period could stay within the question of theological priorities and view major changes from that perspective. The viewpoint developed in this study discloses that there seems to have been a conflict between religious assumptions about providential activity in history and the new scientific orientation which precluded such unsupportable claims. The results of that tension were detrimental to the significance of religious presuppositions whenever historians tried to rely on them in producing satisfactory causal explanations. Yet in a larger context perhaps the changing emphases among church historians might be understood within a methodological framework in religion, not historiography. Decisions regarding the impropriety of old categories about divine providence, spiritual agencies, and the preeminence of confessional standards might be symptoms of a more fundamental shift in theological procedure all along the line. The debate among church historians over a priori theological standards and empirical objectivity might be understood as one segment of a more widespread search for a basis on which to make convincing and authoritative religious pronouncements in the scientific age. There is enough validity in this hypothesis to caution against overemphasizing the religious-secular, confessional-empirical contrasts among historians. The apparent dichotomy in some of these men should be understood in its own light, but one should also not lose sight of the possibility that each of them might have been able to go between the horns of their dilemma rather than choose one side and abandon the other. Even in the case of Emerton this seems to have occurred. No church historian in this study adopted scientific methods and jettisoned all faith assumptions; rather each constructed his theological orientation to correlate his profession and his religious principles. In comparison with Schaff's earlier definition of the issues, there was a definite conflict. But with the different conceptions of religious authority and theological method held by later guildsmen, there was no rupture with a consequent one-sided predominance of theology or science. Since 1895 most church historians have been unwilling to place much emphasis on providential activity, but part of the reason might be that their theological (as well as their historiographical) convictions did not lead them to think in those terms. More research is needed to account for the origins of that theological preference among members of the ASCH.

One should not form an impression that the specific problems studied in these essays were resolved at the turn of this century. The issues considered by those earlier thinkers are very much a part of the self-criticism and careful procedure that mark the reflective publications of historians today. Scientific history, despite its initial popularity, remained an unfulfilled ideal. The search for a more realistic conception of factual evidence, and the historian's function in relation to it, has since gone in many directions. By the time Charles A. Beard and Carl L. Becker added their weight against the old conception of objective facts and impersonal methods, another chapter in historiographical thinking had begun. But in the new phase of discussions, the task of defining church history as part of, or as generically different from, other historical inquiries has not ended.[1] In the intervening years there have been some shifts of emphasis, some new presuppositions have entered, and different working syntheses have emerged as assimilations of new intellectual contexts. But despite the major changes that have taken place in historical investigations, a fundamental crisis of identity has remained at the core of church history. More research might very well be concentrated on patterns of historiographical thought that appeared between 1920 and 1960.

At this juncture it would be difficult to give a detailed projection of the work that needs to be done in this area. One major change requiring analysis is the gradual decline of scientific objectivity as an ideal among historians. Observers of both religious and secular phenomena have finally realized that an unbiased history, written without presuppositions, is epistemologically untenable and a practical impossibility. By the 1920s or shortly thereafter most American historians came to the conclusion that there is no universally applicable scientific method that could be used without regard to the in-

1. This has been a perennial theme among church historians for the past fifty years. Some of the more striking contributions to the debate are the following: James H. Nichols, "Church History and Secular History," *Church History* 13 (June 1944); see also his essay, "The Art of Church History," *Church History* 20 (March 1951); W. Pauck, "The Idea of the Church in Christian History," *Church History* 21 (September 1952); and L. J. Trinterud, "The Task of the American Church Historian," *Church History* 25 (March 1956).

trinsic characteristics of varying subjects. Once the process of historical investigation and interpretation was considered on its own merits, it was found that rational inquiry always involved presuppositions and provisional hypotheses. As one participant stated the self-conscious reaction to the old format, "all historical inquiry is, by definition, . . . 'prejudiced' from the very start—prejudiced because directed. . . . Only in the context of a guided inquiry do the sources speak, . . . 'things' become 'sources,' only when they are . . . exorcised by the inquisitive mind of the historian. . . . Observation itself is impossible without some interpretation, that is, understanding."[2] The historiographically important observation is that the scholar's conception of specific historical problems and his interpretation of data selected as relevant to them are formed within a contemporary framework. That framework, constructed of basic ideas and values which the historian has appropriated, affords a set of working principles for continuing inquiries into the past.[3] It is no longer feasible to argue that historians simply assemble data and let the facts speak for themselves.[4] Evidence must be selected and presented according to some criterion, and that selection "necessarily involves a certain choice of allegiance, an act of faith in one kind of future rather than another. . . ." The historian is a product of the circumstances which fostered his principles, that is, "the history-that-happens itself generates the faiths and allegiances that furnish the principles for selecting what is important in understanding it."[5] The logical direction away from the old frame of mind and its preference for scientific metaphors was to conclude that written his-

2. G. Florovsky, "The Predicament of the Christian Historian," in *Religion and Culture: Essays in Honor of Paul Tillich,* ed. Walter Leibrecht (New York: Harper & Brothers, 1959), p. 144; see also p. 152.

3. For an able and sophisticated treatment of all the nuances of this subject, see Van A. Harvey, *The Historian and the Believer: The Morality of Historical Knowledge and Christian Belief* (New York: Macmillan Co., 1966), pp. 98, 111, 113, 121.

4. C. L. Becker, "What Are Historical Facts?" is probably the best-known example of this line of reasoning. See a recent reprint in Hans Meyerhoff, ed., *The Philosophy of History in Our Time* (Garden City: Doubleday & Co., Anchor Books, 1959), especially p. 130.

5. Taken from J. H. Randall, Jr., and G. Haines, IV, "Controlling Assumptions in the Practice of American Historians," *Theory and Practice in Historical Study: A Report of the Committee on Historiography,* Bulletin 54 (New York: Social Science Research Council, 1946); in S. E. Mead, "Church History Explained," *Church History* 32 (March 1963): 22.

tories are inevitably based upon the allegiances or faith of the historians who produce them.

The continuum employed in the present study will be of no use in subsequent analyses because it is unclear what issues and which priorities divided historians in the years after 1920. Thinkers like Schaff had argued that the subject matter of church history warranted special methods of dealing with it, but scientific historians viewed all topics as parts of a single, human story. This leveling effect was one of the major consequences of the 1876–1918 period, and that general pattern did not change. But the reason originally given for refusing church history a special place (scientific objectivity was applicable to all topics) gradually lost its hold over practicing historians. Most of the new methodological syntheses which took its place reaffirmed the conception of church history as an integral part of historical studies. If all historians are admitted to have allegiances or a faith that gives a particular quality to the work of each individual, then they are to be distinguished by *which* allegiances they have.[6] It is no longer possible to divide historical scholars along methodological lines into groups that "read their presuppositions into the evidence" and a group whose objectivity allowed it to rise above that suspect practice. After 1920 it was admitted that such objectivity was impossible and that all historians came within the former category. Within this wide expanse of relativity and mutual acceptance, however, the problem of reaching a critical self-understanding was still an urgent one.

Many church historians have continued to wrestle with the question of how their chosen topic is to be maintained in the general context of historical studies. A great deal more research needs to be conducted in order to define patterns of church history in the age of relativism, but a few general tendencies may be noted. Most historians of ecclesiastical activity would agree that their "chief business . . . is the re-collection and representation of selected segments of the human past in an intelligible narration based on public data verified by scientific observation."[7] But continuous efforts

6. Mead, "Church History Explained," pp. 22–23; see also Florovsky, "Predicament of the Christian Historians," p. 156.

7. A. C. Outler, "Theodosius' Horse: Reflections on the Predicament of the Church Historian," *Church History* 34 (September 1965): 253; italics omitted.

have been made to define more intelligibly the characteristics of a plausible historical narrative. Many would now agree that a satisfactory result of investigation should supply an interplay between narration and interpretation, that is, to use critically acceptable data as a means of trying to understand the human spirit behind the cold facts. The evidence seems to indicate that many historians in the past half-century have agreed that historical explanation includes an assessment of the ideas and motives of those involved in the activities being studied. As one scholar recently put it: "The actions of people are explained by pointing to the motives that lie back of them. The study of what people said they thought they were doing is the study of their conception of why they were doing it as they did—that is, of their motives. The ascertainment of motives is the chief goal of historical studies because our understanding of the people of the past depends upon our understanding of what motivated them."[8]

Another church historian worked toward the same conclusion, using terminology some historians are reluctant to accept. If the word "metahistorical" is understood to include those aspects of an interpretation that derive more from the historian than from the data, semantic difficulties should not obscure the clarity of his argument. The reasoning is that the historian's business is to represent the human past and that in accomplishing this task "metahistorical judgments are inescapable—[involving] comments that exceed the warrants of verifiability. . . ." To continue, it is "specifically as historians, [that] we are bound to have convictions about what makes history possible and meaningful." Any such convictions "regularly focus on the presuppositions and implications of the historian's recognition that history and metahistory are vitally interdependent."[9] Some church historians have accepted these results of modern his-

8. Mead, "Church History Explained," pp. 19–20. Florovsky ("Predicament of the Christian Historian," p. 155) stated it this way: "No historian can, even in his limited and particular field, within his own competence, avoid raising ultimate problems of human nature and destiny, unless he reduces himself to the role of a registrar of empirical happenings, and forfeits his proper task of 'understanding.' "

9. Outler, "Theodosius' Horse," pp. 257–58. On p. 257 he also makes the observation that "the notion of 'providence' has simply dropped below the mental horizon of modern historiography. In its place, we have a baffling array of metahistorical notions that are consistent only in their common anthropocentrism. At their best, these anthropocentrisms are illuminating. In general, however, they amount to so many pseudo-scientific substitutes for discarded religious beliefs."

toriographical thought and have fashioned new arguments for defining their topic as a special segment of historical inquiry. Basing their new ideas on the newly recognized similarity of methods, some church historians have begun arguing that their choice of topic places them somewhat apart. The metahistorical judgments required in any plausible history of earlier ecclesiastical patterns gives some integrity to their being considered a distinct branch within a common discipline.

One of the most interesting observations regarding this issue is that, while a great number of church historians have discussed the matter between 1920 and 1960, no viewpoint has carried the debate, and no identifiable nexus of ideas has attracted many self-conscious adherents. This can be explained in part by the fact that scores of historians practice their craft without giving much thought to questions of procedure. But even among those who have seriously confronted the task of defining the essential qualities of church history and of distinguishing their branch from related topics—there has been little agreement on methods, priorities, or objectives. There is almost universal agreement now that "the assumptions on which the church historian used to function are no longer valid. His discipline developed at a time when it was a commonly held assumption that the church was a unique institution grounded in the supernatural and fulfilling a transcendent will in history. The church had a special role in society, and so it had a special history."[10] Once that solid body of ideas was removed, a vacuum was created, and nothing approaching its stature has taken its place. It is significant, however, that many insist on keeping the question open and try to fill the vacuum rather than abandoning it entirely.

Most church historians now hold that plausible accounts of topics in their field cannot be concluded without appreciable knowledge of basic Christian convictions. Such knowledge is necessary to compare faith and practice, to measure institutions against their professed ideals, and both categories are recognized as essential to a full historical account. There seems to be no quarrel with the assertion that the church historian must be competent in the critical methods

10. Jerald C. Brauer, "Changing Perspectives on Religion in America," in *Reinterpretation in American Church History*, ed. Jerald C. Brauer (Chicago: University of Chicago Press, 1968), p. 20.

of his craft and that he be theologically knowledgeable in order fully to understand the story he has to tell. Some would take a stand there and hold that the story itself is enough to make church history a distinct area of study:

The peculiar problem of interpreting church history comes from the historian's obligation to rehearse the Christian past in the light of the Christian world view. . . . The special problem is posed by the Christian community's understanding of its origin, mission, and destiny in the world. . . . Christians generally have attributed this identity and continuity to the action of God in history. . . . Any plausible narrative of any part of this history must proceed with this background in view.[11]

One might respond to such a general position by saying it is no different from that taken by historians who study Marxism, democracy, or any other broad topic where ideological systems and institutions have experienced significant alteration. The basic form of their argument would be the same, and mutual acceptance could result from their appreciation of common procedural problems. At the same time their specific topics would, by definition, be enough to give each of them some sense of independent status. Rehearsing the past of any world view involves an obligation to comprehend that ideology at all stages of its development; the historic strength or contemporary importance of such viewpoints carries its own justification as a topic chosen for study.

There are two general directions taken by modern church historians who wish to explicate more fully the contribution they expect their work to make. One type of church historiography tries to enrich the understanding of a particular cultural setting; the other speaks to those trying to understand the Christian faith and its meaning within cultural settings. The function each group tries to perform emerges as the distinguishing factor. In the former category, church historians use the findings of their research into specific ecclesiastical and theological activities as a basic tool for interpreting the fundamental dynamics of a given culture. A major spokesman of this perspective has discussed it in these terms: "We do not interpret the nature and place of religion in our culture merely by writing

11. Outler, "Theodosius' Horse," p. 258; see also Mead, "Church History Explained," p. 29.

stories about the development of religious institutions where 'secular' historians write similar stories of voluntary associations, and of political, economic, or military institutions, but by assessing the place religious beliefs and convictions played in affecting what men did in all their societies, and in their political, economic, and military activities."[12]

The other tendency in modern church historiography seems to be less confined to institutions in cultural environments and more interested in assessing the meaning of religion itself. This latter group of scholars claims that the church is an institution in society, no different from others which play some role in mundane affairs. The study of churches as social institutions is declared open to the research of general historians, and they conclude that there is nothing special about such an inquiry. In contrast to the commonplace, these church historians define their proper topic to be "a dimension of human experience not covered by fellow historians," thereby hoping to preserve an area of study that gives them unique status. The distinguishing feature becomes "the particular dimension of human experience with which the church historian functions." Since the study of institutional activities is not relevant to their conception of meaningful church history, they argue that "we can speak only of historians of Christian religion. At this point the church historian becomes a particular kind of historian—a historian of religion."[13] These two conceptions of the function church history is intended to serve seems to be a major division in historiography today. A short summary of general patterns of thought in this area between 1920 and 1960 might be brought to a close at this point, but one more development must be included.

The problem of faith and reason forces itself on church historians perhaps more than on historians who study other topics be-

12. S. E. Mead, "Reinterpretation in American Church History," in *Reinterpretation in American Church History,* p. 185.
13. Brauer, "Changing Perspectives on Religion in America," pp. 21, 22. On p. 23 he summed it up this way: "If his concern is primarily with an institution taken for granted because of its historical existence, or primarily with abstract ideas in their historical continuity, then such a scholar might well be better off in a history department. He differs not a bit from those fellow historians, and he has nothing distinctive to offer. If the erstwhile church historian sees his essential task as the search to understand the nature of that religious experience called Christianity then he has a special task. His interest in the history of the church is not primarily institutional."

cause it is bound up with the subject matter in a more obvious way. We have already seen how modern historians recognize that the writing of every scholar is shaped according to the beliefs he holds preeminent. In the field of church history students inevitably touch upon Christianity, and they must resolve questions as to how religion affects their thoughts and how their study affects their beliefs. The ramifications involved in this complex set of problems is very much like playing three-dimensional chess where results on one level have implications throughout the system and cannot be easily compartmentalized. Thorough and consistent thinkers insist that the meaning of data verified through scientific methods must be fully thought out and fit into a metaphysical system covering all facets of human experience. Not many want to argue that there is an identifiable set of Christian principles which guide the church historian's procedure. Some hold that there is a fundamental Christian vision of human life and that Christian historians inevitably utilize it as they interpret any aspect of the human past. Still, they are careful to announce that one must be "slow and cautious in detecting the 'providential' structure of actual history." A lasting effect of the 1876–1918 period can be seen in the cautious statement, "Even in the history of the Church 'the hand of Providence' is emphatically hidden." This particular spokesman goes on to confess it would be blasphemous to deny that God is the lord of history, but he does not repeat the nineteenth-century practice of using that faith assumption to draw predetermined conclusions at points of controverted interpretation.[14]

The question of whether there ought to be a reciprocal relationship between beliefs and historical information is one that cannot be avoided. For the past half century church historians have confronted the problem more forthrightly than others in their general profession, but the general difficulty is not confined to their field of inquiry. They have simply made explicit the methodological difficulties inherent in the historian's awesome task; to construct plausible narratives of past experience and to apply them in ways that are relevant to contemporary life. In addition to making a contribution on a general level which includes all types of modern historiography, some church historians suggest that their field may be relevant to con-

14. Florovsky, "Predicament of the Christian Historian," p. 166.

temporary life within the Christian community. One such scholar raises the hope that a critical narrative of the Christian past might convey to its readers a vision of "God's provision and maintenance of the structures and processes of human possibility in the order of creation." While he is careful to state that these ends must be gained without debasing the canons of honest research and evaluation, he holds out for the possibility that "the church in history [can] be delineated, warts and all, with a modesty born of uncertainty and a confidence born of a glimpse of God at work not only in the Scriptures but in all succeeding ages."[15] Another contemporary scholar, impelled to speak because of a basic refusal to avoid the implications of his work, spoke to the issue of history's ultimate value this way:

Granted the assumption that it is the Judeo-Christian religion that has informed our culture, the end of the historian's intellectual quest to understand who and what we most profoundly are, must lead him to the basic precepts of that religion which as Christians we may and do apprehend in faith and celebrate in worship. . . . On these suppositions the paths of both our intellectual and our religious quests lead us to the same point. To the Christian both paths lead to the God preeminently revealed in Jesus Christ, the author of his faith *and* the Lord of all his history.[16]

The debates carried on within the historical guild since the latter part of the nineteenth century have involved fundamental issues regarding the methods and value of human learning. Major points recur under different perspectives as new methods and priorities emerge in our cultural development, but no single viewpoint may be taken as culminating in a final solution. Historiographical analysis can be a valuable study of the ongoing process, as long as it keeps these major issues in view, and church history will be a useful focus for clarifying parts of the problem. The complexity and profundity of writers involved, the various objectives to which they make their work contribute, their honest questions about the meaning of history itself—all these combine to make study in this area a task worth the effort.

15. Outler, "Theodosius' Horse," pp. 260, 261.
16. Mead, "Church History Explained," p. 30.

&APPENDIX
THE AMERICAN SOCIETY
OF CHURCH HISTORY

The American Society of Church History did not serve as the vehicle for changing ideas in church historiography. The history of the institution itself is only tangentially related to major intellectual trends in the latter part of the nineteenth century, but its continued development is not without interest. While the founding of the ASCH and its dissolution after a decade can be understood within a context of differing ideas about the proper approach to writing church history, its reestablishment seems less significant. The reasons for giving the organization a new beginning had no clear connection with methodological considerations. The factors contributing to the emergence of a new ASCH must be made explicit to prevent speculative interpolations and to place events in a more accurate perspective.

On December 27, 1906, after marginal activity for ten years within the cavernous American Historical Association, several members of the small church history division reestablished themselves as a separate and independent organization. The most active figure in that movement was Samuel M. Jackson, secretary of the church historians since 1888 and close friend of the late Philip Schaff. Despite his personal ties with the old order, Jackson was not the intellectual giant or leader of men Schaff had been, and the concerted effort of 1906 did not mark a return to Schaffian principles or to any other unanimous approach regarding problems in church historiography. The revived ASCH differed from its predecessor in its lack of methodological unanimity and its diversity of theological orientations. Many of the strictly "scientific" frame of mind joined; some of the old theological persuasion followed along; vigorous writers who viewed things from new theological positions were there as well. The emergence of a new ASCH as a separate organization indicated a continuing interest in the specialized field of church history, but it did not embody any consensus about the means or ends appropriate to the discipline.

Though they acted for different personal reasons, most members in the new group denied Schaff's well-known ideas about how the study of church history was a unique and religious enterprise. But Schaff's other goals for dedicated practitioners of church historiography—that of furthering church union in the United States and of utilizing traditional creeds for the development of an American theology—were transformed rather than entirely abandoned. Men like McGiffert, Rauschenbusch, and Foster resembled Schaff in their synthesis of theological preconceptions and historical narrative, and they helped sustain an interest in past church activities by concentrating on their readers' commitment to contemporary issues. Many different types of scholarship built around varying interests made themselves felt in the new society, and the diversity of professional opinions made it impossible to return to the format of 1888.

The immediate factor that brought about the reestablishment of a new ASCH, further illustrating its lack of a coherent ideological base, was more the result of emotional conflict than thoughtful conviction. As early as its first meeting in 1888 the ASCH contained members who thought of themselves as working partners with the AHA. Early records indicate that some unidentified church historian even recommended the group merge at once with the larger organization. At the time that suggestion was made, there were no circumstances in the structure of the AHA to discourage such a move. But since the early part of 1889 circumstances had intervened to create an environment that was uncongenial to all historians of the church. So even with the question of conflicting ideologies aside, that change made the 1896 merger a strategic mistake, one that almost ensured the separation which came ten years later. In January, 1889, President Grover Cleveland had signed an act recognizing the AHA as a national organization. The scholarly group was declared a corporation, was encouraged to establish principal offices in the District of Columbia, and was granted the privilege of having its annual reports printed at the government's expense. All such publications routinely went through the office of the secretary of the Smithsonian Institution, and it was that particular circumstance which eventually proved intolerable to the self-appointed leader of church historical interests.

From 1896 to 1906 church historians were faced with the melancholy fact that their papers were not received for publication with the same enthusiasm as essays on other topics. Reasons for that state of affairs lay, officially at least, in the connection the AHA had achieved with the federal government and in the editorial authority delegated by the government to the Smithsonian staff. The assistant secretary at the Smithsonian in charge of editorial duties was Cyrus Adler, a man who took pains to delete everything that was considered "religious matter" from congressional publications. Congress had long been wary of printing discussions about religion at public expense, and Mr. Adler followed the precedent with admirable consistency. Since members of the AHA's church history division produced many papers to be read at each annual meeting, the struggle for getting them published under the auspices of the national organization was a continuing one. Most often it was resolved by a refusal to print any article on a controversial subject that "would perhaps provoke some opposition."[1] Philip Schaff had been asked to present a paper at one early session,[2] and George Park Fisher was elected president of the AHA in 1898. Ephraim Emerton and Williston Walker were able, because of their methodological compatibility, to have some articles published, too, but the relative number of pieces on church history was small. One historian of the day explained the resulting dearth of articles with the wry observation that

the religion of the Hopi or the Ingorrote is deemed a legitimate subject for historical discussion in a scientific publication of the government. Not so the Christian religion. . . . An impartial essay on the Spiritual Franciscans of the thirteenth century . . . would seem to be a perfectly non-explosive compound; but the authorities of the Smithsonian Institution, interpreting the mind of Congress as by long experience they have found it, ruled that such discussions fall outside the line of the *Annual Reports.*[3]

1. Letter from A. H. Clark to H. B. Adams, 22 April 1899, in W. S. Holt, "Historical Scholarship in the United States, 1876–1901: As Revealed in the Correspondence of Herbert Baxter Adams," *JHUS*, 56th ser. (1938), p. 272.

2. Philip Schaff, "Church and State in the United States, or The American Idea of Religious Liberty and its Practical Effects, with Official Documents," *Papers of the AHA* 2 (1888): 391–543.

3. John F. Jameson, "The American Historical Association, 1884–1909," *American Historical Review* 15 (October 1909): 14–15.

Thus church historians were allowed to belong to the AHA but were continuously frustrated in their attempts to publish essays in the weighty *Annual Reports.*[4]

Samuel M. Jackson was provoked to angry outbursts by the state of affairs, and his petulant irascibility destroyed any compromise a more patient and diplomatic individual might have achieved. His pride in the former greatness of church history as a field of study was joined to a considerable amount of self-esteem he thought proper to the status he had attained. These elements proved to be forceful enough to bring the whole controversy out into the open. In 1898 he wrote Herbert Baxter Adams, who was still secretary of the AHA, to protest the apparently uniform policy of excluding topics on church history. His correspondence is worth quoting at length because it reveals how personal pique colored many facets of the interlocking issues:

If my article on the Zwingli country is rejected . . . because it smacks too much of the guide book, or because it is dull . . . or beneath the standard of the A.H.A. I have nothing to say. But if it is rejected because of religious considerations then I protest . . . for there is nothing in it "which would excite any religious animosity." Has it come to this that no member of the A.H.A. is allowed to express the opinion in a governmental publication that Mohammedanism is inferior to Christianity?[5]

In another paragraph Jackson pointed to the futility of pursuing a life of scholarly research that held no promise of possible recognition among fellow practitioners. He flatly declared that such a situation was intolerable to the church history division and foretold separation as the ultimate reprisal against being ignored:

I feel considerable alarm at the rejection of the two papers because it portends the destruction of the Church History section of the Association not only—for if such absolutely colorless papers as . . . mine are unsuited for printing . . . I do not know what will be published and therefore can not ask any one to write for the section—but also is a

---

4. This anxiety over having historical work published can be viewed as added evidence of the vitality among church historians. It also points to a general feeling of equality with general historical studies since the trouble might not have occurred had they still thought of themselves as working in a distinct discipline, producing treatises for selective consumption within denominational circles.

5. Letter from S. M. Jackson to H. B. Adams, 13 June 1898, in the Herbert B. Adams Papers, Johns Hopkins University, Baltimore, Maryland.

blow at Lernfreiheit. Was Dr. Good's paper also rejected? If so then the Church History section is already killed.[6]

The letter ends with a petty invective rarely found among accomplished gentlemen:

But what right has . . . any . . . self-appointed censor to reject a paper which you have sent in?

I think I am entitled to know exactly why the two papers were rejected.

One thing is sure. If the government will not support the Church History section to the extent of printing its papers then it will be withdrawn and the American Society of Church History will be revived.

Why was I deprived of one of my honorary degrees when others were not? E.g. Dr. Faird, Dr. Booth, Sir J. G. Bourinot, Dr. Coe, Dr. Jacobs. They are worthier men but not more betitled than

Very truly yours:
SAMUEL MACAULEY JACKSON[7]

Herbert Adams's answer must have been conciliatory because no break ensued, and Jackson's note four months later indicated how gratified he was to receive assurance that future church history papers would meet fairer treatment. But at the same time he could not refrain from dropping another acid comment regarding "the apparently self constituted printing house censor."[8]

Attempts at conciliation proved to be ineffectual, and the iron logic of circumstances made any lasting or amicable solution impossible. Early in 1899 Jackson, haughty and petulant as ever, wrote Adams another letter filled with peremptory demands and gratuitous invective:

My paper on "Zwingli and the Baptist Party in Zurich" is a chapter in my biography of Zwingli and there I hope it will appear. I had not intended to submit it to Mr. Cyrus Adler's censorship. Dr. Norcross's paper on "Erasmus" will not be published by the Association, nor should it be as it is not scholarly enough.[9] I told Dr. Richards [who wrote a

6. Ibid.
7. Letter from Jackson, June 1898, Adams Papers.
8. Letter from Jackson, 30 October 1898, Adams Papers.
9. The article was published over Jackson's objections. See G. Norcross, "Erasmus, the Prince of the Humanists," *Annual Reports of the American Historical Association for the Year 1898* (Washington, D.C.: Government Printing Office, 1899), pp. 365–80.

treatise on Protestant worship] to send it on and I hope Mr. Adler will kindly allow it to be printed.[10]

If he does not then it will be incumbent upon me to announce to my clerical friends whom I ask to write papers for the Association that their papers will not be published because a Jew says they must not be!

Allow me to call your attention to a rule stating "The programme committee . . . of which the secretary of the (Church History) section shall be ex officio a member, and no such paper will be published without his consent." This clause had been entirely overlooked. I had no part in the programme or publications in 1897 and 1898.[11]

Such was the condition of things at the turn of the century. The AHA continued to work in conjunction with the federal printing house, and the rather one-sided interpretation of governmental publishing policy made by the Smithsonian staff remained in force. To make matters worse Herbert Adams, apparently the one cool head in the entire episode, resigned as secretary of the association in 1900. Without his diplomatic presence the break came soon.

The revival of the ASCH in 1906 appears to have been as much an act of exasperation as it was an attempt to provide more opportunity for research and publication in a scholarly discipline. Led by the fitful Jackson, several former members of the old ASCH reasserted their determination to exist as an independent organization, but they were unable to reach agreement on a standard format to guide future work in the area of church history. Whereas the events of 1896 indicated a general trend in intellectual history, the developments of 1906 afford the historian more modest conclusions. All one can say about the second ASCH is that it had no consensus and that many of the internal divisions and conflicting ideologies were carried over into the new group. In the old ASCH Schaff had sponsored an organization in hopes of furthering certain ideas about historiographical method and ecumenicity. By 1896 that viewpoint and its institutional expression had fragmented into a variety of perspectives, and

10. Jackson's dictation was contravened in both instances because Richards's paper was not printed. The following letter from A. H. Clark of the Smithsonian staff, 22 April 1899, shows the policy still at work: "The Secretary decided to leave out Professor Richards' paper as there was doubt about the advisability of printing it.—It is interesting but would perhaps provoke some opposition" (Adams Papers).
11. Letter from Jackson, 13 February 1899, Adams Papers.

any attempted synthesis in 1906 or later proved an impossible task. That lack of unanimity, however, proved to be a strength rather than a weakness.

The ASCH has continued to exist as a separate professional society to the present day, and it has always maintained within itself a variety of ideas about church history. In 1906 critical church historians such as Emerton and Walker joined the revived ASCH, representing one line of thought which still survives, but they also retained membership in the AHA and felt at ease in both organizations. There were some historians who continued to uphold both the principles and distinctive ideas Schaff had defended so eloquently, but they seem to have constituted a minority as the age of science continued to hold sway. Liberal theologians such as McGiffert continued to function with a more religiously oriented perspective, but no one tried to reestablish the evangelical platform of the earlier period. No single conception has ever dominated all thinkers since the turn of the century, and that open-ended search for truth has produced a great deal of fruitful debate and a beneficial exchange of ideas. The continued vitality of the ASCH during this later era can be taken as evidence of man's interest in religion and his persistence in trying to understand its past.

&BIBLIOGRAPHY

CHAPTER I

Books

Ausubel, Herman. *Historians and Their Craft: A Study of the Presidential Addresses of the American Historical Association, 1884–1945.* New York: Columbia University Press, 1950.

Bassett, John S. *The Middle Group of American Historians.* New York: Macmillan Co., 1917.

Becker, Carl L. *Cornell University: Founders and the Founding.* Ithaca: Cornell University Press, 1943.

Bellot, H. Hale. *American History and American Historians.* London: Athlone Press, 1952.

Burgess, John W. *Reminiscences of an American Scholar: The Beginnings of Columbia University.* New York: Columbia University Press, 1934.

Dunlap, Leslie W. *American Historical Societies, 1790–1860.* Madison, Wisconsin: Privately printed, 1944.

Eliot, Charles W. *Educational Reform: Essays and Addresses.* New York: Century Co., 1901.

Franklin, Fabian. *The Life of Daniel Coit Gilman.* New York: Dodd, Mead & Co., 1910.

Gooch, G. P. *History and Historians in the Nineteenth Century.* New York: Longmans, Green & Co., 1913.

Hall, G. Stanley, ed. *Methods of Teaching History.* Pedagogical Library, vol. 1. Boston: Ginn, Heath and Co., 1883.

Hawkins, Hugh. *Pioneer: A History of the Johns Hopkins University, 1874–1889.* Ithaca: Cornell University Press, 1960.

Herbst, Jurgen. *The German Historical School in American Scholarship: A Study in the Transfer of Culture.* Ithaca: Cornell University Press, 1965.

Hewett, Waterman T. *Cornell University: A History.* 4 vols. New York: University Publishing Society, 1905.

Higham, John, Krieger, Leonard, and Gilbert, Felix, eds. *History.* Englewood Cliffs, N.J.: Prentice-Hall, 1965.

Hinsdale, Burke A. *History of the University of Michigan.* Ann Arbor: Published by the University, 1906.

Hofstadter, Richard, and Smith, Wilson, eds. *American Higher Education: A Documentary History.* 2 vols. Chicago: University of Chicago Press, 1961.

Hutchinson, William T., ed. *The Marcus W. Jernegan Essays in American Historiography.* Chicago: University of Chicago Press, 1937.

Iggers, Georg G. *The German Conception of History: The National Tradition of Historical Thought from Herder to the Present.* Middletown, Conn.: Wesleyan University Press, 1968.

Jameson, John F. *The History of Historical Societies.* Savannah, Ga.: Morning News Print, 1914.

———. *The History of Historical Writing in America.* Boston: Houghton Mifflin Co., 1891.

Kraus, Michael. *A History of American History.* New York: Farrar and Rinehart, 1937.

———. *The Writing of American History.* Norman: University of Oklahoma Press, 1953.

Levin, David. *History as Romantic Art: Bancroft, Prescott, Motley, and Parkman.* Stanford: Stanford University Press, 1959.

Lovejoy, Arthur O. *Essays in the History of Ideas.* Baltimore: Johns Hopkins Press, 1948.

Morison, Samuel E., ed. *The Development of Harvard University since the Inauguration of President Eliot, 1869–1929.* Cambridge, Mass.: Harvard University Press, 1930.

Persons, Stow. *American Minds: A History of Ideas.* New York: Henry Holt and Co., 1958.

Saveth, Edward N., ed. *Understanding the American Past.* Boston: Little, Brown & Co., 1954.

Schlesinger, Arthur M., Jr., and White, Morton, eds. *Paths of American Thought.* Boston: Houghton Mifflin Co., 1963.

Skotheim, Robert A. *American Intellectual Histories and Historians.* Princeton: Princeton University Press, 1966.

Storr, Richard J. *The Beginnings of Graduate Education in America.* Chicago: University of Chicago Press, 1953.

Tewksbury, Donald G. *The Founding of American Colleges and Universities before the Civil War with Particular Reference to the Religious Influences Bearing upon the College Movement.* New York: Teacher's College, Columbia University, 1932.

Tripathi, Amales. *Evolutions of Historiography in America, 1870–1910.* Calcutta: World Press Private, 1956.

Veysey, Laurence R. *The Emergence of the American University.* Chicago: University of Chicago Press, 1965.

White, Edward A. *Science and Religion in American Thought: The Impact of Naturalism.* Stanford: Stanford University Press, 1952.

Wish, Harvey. *The American Historian: A Social-Intellectual History of the Writing of the American Past.* New York: Oxford University Press, 1960.

Youmans, E. L., ed. *The Culture Demanded by Modern Life: A Series of Addresses and Arguments on the Claims of Scientific Education.* New York: D. Appleton and Co., 1867.

Articles

Adams, Charles Francis. "The Sifted Grain and the Grain Sifters." *American Historical Review* 6 (January 1901): 197–234.

Adams, George Burton. "Methods of Work in Historical Seminaries." *American Historical Review* 10 (April 1905): 521–33.

Andrews, Charles M. "These Forty Years." *American Historical Review* 30 (January 1925): 225–50.

Berlin, Isaiah. "History and Theory, The Concept of Scientific History." *History and Theory, Studies in the Philosophy of History* 1 (1960): 1–31.

Channing, Edward. "Justin Winsor." *American Historical Review* 3 (January 1898): 197–202.

Ford, Paul L. "Bibliography of the American Historical Association." *Papers of the American Historical Association* 4 (October 1890): 99–103.

Freeman, Edward A. "An Introduction to American Institutional History." *Johns Hopkins University Studies in Historical and Political Science* 1 (1883): 13–39.

Gilman, Daniel C. "The Johns Hopkins University, 1876–1891." *Johns Hopkins University Studies in Historical and Political Science,* 9th ser., nos. 3–4 (March–April 1891), pp. 183–217.

Greene, Evarts B. "Our Pioneer Historical Societies." *Indiana Historical Society Publications* 10 (1931): 83–97.

Holt, W. Stull, ed. "Historical Scholarship in the United States, 1876–1901: As Revealed in the Correspondence of Herbert Baxter Adams." *Johns Hopkins University Studies in Historical and Political Science,* ser. 56, no. 4 (1938), pp. 7–300.

Iggers, Georg G. "The Image of Ranke in American and German Historical Thought." *History and Theory, Studies in the Philosophy of History* 2 (1962): 17–40.

Jameson, John F. "The American Historical Association, 1884–1909."
    American Historical Review 15 (October 1909): 1–20.
——. "Early Days of the American Historical Association, 1884–
    1895." *American Historical Review* 40 (October 1934): 1–9.
——. "The Johns Hopkins Anniversary." *Dial* 32 (1 March 1902):
    143–46.
Laughlin, J. L. "Some Recollections of Henry Adams." *Scribner's Maga-
    zine* 69 (May 1921): 576–85.
Lovejoy, Arthur O. "The Meaning of Romanticism for the Historian of
    Ideas." *Journal of the History of Ideas* 2 (June 1941): 257–78.
Ratner, Sidney. "Evolution and the Rise of the Scientific Spirit in
    America." *Philosophy of Science* 3 (January 1936): 104–22.
Saveth, Edward N. "Race and Nationalism in American Historiography:
    The Late Nineteenth Century." *Political Science Quarterly* 54 (Sep-
    tember 1939): 421–41.
Scudder, Horace. "Memoir of Justin Winsor, LL.D." *Proceedings of
    the Massachusetts Historical Society,* 2d ser. 12 (February 1899):
    457–82.
Webb, Walter P. "The Historical Seminar: Its Outer Shell and Its Inner
    Spirit." *Mississippi Valley Historical Review* 42 (June 1955): 3–23.
Winsor, Justin. "The Perils of Historical Narrative." *Atlantic Monthly*
    66 (September 1890): 289–97.
Woodburn, James A. "Promotion of Historical Study in America fol-
    lowing the Civil War." *Journal of the Illinois State Historical Society*
    15 (April–July 1922): 439–59.

Works Concerning Charles Kendall Adams

The one good secondary reference for Charles Kendall Adams is Charles
F. Smith, *Charles Kendall Adams: A Life-Sketch* (Madison: University of Wisconsin Press, 1924). The principal primary sources by Adams
utilized in this study are the following:

Books

Adams, Charles K. *Christopher Columbus: His Life and His Work.*
    New York: Dodd, Mead & Co., 1892.
——. *Democracy and Monarchy in France, from the Inception of the
    Great Revolution to the Overthrow of the Second Empire.* New York:
    Henry Holt and Co., 1874.
——. *A Manual of Historical Literature, Comprising Brief Descrip-
    tions of the Most Important Histories in English, French, and German:*

Together with Practical Suggestions as to Methods and Courses of Historical Study. New York: Harper & Brothers, 1882.

————. *The Present Obligations of the Scholar.* Madison, Wisconsin: Democrat Printing Co., 1897.

Articles

Adams, Charles K. "Recent Historical Work in the Colleges and Universities of Europe and America." *Papers of the American Historical Association* 4 (1890): 39–65.

Works Concerning Herbert Baxter Adams

Manuscripts

Baltimore. Johns Hopkins University. Herbert B. Adams papers.
Durham, N.C. Duke University. John C. C. Newton papers.

Books

Herbert B. Adams, Tributes of Friends: With a Bibliography of the Department of History, Politics and Economics of the Johns Hopkins University, 1876–1901. Baltimore: Johns Hopkins Press, 1902.

Articles

Adams, Herbert B. "The Church and Popular Education." *Johns Hopkins University Studies in Historical and Political Science,* 18th ser. 8–9 (1900): 399–476.

————. "The College of William and Mary." *Bureau of Education Circular of Information,* no. 1 (1887).

————. "Columbus and His Discovery of America." *Johns Hopkins University Studies in Historical and Political Science,* ser. 13 (1894), pp. 471–503.

————. "Co-operation in University Work." *Johns Hopkins University Studies in Historical and Political Science* 1 (1883): 79–97.

————. "Is History Past Politics?" *Johns Hopkins University Studies in Historical and Political Science,* ser. 13 (1894), pp. 189–203.

————. "A New Historical Movement." *Nation,* 18 September 1884, p. 240.

————. "New Methods of Study in History." *Johns Hopkins University Studies in Historical and Political Science,* 2d ser. 1–2 (1884): 25–137.

————. "New Methods of Study in History." *Journal of Social Science* 18 (May 1884): 213–65.

————. "Seminary Libraries and University Extension." *Johns Hopkins*

University Studies in Historical and Political Science 5 (1887): 443–69.

———. "Special Methods of Historical Study." *Johns Hopkins University Studies in Historical and Political Science,* 2d ser. 1–2 (1884): 5–23.

———. "The Study of History in American Colleges and Universities." *Bureau of Education Circular of Information,* no. 2 (1887).

———. "The Teaching of History." *Annual Report of the American Historical Association for the Year 1897* (Washington, D.C.: Government Printing Office, 1898), 1: 245–55.

Works Concerning Justin Winsor and Moses Coit Tyler

For the Harvard librarian and history editor Justin Winsor, see Joseph A. Borome, "The Life and Letters of Justin Winsor" (Ph.D. dissertation, Columbia University, 1950). For the best secondary work on Tyler, see Howard M. Jones, *The Life of Moses Coit Tyler* (Ann Arbor: University of Michigan Press, 1933). See also *Moses Coit Tyler: Selections from His Letters and Diaries,* edited by Jessica Tyler Austen (Garden City: Doubleday, Page and Co., 1911). Some insight may also be gained by reading Tyler's masterpiece, *The Literary History of the American Revolution, 1763–1783* (1897; reprint ed. New York: Barnes and Noble, Facsimile Library, 1941).

CHAPTER 2

Books

Bainton, Roland H. *Yale and the Ministry: A History of Education for the Christian Ministry at Yale from the Founding in 1701.* New York: Harper & Brothers, 1957.

Binkley, Luther J. *The Mercersburg Theology.* Manheim, Pa.: Sentinel Printing House, 1953.

Dewitt, John. *Church History, as a Science, as a Theological Discipline and as a Mode of the Gospel.* Cincinnati: Elm Street Printing Co., 1883.

Hitchcock, Roswell D. *The True Idea and Uses of Church History: An Inaugural Address.* New York: J. F. Trow, Printer, 1856.

Kelly, Robert L. *Theological Education in America: A Study of One Hundred Sixty-One Theological Schools in the United States and Canada.* New York: George H. Doran Co., 1924.

Klein, H. M. *A Century of Education at Mercersburg.* Lancaster, Pa.: Lancaster Press, 1936.

McCosh, James. *Christianity and Positivism: A Series of Lectures to the Times on Natural Theology and Apologetics.* New York: Robert Carter and Brothers, 1871.

Miller, Samuel. *The Life of Samuel Miller, D.D., LL.D., Second Professor in the Theological Seminary of the Presbyterian Church, at Princeton, New Jersey.* Philadelphia: Claxton, Remsen and Haffelfinger, 1869.

Nichols, James H. *Romanticism in American Theology: Nevin and Schaff at Mercersburg.* Chicago: University of Chicago Press, 1961.

————, ed. *The Mercersburg Theology.* New York: Oxford University Press, 1966.

Niebuhr, Helmut R., and Williams, Daniel D., eds. *The Ministry in Historical Perspectives.* New York: Harper & Brothers, 1956.

Prentiss, George L. *The Theological Seminary of the City of New York: Historical and Biographical Sketches of Its First Fifty Years.* New York: Anson D. F. Randolph and Co., 1889.

————. *The Union Theological Seminary in the City of New York: Its Design and Another Decade of Its History.* Asbury Park, N.J.: M., W. and C. Pennypacker, 1899.

Richards, George W. *History of the Theological Seminary of the Reformed Church in the United States, 1825–1934, Evangelical and Reformed Church, 1934–1952.* Lancaster, Pa.: Rudisill and Co., 1952.

Rowe, Henry K. *History of Andover Theological Seminary.* Newton, Mass.: Thomas Todd Co., 1933.

Shriver, George H., ed. *American Religious Heretics: Formal and Informal Trials.* Nashville: Abingdon Press, 1966.

Smith, Henry B. *Nature and Worth of the Science of Church History: An Inaugural Address, Delivered before the Directors of the Union Theological Seminary, New York, Feb. 12, 1851.* Andover: Warren F. Draper, 1851.

Smyth, Egbert C. *Value of the Study of Church History in Ministerial Education.* Andover: Warren F. Draper, 1851.

Williams, George H., ed. *The Harvard Divinity School: Its Place in Harvard University and in American Culture.* Boston: Beacon Press, 1954.

Woods, Leonard. *History of the Andover Theological Seminary.* Boston: James R. Osgood and Co., 1885.

Articles

Shriver, George H. "Philip Schaff as a Teacher of Church History." *Journal of Presbyterian History* 47 (March 1969): 74–92.

Smylie, James H. "Philip Schaff Ecumenist: The Reunion of Protestantism and Roman Catholicism." *Encounter* 28 (1967): 3–16.

Unpublished Materials
Penzel, Klaus. "Church History and the Ecumenical Quest: A Study of
the German Background and Thought of Philip Schaff." Th.D. disser-
tation, Union Theological Seminary, New York, 1962.
Shriver, George H. "Philip Schaff's Concept of Organic Historiography
Interpreted in Relation to the Realization of an 'Evangelical Cathol-
icism' within the Christian Community." Ph.D. dissertation, Duke
University, 1960.
Trost, Theodore L. "Philip Schaff's Concept of the Church, with Special
Reference to His Role in the Mercersburg Movement, 1844–1864."
Ph.D. dissertation, New College, Edinburgh University, 1958.

Works Concerning Philip Schaff

The best biography of Philip Schaff is still that written by his son, David
S. Schaff, *The Life of Philip Schaff: In Part Autobiographical* (New
York: Charles Scribner's Sons, 1897), of which pages 511–18 contain
the most complete printed bibliography. The works listed below are the
most valuable for understanding Schaff's ideas about church history, its
content, and its goals.

Books
Schaff, Philip. *America: A Sketch of the Political, Social and Religious
Character of the United States of North America.* 1855. Reprint ed.
Edited by Perry Miller. John Harvard Library Series. Cambridge, Mass.:
Harvard University Press, Belknap Press, 1961.
———. *Christ and Christianity.* London: James Nisbet and Co., 1885.
———. *Germany: Its Universities, Theology and Religion, With Sketches
of Distinguished Divines of the Age.* Philadelphia: Lindsay and
Blakiston, 1857.
———. *History of the Apostolic Church: With a General Introduction
to Church History.* Translated by Edward D. Yeomans. New York:
Charles Scribner and Co., 1853.
———. *History of the Christian Church.* 6 vols. New York: Charles
Scribner's Sons, 1882–92.
———. *The Person of Christ: The Perfection of His Humanity Viewed
as a Proof of His Divinity.* New York: American Tract Society, 1880.
———. *Principle of Protestantism, as Related to the Present State of the
Church.* 1845. Reprint ed. Edited by Bard Thompson and George H.

Bricker. Lancaster Series on Mercersburg Theology, vol. 1. Philadelphia: United Church Press, 1964.

————. *The Reunion of Christendom.* New York, 1893.

————. *Saint Augustine, Melanchthon, Neander: Three Biographies.* New York: Funk and Wagnalls, 1886.

————. *Theological Propaedeutic: A General Introduction to the Study of Theology, Exegetical, Historical, Systematic, and Practical, Including Encyclopedia, Methodology and Bibliography.* New York: Christian Literature Co., 1892.

————. *What Is Church History? A Vindication of the Idea of Historical Development.* Philadelphia: J. B. Lippincott Co., 1846.

Articles

Schaff, Philip. "Church and State in the United States, or the American Idea of Religious Liberty and Its Practical Effects, with Official Documents." *Papers of the American Historical Association* 2 (1888): 391–543.

CHAPTER 3

Books

Cadden, John P. *The Historiography of the American Catholic Church, 1785–1943.* Washington, D.C.: Catholic University of America Press, 1944.

Ellis, John T. *Perspectives in American Catholicism.* Baltimore: Helicon Press, 1963.

Guy, Francis S. *Edmund Bailey O'Callaghan: A Study in American Historiography, 1797–1880.* Washington, D.C.: Catholic University of America Press, 1934.

McAvoy, Thomas T. *The Great Crisis in American Catholic History, 1895–1900.* Chicago: Henry Regnery Co., 1957.

————, ed. *Roman Catholicism and the American Way of Life.* Notre Dame: University of Notre Dame Press, 1960.

MacCaffrey, James. *History of the Catholic Church in the Nineteenth Century, 1789–1908.* Dublin: M. H. Gill and Son, 1910.

Articles

Brown, Thomas N. "The Origins and Character of Irish-American Nationalism," *Review of Politics* 18 (July 1956): 327–58.

English, Adrian T. "The Historiography of American Catholic History

(1785–1884)." *Catholic Historical Review,* n.s. 5 (January 1926): 561–98.

Guilday, Peter. "The American Catholic Historical Association." *Catholic Mind* 18 (June 22, 1920): 227–36.

Leland, Waldo G. "Concerning Catholic Historical Societies." *Catholic Historical Review* 2 (January 1917): 386–99.

Lilly, Edward P. "A Major Problem for Catholic American Historians." *Catholic Historical Review* 24 (January 1939): 427–48.

McAvoy, Thomas T. "The American Catholic Minority in the Later Nineteenth Century." *Review of Politics* 15 (July 1953): 275–302.

———. "Orestes A. Brownson and American History." *Catholic Historical Review* 40 (October 1954): 257–68.

Tourscher, F. E. "Catholic Scholarship in the United States." *Catholic Historical Review,* n.s. 7 (October 1927): 470–79.

Walsh, James J. "Edmund Bailey O'Callaghan, of New York: Physician, Historian and Antiquarian, A.D. 1797–1880." *Records of the American Catholic Historical Society of Philadelphia* 16 (1905): 5–33.

Works Concerning John Gilmary Shea

There have been only two serious attempts at publishing full-length studies of Shea: James J. Walsh, "John Gilmary Shea," *American Catholic Quarterly Review* 38 (April 1913): 185–203; and Peter Guilday, *John Gilmary Shea: Father of American Catholic History, 1824–1892* (New York: United States Catholic Historical Society, 1926), by far the better of the two references and the one with the better bibliography. The following works are the most useful of Shea's printed materials:

Books

Shea, John G. *Discovery and Exploration of the Mississippi Valley: With the Original Narratives of Marquette, Allouez, Membre, Hennepin and Anastase Douay.* New York: J. S. Redfield, 1852.

———. *A History of the Catholic Church within the Limits of the United States: From the First Attempted Colonization to the Present Time.* 4 vols. New York: John Gilmary Shea, 1886–92. Vol. 1, *The Catholic Church in Colonial Days . . . 1521–1763,* 1886; Vol. 2, *Life and Times of the Most Rev. John Carroll, Bishop and First Archbishop of Baltimore . . . 1763–1815,* 1888; Vol. 3, *From the Division of the Diocese of Baltimore, 1808, and Death of Archbishop Carroll, 1815, to the Fifth Provincial Council of Baltimore, 1843,* 1890; Vol. 4, *From the Fifth Provincial Council of Baltimore, 1843, to the Second Plenary Council of Baltimore, 1866,* 1892.

————. *History of the Catholic Missions among the Indian Tribes of the United States, 1529–1854*. New York: Edward Dunigan and Brother, 1855.

Articles

Shea, John G. "Bancroft's History of the United States." *American Catholic Quarterly Review* 8 (October 1883): 672–88.

————. "The Boston of Winthrop." *American Catholic Quarterly Review* 12 (April 1887): 193–209.

————. "The Catholic Church in American History." *American Catholic Quarterly Review* 1 (January 1876): 148–73.

————. "The Catholic Church in the United States in the Recent Translation of Alzog." *American Catholic Quarterly Review* 4 (January 1879): 138–42.

————. "Christopher Columbus: This Century's Estimates of His Life and Work." *American Catholic Quarterly Review* 12 (July 1887): 385–408.

————. "Columbus Centenary of 1892." *American Catholic Quarterly Review* 14 (October 1889): 691–700.

————. "The Coming Plenary Council of Baltimore." *American Catholic Quarterly Review* 9 (April 1884): 340–57.

————. "Edmund Bailey O'Callaghan MD, LL.D., Historian of New Netherland and New York." *Magazine of American History* 5 (July 1880): 77–80.

————. "Is Froude a Historian?" *American Catholic Quarterly Review* 5 (January 1880): 113–37.

————. "Notes on the Early History of the Catholic Church in New England." *Historical Magazine* 5, 2d ser., no. 5 (May 1869): 313–17.

————. "The Progress of the Church in the United States, From the First Provincial Council to the Third Plenary Council of Baltimore." *American Catholic Quarterly Review* 9 (July 1884): 471–97.

————. "The Proposed American Catholic University." *American Catholic Quarterly Review* 10 (April 1885): 312–25.

————. "Romance and Reality of the Death of Father James Marquette, and the Recent Discovery of His Remains." *Catholic World* 26 (November 1877): 267–81.

————. "Vagaries of Protestant Religious Belief." *American Catholic Quarterly Review* 10 (July 1885): 432–43.

————. "What Right Has the Federal Government to Mismanage the Indians?" *American Catholic Quarterly Review* 6 (July 1881)· 520–41.

Translations
Charlevoix, P. F. X. *History and General Description of New France.*
    Translated and annotated by John G. Shea. 6 vols. New York: Pri-
    vately published, 1866–72.
De Courcy de Laroche-Heron, Henry. *The Catholic Church in the
    United States: Pages of Its History.* Translated and enlarged by John
    G. Shea. 2d ed. New York: T. W. Strong, 1857.
Martin, Felix. *The Life of Father Isaac Jogues: Missionary Priest of the
    Society of Jesus, Slain by the Mohawk Iroquois, in the Present State
    of New York, Oct. 18, 1646.* Translated by John G. Shea. New York:
    Benziger Brothers, 1885.

CHAPTER 4

Works Concerning Ephraim Emerton

There is a dearth of information on Ephraim Emerton. His own essay,
"History," in *The Development of Harvard University since the Inauguration of President Eliot, 1869–1929,* ed. Samuel E. Morison (Cambridge,
Mass.: Harvard University Press, 1930), pp. 150–66, is helpful, but the
only serious attempt to bring this extremely important thinker out of
obscurity was made by George H. Williams, "A Century of Church History at Harvard, 1857–1957," *Harvard Divinity School Bulletin* 55
(April 1958): 87–101. The following works should facilitate further
study.

Books
Emerton, Ephraim. *Desiderius Erasmus of Rotterdam.* New York: G. P.
    Putnam's Sons, 1899.
————. *Humanism and Tyranny: Studies in the Italian Trecento.*
    Cambridge, Mass.: Harvard University Press, 1925.
————. *An Introduction to the Middle Ages, 375–814.* Boston: Ginn
    and Co., 1888.
————. *Learning and Living: Academic Essays.* Cambridge, Mass.:
    Harvard University Press, 1921.
————. *Mediaeval Europe, 814–1300.* Boston: Ginn and Co., 1894.
————. *Unitarian Thought.* New York: Macmillan Co., 1911.

Articles
Emerton, Ephraim. "Calvin and Servetus." *Harvard Theological Review* 2
    (April 1909): 139–60.

————. "The Chronology of the Erasmus Letters." *Annual Report of the American Historical Association for the Year 1901.* Washington, D.C.: Government Printing Office, 1902. Pp. 175–86.

————. "The Defensor Pacis of Marsiglio of Padua." *Harvard Theological Studies* 8 (1920): 1–81.

————. "A Definition of Church History." *Papers of the American Society of Church History,* 2d ser. 7 (1923): 55–68.

————. "The Religious Environment of Early Christianity." *Harvard Theological Review* 3 (April 1910): 181–208.

————. "The Study of Church History." *Unitarian Review and Religious Magazine* 19 (January 1883): 1–18.

Translations

Boniface, Saint. *The Letters of Saint Boniface.* Translated by Ephraim Emerton. New York: Columbia University Press, 1940.

Gregory VII, Pope. *The Correspondence of Pope Gregory VII: Selected from the Registrum.* Translated by Ephraim Emerton. New York: Columbia University Press, 1932.

CHAPTER 5

Works Concerning Williston Walker

Books

Walker, Williston. *The Creeds and Platforms of Congregationalism.* 1893. Reprint ed. Boston: United Church Press, Pilgrim Press, 1960.

————. "The Early Development of Church Officers." In *Approaches towards Church Unity,* edited by Newman Smyth and Williston Walker, pp. 11–35. New Haven: Yale University Press, 1919.

————. *The First Ecclesiastical Society in Hartford, 1670–1903.* Hartford: First Church of Christ, 1903.

————. *Great Men of the Christian Church.* Chicago: University of Chicago Press, 1908.

————. *A History of the Christian Church.* 1918. Rev. ed. Edited by C. C. Richardson et al. New York: Charles Scribner's Sons, 1959.

————. *A History of the Congregational Churches in the United States.* New York: Christian Literature Co., 1894.

————. *John Calvin: The Organiser of Reformed Protestantism, 1509–1564.* New York: G. P. Putnam's Sons, 1906.

————. *On the Increase of Royal Power in France under Philip Augustus, 1179–1223.* Leipzig: Gressner and Schramm, 1888.

————. *The Reformation.* New York: Charles Scribner's Sons, 1915.

————. *Ten New England Leaders.* New York: Silver, Burdett and Co., 1901.

————. *Three Phases of New England Congregational Development.* Hartford: Hartford Seminary Press, 1893.

————. *The Validity of Congregational Ordination.* Hartford: Case, Lockwood and Brainard Co., 1898.

Articles

Walker, Williston. "The Current Outlook in Church History." *Papers of the American Society of Church History,* 2d ser. 1 (1913): 17–32.

————. "The Genesis of the Common Form of Public Worship in Our Non-Liturgical Churches." *Papers of the American Society of Church History,* 2d ser. 1 (1913): 81–91.

————. "The 'Heads of Agreement,' and the Union of Congregationalists and Presbyterians Based on Them in London, 1691." *Papers of the American Society of Church History* 4 (1892): 29–52.

————. "The Sandemanians of New England." *Annual Report of the American Historical Association for the Year 1901.* Washington, D.C.: Government Printing Office, 1902. Pp. 133–62.

————. "The Services of the Mathers in New England Religious Development." *Papers of the American Society of Church History* 5 (1893): 61–85.

————. "A Study of a New England Town." *Yale Review* 1 (February 1893): 368–80.

————. "Why Did Not Massachusetts Have a Saybrook Platform?" *Yale Review* 1 (May 1892): 68–86.

CHAPTER 6

Works Concerning Arthur C. McGiffert

The most complete bibliography on Arthur C. McGiffert is to be found in *A Bibliography of the Faculty of Political Science of Columbia University, 1880–1930* (New York: Columbia University Press, 1931), pp. 185–88. McGiffert's publications below were selected for their value in understanding his ideas about church historiography.

Books and Articles on the Heresy Question

Birch, G. W. F. *Appeal to the General Assembly to Meet in St. Louis, Mo., May 17, 1900: From the Final Judgment of the Presbytery of*

New York, Made February 12, 1900, n.p., n.d. Pamphlet Collection, Speer Library, Princeton Theological Seminary.

Duffield, J. T. *The McGiffert Case.* New York, n.p., n.d. Pamphlet Collection, Speer Collection, Princeton Theological Seminary.

Johnson, Herrick. "Dr. McGiffert's 'Apostolic Age.'" *Evangelist,* 5 May 1898.

Loetscher, Lefferts A. *The Broadening Church: A Study of Theological Issues in the Presbyterian Church Since 1869.* Philadelphia: University of Pennsylvania Press, 1954.

Moore, Dunlop. *Prof. A. C. McGiffert and the Next General Assembly,* n.p., n.d. Pamphlet Collection, Speer Library, Princeton Theological Seminary.

Orr, James. "Dr. McGiffert on Apostolic Christianity." *Presbyterian and Reformed Review* (April 1898), pp. 193–213.

Presbytery of New York: In the Matter of the Rev. Arthur C. McGiffert, D.D. New York: Printed by order of the Presbytery, 1899.

Vernon, Ambrose W. "Arthur Cushman McGiffert." *Hibbert Journal* 32 (January 1934): 283–91.

Books

McGiffert, Arthur C. *The Apostles' Creed, Its Origin, Its Purpose, and Its Historical Interpretation: A Lecture with Critical Notes.* New York: Charles Scribner's Sons, 1902.

———. *History and Theology: An Address Delivered before the Presbyterian Ministers' Association of Philadelphia on April 25th, 1898,* n.p., n.d.

———. *A History of Christianity in the Apostolic Age.* New York: Charles Scribner's Sons, 1897.

———. *A History of Christian Thought.* 2 vols. New York: Charles Scribner's Sons, 1932.

———. *Martin Luther: The Man and His Work.* New York: Century Co., 1911.

———. *Primitive and Catholic Christianity.* New York: John C. Rankin Co., 1893.

———. *The Problem of Christian Creeds as Affected by Modern Thought.* Buffalo: Peter Paul and Co., 1901.

———. *Protestant Thought before Kant.* London: Gerald Duckworth and Co., 1911. Reprint ed. New York: Harper & Row, 1962.

———. "Protestantism." In *The Unity of Religions: A Popular Discussion of Ancient and Modern Beliefs,* edited by J. H. Randall and J. G. Smith, pp. 261–74. New York: Thomas Y. Crowell and Co., 1910.

————. *The Rise of Modern Religious Ideas.* New York: Macmillan Co., 1915.

————. "Theological Reconstruction." In *The Christian Point of View: Three Addresses.* New York: Charles Scribner's Sons, 1902. Pp. 31–48.

Articles

McGiffert, Arthur C. "Christianity in the Light of Its History." *Hibbert Journal* 11 (1913): 717–32.

————. "The Christianity of Ignatius of Antioch." *New World: A Quarterly Review of Religion, Ethics and Theology* 7 (September 1898): 470–83.

————. "Divine Immanence and the Christian Purpose." *Hibbert Journal* 5 (1907): 768–83.

————. "The Gospel of Peter." *Papers of the American Society of Church History* 6 (1894): 101–19.

————. "The Historical Study of Christianity." *Bibliotheca Sacra* 50 (January 1893): 150–71.

————. "How May Christianity Be Defended Today?" *Hibbert Journal* 7 (1908): 152–62.

————. "The Influence of Christianity upon the Roman Empire." *Harvard Theological Review* 2 (January 1909): 28–49.

————. "Luther and the Unfinished Reformation." *Union Theological Seminary Bulletin* 1 (January 1918): 18–26.

————. "Modernism and Catholicism." *Harvard Theological Review* 3 (January 1910): 24–46.

————. "Mysticism in the Early Church." *American Journal of Theology* 11 (July 1907): 407–27.

————. "The Progress of Theological Thought during the Past Fifty Years." *American Journal of Theology* 20 (July 1916): 321–32.

————. "The Study of Early Church History." *New World: A Quarterly Review of Religion, Ethics and Theology* 8 (March 1899): 1–22.

————. "A Teaching Church." *Hibbert Journal* 19 (1920): 123–32.

————. "Theological Education." *American Journal of Theology* 15 (January 1911): 1–19.

————. "Was Jesus or Paul the Founder of Christianity?" *American Journal of Theology* 13 (January 1909): 1–20.

Translations

Eusebius. "Eusebius: Church History." Translated by Arthur C. McGiffert. In *A Select Library of Nicene and Post-Nicene Fathers of the Christian Church,* edited by Philip Schaff and Henry Wace. 2d ser., vol. 1. New York: Christian Literature Co., 1890.

Publications by Arthur C. McGiffert, Jr.
McGiffert, Arthur C., Jr. "The Making of an American Scholar: Biography in Letters." *Union Seminary Quarterly Review* 24 (Fall 1968): 31–46.
————. "A 'Mischievous' Book: Further Correspondence of A. C. McGiffert." *Union Seminary Quarterly Review* 24 (Summer 1969): 365–75.
————, ed. *Christianity as History and Faith by Arthur Cushman McGiffert.* New York: Charles Scribner's Sons, 1934.

CHAPTER 7

Works Concerning Walter Rauschenbusch

Studies of Walter Rauschenbusch are more plentiful, though none is directly related to historiographical research. The following titles, however, are useful for that purpose: Dores R. Sharpe, *Walter Rauschenbusch* (New York: Macmillan Co., 1942); and Vernon P. Bodein, *The Social Gospel of Walter Rauschenbusch and Its Relation to Religious Education* (New Haven: Yale University Press, 1944). Other valuable studies include Reinhart Müller, *Walter Rauschenbusch, ein Beitrag zur Begegnung des deutschen und des amerikanischen Protestantismus* (Leiden/Köln: E. J. Brill, 1957); Robert T. Handy, ed., *The Social Gospel in America, 1870–1920* (New York: Oxford University Press, 1966), pp. 253–389; Sydney Ahlstrom, ed., *Theology in America* (New York: Bobbs-Merrill Co., 1967), pp. 351–586; and Arthur C. McGiffert, Jr., "Walter Rauschenbusch: Twenty Years After," *Christendom* 3 (Winter 1938): 96–109.

Manuscripts
Rochester, N.Y. American Baptist Historical Society. Walter Rauschenbusch papers.

Books
Rauschenbusch, Walter. *Christianity and the Social Crisis.* New York: Macmillan Co., 1907.
————. *Christianizing the Social Order.* New York: Macmillan Co., 1912.
————. *Die Geschichte der Idee des Reiches Gottes: Als Rede gehalten beim Schulanfang der deutschen Abteilung des theologischen Seminars in Rochester, N.Y., am 12, September 1902,* n.p., n.d.

――――. (Sections on North and South America.) In *Handbuch der Kirchengeschichte*, edited by Gustav Krüger. Tübingen, 1909. Vol. 4, pp. 25–27, 100–104, 125–26, 165–66, 169–71, and 270–84.

――――. "The Social Awakening in the Churches of America." In *Proceedings and Papers of the Fifth International Congress of Free Christianity and Religious Progress, Berlin, August 5–10, 1910*, edited by Charles W. Wendte, pp. 561–67. Berlin-Schönberg, 1911.

――――. *The Social Principles of Jesus.* New York: Association Press, 1916.

――――. *A Theology for the Social Gospel.* 1917. Reprint ed. New York Abingdon Press, 1945.

Articles

Rauschenbusch, Walter. "The Influence of Historical Studies on Theology." *American Journal of Theology* 11 (January 1907): 111–27.

――――. "The New Evangelism." *Independent* 56 (May 12, 1904): 1055–59.

――――. "The Stake of the Church in the Social Movement." *American Journal of Sociology* 3 (July 1897): 18–30.

――――. "The True American Church: Great Christian Groups Which Belong Together." *Congregationalist,* 23 October 1913, pp. 1–8.

――――. "The Value and Use of History." *Record* (November 1914), pp. 31–41.

CHAPTER 8

Works Concerning Frank Foster

Very little work has been done on Frank Foster, and he deserves better at the hands of contemporary scholars. One significant contribution has recently been made by Henry C. Brockmann in "Frank Hugh Foster: A Chapter in the American Protestant Quest for Authority in Theology" (Ph.D. dissertation, Union Theological Seminary, New York, 1967). In addition to referring to that work, the following list of Foster's publications may facilitate study of his theological ideas and historiographical activity.

Books

Foster, Frank. *Christian Life and Theology.* New York: Fleming H. Revell Co., 1900.

――――. *The Fundamental Ideas of the Roman Catholic Church Ex-*

plained and Discussed for Protestants and Catholics. Philadelphia: Presbyterian Board of Publication and Sabbath-School World, 1899.

―――. *A Genetic History of the New England Theology.* New York: Russell and Russell, 1907.

―――. *The Life of Edwards Amasa Park, S.T.D., LL.D.: Abbot Professor, Andover Theological Seminary.* New York: Fleming H. Revell Co., 1936.

―――. *The Modern Movement in American Theology: Sketches in the History of American Protestant Thought from the Civil War to the World War.* New York: Fleming H. Revell Co., 1939.

―――. *The Seminary Method of Original Study in the Historical Sciences: Illustrated from Church History.* New York: Charles Scribner's Sons, 1888.

―――. "Zwingli's Theology, Philosophy and Ethics." In *Huldreich Zwingli: The Reformer of German Switzerland, 1484–1531,* edited by Samuel M. Jackson. New York: G. P. Putnam's Sons, 1900.

Articles

Foster, Frank. "The Argument from Christian Experience for the Inspiration of the Bible." *Bibliotheca Sacra* 40 (January 1883): 97–138.

―――. "The Authority and Inspiration of the Scriptures." *Bibliotheca Sacra* 52 (January–April 1895): 69–96 and 232–58.

―――. "The Benevolence Theory of the Atonement." *Bibliotheca Sacra* 47 (October 1890): 567–88.

―――. "The Christology of a Modern Rationalist." *American Journal of Theology* 15 (October 1911): 584–98.

―――. "The Eschatology of the New England Divines." *Bibliotheca Sacra* 43 (January–October 1886): 1–32, 287–303, and 711–27; 45 (October 1888): 669–94; 46 (January 1889): 95–123.

―――. "Evolution and the Evangelical System of Doctrine." *Bibliotheca Sacra* 50 (July 1893): 408–28.

―――. "The Experiential Theology." *American Journal of Theology* 12 (October 1908): 623–27.

―――. "The Gospel of Paul." *Bibliotheca Sacra* 53 (January 1896): 89–99.

―――. "Is Eternal Punishment Endless?" *Bibliotheca Sacra* 35 (April 1878): 353–80.

―――. "Melanchthon's 'Synergism.'" *Papers of the American Society of Church History* 1 (1888): 185–204.

―――. "The New Testament Miracles: An Investigation of Their Function." *American Journal of Theology* 12 (July 1908): 369–91.

————. "Studies in Christology." *Bibliotheca Sacra* 52 (July 1895): 531–48.

————. "Studies in Christology: With Criticisms upon the Theories of Professor Adolf Harnack." *Bibliotheca Sacra* 49 (April 1892): 240–75.

————. "Theological Obscurantism." *American Journal of Theology* 15 (January 1911): 96–106.

————. "The Theology of the New Rationalism." *American Journal of Theology* 13 (July 1909): 405–13.

————. "Two Histories of Christian Doctrine." *Bibliotheca Sacra* 45 (January and July 1888): 163–85 and 506–14.

Translations

Grotius, Hugo. *A Defense of the Catholic Faith Concerning the Satisfaction of Christ Against Faustus Socinus of Sienna.* Translated by Frank Foster. Andover: W. F. Draper, 1889. [Originally published in *Bibliotheca Sacra* 36 (1879).]

&INDEX

A

Adams, Charles Kendall, 8, 11–12, 17–18, 22, 28
Adams, Henry, 12, 24, 40, 94
Adams, Herbert Baxter, xiii, 8, 27, 46, 55–57, 77, 95, 105, 115, 225, 242–44; on empiricism, 10, 20; on naturalism, 24; course on church history, 26–27
Adler, Cyrus, 241, 243
American Historical Association, 28–30, 58, 60, 77, 226, 239–45
American Society of Church History, 58–61, 226; ecumenical goal, 59; dissolution, 66–68; renewal, 239–45
Andover Theological Seminary: church history at, 36–37, 40
Archivists, 5–6, 28, 71

B

Bancroft, George, 4, 74, 89
Becker, Carl L., 230–31
Berg, Joseph F., 33–35
Birch, G. W. F., 139–41
Brauer, Jerald C., 234, 236
Buckle, Henry Thomas, xiii–xiv, 17, 22

C

Cornell University: history seminars at, 12

E

Edwards, Jonathan, 217–18
Eliot, Charles W., 6–8
Emerton, Ephraim: on iconoclasm, 96–97; on historical objectivity, 97–99; on naturalism, 99, 106–7; on theological church history,

100–101, 103; on divine agency in history, 101, 106, 108–10; definition of church history, 102, 105, 110; definition of religion, 104; definition of church, 104–5; interpretation of medieval Christianity, 111–12; interpretation of Protestant Reformation, 112–13
Empiricism: element in "scientific history," xiii–xiv, 225; and von Ranke's methods, 10; and the "new breed of American scholars," 19–21; and "naturalistic" values, 23–24; Schaff's views, 50–51, 56; Shea's methods, 71–72, 74, 76, 81; Emerton's views, 97–100; Walker's views, 118–22; McGiffert's views, 144; Rauschenbusch's views, 174–75; Foster's views, 197, 199

F

Fisher, George Park, 66
Florovsky, Georges, 231, 237
Force, Peter, 5, 28
Foster, Frank Hugh: and scientific history, 197–99; on Schaff's work, 200; on theological church history, 200–201; definition of church history, 201–2; on historical insight, 202; on history and theology, 203–4, 207, 222–23; on historical development, 203–4, 207–8; on modern science and theology, 208–13, 223–24; definition of theology, 209–11, 213–14; interpretation of early Christianity, 212; interpretation of declining Calvinism, 216–21